Have You Got Good Religion?

Have You Got Good Religion?

Black Women's Faith, Courage, and Moral Leadership in the Civil Rights Movement

ANNEMARIE MINGO

UNIVERSITY OF ILLINOIS PRESS
Urbana, Chicago, and Springfield

Cataloging data available from the Library of Congress
ISBN 978-0-252-04565-3 (hardcover)
ISBN 978-0-252-08776-9 (paperback)
ISBN 978-0-252-05534-8 (ebook)

For my parents, Gwenuel and Cynthia Mingo,
whose love anchors me; and my Godchildren, Brianna,
Corrin, and Ryan, whose hope propels me forward

Contents

Acknowledgments

This book is the result of a community of supporters who helped provide time, space, and resources, which enabled me to complete this project. I offer sincere thanks to many in my village who helped make this possible.

The love and support of my parents, Dr. G.W. and Mrs. Cynthia Mingo, is unparalleled! They were my first and remain my best teachers, historians, theologians, and ethicists. My parents are my greatest supporters, and words are not adequate to express the love and gratitude I have for them. I am who I am because of them. They know being near the ocean is important to me and I am thankful for the space they created for me to write in Key West for months at a time where I made the most progress on writing this book.

My younger brother Gerald Mingo, whose free spirit continues to soar, joins me in the commitment to social change that has been passed to us through our parents as he carves his own path. Our parents have always charged us to "Represent for the Mingos," and Gerald and I try our best in our different areas of work and impact to do just that.

My four-legged son, Duke Ellington, is such a blessing to me and all whom he encounters. Since the moment he entered my life as a rescue puppy while I finished my dissertation he has brought extra love and balance for which I am grateful.

I have been a student of history for all of my life with interests in Black freedom movements often taking center stage. This book began during the first year of my PhD program at Emory University when I wrote a paper for Alton Pollard about the role of unnamed Black women and children as frontline socio-political martyrs in the Civil Rights Movement. That paper along with the departure of Pollard and Robert Franklin after my first year, both of whom I went to Emory to study with, shifted my focus and sparked what has become an important part of my life's work. I am thankful for my dissertation committee—Elizabeth Bounds, Marcia Y. Riggs, Carol Anderson, and Dianne Stewart—who guided me through the early scholarship this book builds upon.

The research that grounds this book would not have been possible without critical financial support throughout the years from various organizations including the Laney Graduate School at Emory University, the Forum for Theological Exploration, the Andrew W. Mellon Graduate Teaching Fellowship, Emory's Graduate Division of Religion's Initiative in Religious Practices and Practical Theology, Emory University Center for Creativity and Arts, CrossCurrents' Summer Research Colloquium, the Calvin Institute for Christian Worship, and others. I could not have imbedded myself in the community to do research in Harlem without the generous support of Liz Bounds, who allowed me to stay at her mother's apartment for two months at a time during two summers, and at other times when I needed to be present with the women in New York.

Students who took variations of my course on Black women in the Civil Rights Movement at Emory University, Morehouse College, University of California, Santa Barbara, and Penn State University have heard me teach about women whose names and experiences were well-known along with those who were virtually unknown in the Movement. Their questions and interests inspired me to make the narratives come alive for the many of us who were not present in the 1950s and 1960s. The students who have been open to being stretched in my classroom are seeds of hope I have sown, and I expect them to continue to bloom where they are planted and do their part to make our world a more just place. Special thanks to Ashley Lamarre who came on board as my graduate research assistant at the end of this project to help me track down some of the visual elements for the book. I look forward to her scholarship as she carves a critical and creative path in the academy.

From the early through final stages of the writing of this book, I have been blessed with the support of family and friends who have helped me, including Saundra Burgess, Calvin Burgess, Michael Killings, Nekisha Killings, my young cousins (A, H, Z, and S) in the Killings Pride, Charles Morris, James Harris, Stephanie Mingo McKoy, Taydra Mitchell Jackson, Rob Hardy, Shaun Hardy, Robert Hardy, Brooke Hobbs, Chuck Hobbs, Anika Khan, Rahman Khan, Telluric 41, Bishop Adam J. Richardson, Connie Speights Richardson, William D. Watley, Muriel Watley, Marian "Gran" Watley, Jennifer Watley Maxell, Mae McCoy McDonald, Tiffany McDonald Pittman, Audrey Jackson, Woodrow Jackson, Brian Hart, and my aunts, uncles, and cousins who gave me space to simply be myself. I am thankful for the Women of Allen from my home church, Mt. Olive A.M.E. in Gainesville, who sent care packages at just the right time, and my many church families who created space for my spiritual well-being, including St. Mark A.M.E. (Orlando), St. James A.M.E. (Newark), Calvary Baptist (Morristown), Big Bethel A.M.E. (Atlanta), Ebenezer Baptist (Atlanta), The Breakthrough Fellowship (Atlanta), St. Paul A.M.E. (Santa Barbara), New Covenant Worship Center (Santa Barbara), and Albright-Bethune United Methodist (State College).

Special colleagues and sojourners in the life of the mind have journeyed with me at different times of this work, and I am thankful for the friendship and support of Angela D. Sims, Stephanie M. Crumpton, Terri Laws, Elise Edwards, Thelathia "Nikki" Young, Bradley Burroughs, Letitia Campbell, Daryl Roberts, Brittney Cooper, Sheri Davis, Kwesi DeGraft-Hanson, Donna Mote, John Senior, R. Candy Tate, Vincent Willis, Wynnetta Wimberly, Kirk Lyons, Matthew W. Williams, Patrick Reyes, Teresa Fry Brown, Michael Waters, Cheryl Kirk-Duggan, Vanessa Lovelace, Ruby Sales, Paul C. Taylor, Keith Gilyard, Vincent Colapietro, Nan Woodruff, Shirley Moody-Turner, Crystal Sanders, the Wells Women, and many others whose conversations provided support, critique, and encouragement.

I have deep appreciation for my former colleagues in the African American Studies and Women's, Gender, and Sexuality Studies departments at Penn State, the Africana Research Center, and the Faculty Writing Group at Penn State, along with the Write-on-Site writing group at UCSB. I am thankful for new colleagues at Pittsburgh Theological Seminary who have warmly welcomed me and the interdisciplinary work I do.

It was my desire to learn from women who risked their own safety to create opportunities for others to live more freely. I needed to know the stories of the many women whose images I saw in photographs from the Civil Rights Movement, walking, sitting in, protesting, but no one identified them. A driving question for me is what role faith plays in social activism, so I sought out churches in Atlanta, Georgia, and Harlem, New York, where I could do a deeper dive. I offer special thanks to the pastors (during the time of my core research), staffs, and congregations of the four churches, which served as my primary research sites: Rev. Dr. Gregory V. Eason and Big Bethel A.M.E. Church; Rev. Dr. Raphael G. Warnock and Ebenezer Baptist Church; Rev. Dr. Henry A. Belin, III and First A.M.E. Bethel Church; and Rev. Dr. Calvin O. Butts, III and Abyssinian Baptist Church.

I share a love for the people with elder mentors and comrades in struggle, some who remain with me now and others who have become ancestors, including Vincent Harding, Francis Kennedy, and Katie Geneva Cannon, whose generosity of spirit provided guidance to me along the way.

I created the organization Sister Scholars in 2008 to meet a need I saw for community and support among Black women pursuing doctorates. Today, the women who are a part of Sister Scholars continue to shift the academy through their bold and brilliant presence and their commitment to support other sisters along the way. Key parts of this book were written in spaces with women in the Sister Scholars community as we encouraged each other to do the work we are called to do while making intentional choices to be healthy and whole in the process. Thank you, Sister Scholars!

My State College crew including Teresa Hamilton, Stephanie D. Preston, Daisha Hankle, Mia Wood, Rasa Drane, April Sams Bernard, Timeka N. Tounsel, Wally Richardson, Reggie Hamilton, Dawn Witherspoon, Shannon Holliday, Charima Young, and Julia Bryan gave me room to be AnneMarie and not Dr. Mingo and helped me find places of joy in a difficult space. There were a few couples who have lived in State College for decades who embraced me and created additional depth to my village, including Cathy and Blannie Bowen, Jo Ann and Charles Dumas, and Barbara and Edgar Farmer. I am thankful to each of them.

Once I finally figured out the path I wanted to take with this book, I worked with two wonderful editors who encouraged me to keep telling the stories. Cecelia A. Cancellaro helped ensure I developed my larger arguments, and later Stephanie Gilmore made sure I made the smaller connections I desired. My acquisitions editor at the University of Illinois Press, Dominique Moore, took time to wait for the availability of persons she knew were critical voices in the field so my book could receive thorough reviews for me to respond to. I am thankful to the three anonymous reviewers who took the time to read and comment on the full manuscript. This work is stronger because of their feedback, and I take responsibility for any areas where it falls short.

This book would not exist without the many women who shared openly with me through focus groups, surveys, and one-on-one interviews. They invited me into their homes, churches, and lives as they shared their lived experiences in the freedom struggles primarily throughout the southern and northeastern portions of the United States. Their faith, courage, and moral imagination are only partially captured in the pages of this book. Their commitment to create the atmosphere necessary for social and political change continues to be felt nearly sixty years after most of their direct actions during the Civil Rights Movement as well as those that continue during the Movement for Black Lives. I am grateful to foot soldiers I interviewed, including Barbara Ann Adams, Shirley Ann Barnhart, Lillian Sue Bethel, Rosa Brown, Doris Virginia Brunson, Mary Stephens Dansby, Margie Davis, Pearlie Craft Dove, Patricia Pates Eaton, Margaret L. Evans, Ruth N. Fofana, Emma Franklin, Maxine Frere, Sarah P. Frierson, Mary S. Gipson, Ernestine Lee Henning, Azira Hill, Linda L. Jolly, Grace L. Jones, J. Louise Ketchen, Peggy Lucas, Pat Mabry, Juliette S. Mamby, Esther McCall, Caryl McCalla, Lillie McGowan, Cynthia Mingo, Genevevie Mitchell, Paschell C. Mix, Inez Montgomery, Edsel Dolores Evans O'Connor, Alicia Roberts, Rose Davis Schofield, Paulette Jones Scott, Bessie S. Sellaway, Ann P. Sheriff, Patricia Small, Marjorie Wallace Smyth, Beatrice Perry Soublet, Deborah Stuckey, A. Lenora Taitt-Magubane, Johnsie Williams Thomas, Nellie Thomas, Hilda Thompson, Lydia Walker, and Jayme Coleman Williams, as well as contemporary movement pastors Reverends Karen Anderson, Traci Blackmon, Leslie D. Callahan, Cassandra Gould, and Pamela Lightsey. Although I have not been able to name and include all of their experiences directly within the pages of this book, each of these women shaped my understanding of the civil rights era and a theology of movement through their eyes, and I am forever grateful for each of them.

It is my hope that the future work that arises from this research will continue to equip and empower those participating in the fight for justice and freedom today.

"We who believe in freedom cannot rest until it comes."—Ella Baker

Have You Got
Good Religion?

"Ain't Gonna Let Nobody Turn Me Around"

A Legacy of Self-Determination in Black Freedom Struggles

George Calvin Bess Jr.'s body was found in a creek in West Point, Mississippi, on August 6, 1967. The official report indicated that at six feet tall, he had "accidentally drowned" in a mere three feet of water.[1] . . . Calvin, as he was known, left Tallahassee in the summer of 1967 to participate in voter registration activities with the Student Nonviolent Coordinating Committee (SNCC) throughout the South. He went missing, and as my mother recalls, "everybody was scared to say anything or ask anything. You just didn't know anything."[2] As I grew up, my mother, Cynthia Mingo, often recounted the story of Calvin's death and it always troubled me. They had grown up together doing Easter and Christmas speeches at church. Calvin and my mother had been influenced by the same Sunday School teacher, Daisy O. Young, and pastor, Reverend King Solomon DuPont, who helped organize carpools and declared he "would die and go to hell before he would ride the bus again."[3] Calvin's death was a reminder of the danger associated with organizing. And, though it was a reminder, it was not a deterrent for my mother and countless other women in my community.

Growing up in North Central Florida, a region with a history of racist activities that were as evident as Spanish moss swaying from southern trees yet as elusive as the wind, created a fascinating backdrop for frequent living history lessons from my parents. Like me, my parents are also Florida natives, however the eras that shaped us in this overlooked *southern* state differ greatly. Their experiences growing up in northern and southern Florida from the 1940s to the 1960s grounded them in racial realities of the "Sunshine State" that included vestiges of dark periods from Rosewood to Ocoee[4] of which they made sure my younger brother and I were always aware.

The stories, like this one of Calvin Bess, that captivated me most as a child were from my mother, who was born and raised in Tallahassee. In the shadow of Florida's capital building, she and other Blacks faced the disturbing realities of Jim and Jane Crow on a daily basis. She explained how when riding the city bus, they were forced to pay at the front and then enter from the back, only to be left on the side of the road after paying if they did not make it to the rear entrance before the driver sped off. She told me how saleswomen followed them around department stores such as Lerner Shops and prevented them from trying on clothes, shoes, and other items in downtown stores that would take Black people's money without the assurance of satisfaction with their purchase. She also described how Blacks were required to stand and eat at a counter in the rear of restaurants, despite paying the same amount of money for food as White patrons who ate leisurely while seated at nice tables in the front. My mother shared stories of these daily discriminations so my brother and I could better understand and appreciate our ways of being in relation to our parents' rather recent past.

In her early teens, my mother watched adults in her community from Rev. Charles Kenzie Steele, pastor of Bethel Baptist Church, to Mr. Sam Johnson, her Sunday School superintendent, create a transportation network that enabled persons including her father to get to and from their places of employment during the eight-month bus boycott between 1956 and 1957. She listened as students on Florida A&M University's (FAMU) campus made plans to actively challenge and push against the unjust system of segregation by boycotting, protesting, and marching. Mass meetings at her home congregation, Fountain Chapel A.M.E. Church, pastored by Rev. King Solomon DuPont, reinforced her need to do what she could when she could to thwart segregation, even if it meant risking physical violence. After nearly eighty years of the degradation of Jim and Jane Crow, it was time for action. It was time for the seeds of justice planted in my mother and others to grow.

My mother's mother, Annie Lee, was very strict.[5] Although my grandfather had participated daily in the Tallahassee bus boycott, started in May of 1956 by two young women who were FAMU students,[6] my grandmother was firmly against my mother and her older sister Eunice's participation in the 1960 sit-ins just a few years later.[7] Knowing the authoritarian way in which my grandmother ruled the home, it was always intriguing to me that my mother and aunt participated in the sit-ins during my mother's freshman year of college, against my grandmother's wishes and without her knowledge. My mother admits she was more afraid of a neighbor seeing her and telling her mother what she was doing than any potential retaliation from Whites

Florida A&M student protesting in downtown Tallahassee 1964. Source: ©Bob Adelman

who did not want them at the lunch counter. As a child, I wondered why my mother and aunt would risk possible violence from segregationists at the McCrory's five and dime stores and perhaps even worse punishment from their mother at home.

That question never left me.

My mother and her sister defied their unapologetically strict mother to participate in sit-ins during a time when the consequences of standing for justice could be life-threatening, yet they did it anyway. Their commitment to seek justice, despite the risk, helped shape me from an early age. As a young woman, my mother committed to doing her small part to make sure that segregation and injustice would not always exist. My mother is a civil rights activist, but like so many other women, her name and story are unknown in the narratives of civil rights in the United States.

Almost thirty years after my internal questioning of why my mother would risk what she did to sit in and protest at the McCrory's in Tallahassee, I found myself in the presence of another woman whose story would make the links clear for me. I scribbled feverishly in my little notebook as I listened to

Rosa "Nana Rosa" Brown, at that time an octogenarian Black woman and member at Big Bethel A.M.E. Church in Atlanta, Georgia.[8] She described to me her experiences during the Civil Rights Movement, explaining how she was working at the Atlanta Life Insurance Company while her husband was one of the few Black men working at the US Post Office. Nana Rosa explained how each week she and other women colleagues spent their lunch hour protesting in front of the Post Office for its lack of representative hiring and advancement of Blacks. I paused in my note taking to verify the timing of when this weekly protesting was happening, and that is when I had an "ah-ha moment."

I asked, "Were you protesting in front of the Post Office at the same time that your husband was one of the few Black men to work there?" Her immediate response was, "It didn't matter; it was bigger than that." I heard in her story the stories I had grown up hearing from my mother and other women in my home church.[9] Nana Rosa, my mother, and others like them were the types of women who worked as both Martin and Coretta King said, to "redeem the soul of America."[10]

They did not simply focus on individual success and advancement, but the moral transformation of a whole society. For them, the struggle for freedom and justice would not be deterred by disapproving parents or silenced in the face of possible reprisals against a spouse. Their actions were rooted in the belief that what they were doing "was bigger than" themselves. For these women, becoming active in the Movement was something they simply had to do.

I came to discover the historical narratives of women like Nana Rosa and Cynthia Mingo as rich resources for understanding the motivation behind the risk taking involved in direct nonviolent activism. I leveraged their stories to understand a lived religion at work and to construct ethical categories from the lives of Black Churchwomen.[11] My research draws primarily from women associated with Ebenezer Baptist Church and Big Bethel A.M.E. Church in Atlanta, and Abyssinian Baptist Church and First A.M.E. Bethel Church in Harlem. As a social ethicist and oral historian, I employed methods in the communities in which my research participants currently live that expand beyond traditional participant observation of ethnography, by pairing observations of Civil Rights era women in their twenty-first-century ongoing social justice work with oral histories that reveal their formation in the past. I utilize methods similar to what Tracey Hucks describes as participant engagement,[12] for the contemporary Movement leaders who are active during the twenty-first-century Movement for Black Lives and what I categorize as working as an *inside-outsider*. An inside-outsider is an individual who is able to easily connect and join with the established group in a way that provides a closeness to practices that would not be obvious or accessible to persons who are not considered to be inside the group, yet the person remains in a non-member status that enables them to critically observe and analyze the practices. The insider status is more than simply collegiality toward the researcher, they are accepted and looked upon as "one of them" by the group being studied. Years after beginning my research at Ebenezer Baptist, I had a conversation with a member and while talking she said, "well you were immediately accepted at Ebenezer because you are old school church. They [the older members of Ebenezer] don't accept everybody, but they accepted you right away because you know how things work."[13] This reminded me of the importance of my inside-outsider status in gaining access to the women who would share their experiences with me from that and other churches.

Over the course of two years, I lived within the communities in which I conducted my research in Atlanta and Harlem and became a regular participant in many aspects of their religious lives. I was often "adopted" into their families as a surrogate daughter, niece, or granddaughter. I approached this research as an inside-outsider raised within a strong Black American Christian culture, knowing the language, and the sacred traditions, while still not being native to some of the specific iterations in the research areas. As an inside-outsider I entered the space through personal connections that could influence the "doorkeepers" in the congregations. This enabled me to be welcomed at a level more akin to a member than a visitor, and certainly not solely as an outside researcher. For multiple Sundays, the pastors at each of the churches would have me stand and from the pulpit they said something such as, "Now, this is Reverend AnneMarie Mingo, she's here to do some research and we want to make sure we help her get what she needs. If you are a woman who was involved in the Civil Rights Movement make sure you see her after service."

This public endorsement from the pastor gave my presence and research further credence within the church community, which encouraged women to open the doors of their homes for me to come and interview them. Through adoption by various women in each congregation I was able to gain access to information that would often remain elusive from external researchers and often had not even been shared with other biological family members. Inherent within this method is the challenge of becoming too closely involved to be a critical observer; however, I entered the relationships conscious of this challenge, and through classic methods of ethnography, including participant observation, interviewing, note taking, and writing thick descriptions of experiences, I made intentional efforts to maintain space for critique and analysis.

By building on previous scholarship about Civil Rights Movement history, liberation theologies, and ethics, along with my new oral histories from "everyday" Black Churchwomen of the civil rights era, I offer new understandings of religious and moral motivations for social activism during the Civil Rights Movement.[14] I retrieve a lived religion from the experiences, songs, scriptures, and prayers that formed a critical engagement with God in moments of socioreligious contestation. By the words they used—their own or others'—these women articulated their theological understanding of how God was present and active in the lives of those fighting for justice and freedom. This lived religion clarifies the women's "doing of justice" and articulates their liberating morality and social ethic rooted in virtues of freedom, courage, and imagination. I make the case that the lived religion of these women is derived from a liberative theology differing from the traditional Latin American liberation theology and Black liberation theology articulated by men during roughly the same period of time in the 1950s and 1960s.

The retrieval is necessary to provide a fuller understanding of how the Civil Rights Movement's success was the result of more than the courage, dream, and sacrifice of one eloquent man. Each January in schools and communities throughout the United States, young and old alike pause to commemorate the life and legacy of the most prominent charismatic male leader of the Civil Rights Movement, Martin Luther King Jr. They sing songs, recite lines from his famous speeches, color pictures, attend talks, and commit to doing a day of service in King's honor. This sole focus on King helps to simultaneously bolster his position as *a* leader within the Movement while conflating his involvement in ways that imply that he was the *only* leader, erasing the many other women, men, and children who led during the Movement and continued the work after King's death. More than fifty years after the Civil Rights Movement, historical media accounts focus almost solely on the experiences and perspectives of men who spoke at mass meetings, occupied the front lines of marches, and openly challenged city, county, state, and federal leadership. Since these accounts often omit the women who helped both organize and sustain the Movement, they have continuously reinscribed the male-savior narratives of the Civil Rights Movement. It has been the work of scholars and practitioners such as Bettye Collier-Thomas, Vicki Crawford, Joanne Grant, Belinda Robnett, Rosetta Ross, Deborah Gray White, Danielle McGuire, Barbara Ransby, Jacqueline Rouse, and others to ensure that the women of the Movement are reclaimed from their places of relative obscurity.[15]

Widening the Scope and Influences
of the Movement

Almost without fail, whenever you ask someone to name people from the Civil Rights Movement the first name mentioned is Martin Luther King Jr. and the second is Rosa Parks. Even with limited knowledge about her long-standing commitments to justice work, they mark Parks as a key figure from the beginning of the Movement. The bus boycott that Parks's actions sparked was organized by the Women's Political Council in Montgomery who also had a long-term commitment to fighting for equality. The boycott was effective because of the economic impact when Black women stayed off the buses that most Black men had already stopped riding to avoid confrontation with racist drivers and patrons. Footage from the Montgomery boycott shows hundreds of women and young girls walking, yet we do not know them. Women feature prominently in historic photographs and documentaries from the Civil Rights Movement, particularly inside Black churches at mass meetings, in the streets protesting, singing to keep their spirits up, and even as they were being arrested. Often dressed in their Sunday best, the faces of these women are clearly visible, making their involvement in the Movement undeniable, yet their names and particular stories are unknown. Even though newer scholarship challenges the narrative of universal struggles that male Movement leaders addressed and includes perspectives of female community organizers, there is still little information about one particular group of women whose beliefs and actions were critical to the Movement—Black Churchwomen.[16] Virtually barred from formal leadership in the Black community's most dominant organ, the Black Church, these women often acted as the informal or "bridge" leaders as Belinda Robnett categorizes them, maintaining significant organizational power within their communities.[17]

The male-dominated media reinforced the patriarchal leadership profiles by looking for a man to speak with to capture sound bites. Yet, at the grassroots level, many men and women during the Movement recognized that leadership was not associated with gender but with persons who were willing to stand up for justice, and who were not afraid to risk the consequences that such a stand could generate. The title of pastor or minister was not a prerequisite for leadership, although it made men easily identifiable to the media and full-time clergy relished a different form of independence that the clerical collar offered, which could often endure economic retaliation. Wanting to be a part of movements for social change caused many young women to ignore societal norms that encouraged them to sit back, be careful, and adhere to the community's unwritten politics of respectability. Girls and women accepted risks associated with standing up against persons whose actions they deemed unjust. They proudly went to jail, and boldly spoke up for themselves and others as they fought for causes they believed were bigger than their individual experiences. Regardless of negative perceptions of many older leaders about the student-led direct-action approach, they believed themselves to be doing God's work and found respectability in that. Young women who had grown up in Black churches were taught about a God of love and justice who would not continually turn a blind eye to the injustices they faced, but would be with them in a righteous fight. They boldly acted on that belief.

As a consequence of ignoring the stories of Black Churchwomen in the Civil Rights Movement, vital resources for current and future social activists are quietly making their way to the grave. In many ways, this book was a race against the clock to capture the experiences of women who have not had the privilege of numerous researchers seeking them out like better-known women such as Rosa Parks, Coretta Scott King, Ella Baker, Fannie Lou Hamer, and Septima P. Clark. In this book, I explore the oral histories of Black Churchwomen in an attempt to better understand how their actions contributed to the Movement.

My research uncovers a lived religion and liberation ethic born out of the concrete experiences of Black women as they participated in various struggles during the Civil Rights Movement. This lived religion was not limited to traditional construction, but was developed by, articulated from, and embodied through Black women's tangible experiences with God during periods of struggle and public contestation of rights. God was not merely a distant cosmic being linked to a future hope, God was known as "a present help in times of trouble," as described in Psalm 46. God's presence was felt in the midst of difficulties, which despite not being able to touch physically made God real to many of the women in ways that defied typical explanations. Black Churchwomen's challenge of racist, sexist, and classist limitations in their fight to enflesh the word of God and embrace their marginalized lives as sacred beings that created *imago dei* can be seen in their activism during the Civil Rights Movement. They encountered and understood God as a divine living being always acting with and on behalf of those facing mistreatment and oppression. Many religious Black women during the Civil Rights Movement understood their beliefs as connected to their social responsibility and acted accordingly.

Samuel K. Roberts argues that African American Christians developed a unique ethical consciousness as a result of the particular aspects of their culture and history within the United States, and they created ways to resolve the paradox of a God introduced to them by White oppressors, yet not limited by the perspectives of any humans.[18] As I began my study, I was driven to understand the lived experiences of Black religious women during the Civil Rights Movement, to learn how their understanding of God (their theology) impacted their actions towards forming a more just society (their ethics). To be clear, all of the women who participated in this study, as well as myself, identify as religious today, believing that God exists and plays an active role in their lives, and only one currently identifies as non-Christian (although she grew up in a Baptist church). As we experience mid-twentieth century Black freedom struggles through the lens of the women I interviewed, we also gain insights into various aspects of a non-monolithic Christianity through their narratives and sources of faith they drew from. As a result, there is not a fixed theological perspective that the women have, however there are some commonalities regarding a belief and understanding that a God existed who they could be in relationship with who was on the side of the oppressed as many Black liberation theologies espouse.[19] This God differed from the God of those who were oppressing them, a concept I explore a little more in chapter 4. For these women, and others like them, faith was intentionally fashioned as a tool of liberation and not the reification of oppression.

Traci C. West's liberative social ethics, which she describes as a range of interconnected moral concerns, with components of embodied spiritual quest, seeking out the margins, historical consciousness, strategic resistance, and scrutiny of institutions, shapes a portion of my ethical theory.[20] In this book, I understand liberative social ethics as a collection of communal values and virtues that shape actions of Black women based on an inherited faith, critical assessment of experiences, and resistance to oppression to recreate the world more justly.

Using aspects of Katie G. Cannon's womanist virtue ethical method as identified by Melanie L. Harris,[21] I expand our understanding of how virtues can be employed in contemporary social justice work by centering virtue ethics drawn from the lived experiences of the Black women who through their understanding of God's alignment with them chose to risk their individual lives to create collective change for the broader society. I offer moral exemplars throughout the book with the hope that their examples will spark desires in the reader to find their own virtuous path for particular and universal impact.

Similar to the way that I wondered why my mother and aunt would take the risk to sit-in at lunch counters, I want to better understand the motivations of civil rights era Black Churchwomen who showed up in the face of difficulties and horrors throughout the South and certain parts of the North.

As the narrative of Nana Rosa suggests, some women who participated in the Civil Rights Movement did so because of a greater "calling" they felt on their lives; they participated despite any fears or concerns for themselves individually. In critical Movement moments, their faith in and commitment to justice and freedom was shaped, challenged, defined, and/or dashed. Yet, many women continued to press forward.

Expanding the Movement

There is much more to the Movement than can be reflected in sound bites of "We Shall Overcome," and "I Have a Dream." Atlanta Student Movement civil rights veteran Charles Black explains that what many people do not understand about the Civil Rights Movement is that it was "long, wide, and deep."[22] As scholars explore areas of the Civil Rights Movement beyond the traditional narrative of Martin Luther King, we are able to see the expansiveness of the Movement that brought significant changes throughout the United States and inspired changes in other parts of the world. Expanding the length, breadth, and depth of the historical period of the Movement enables us to understand its historic, religious, and moral lessons.

While the analyses and critiques of many long views of the Movement lean more toward the influence of labor and the left, I resurrect the role of Black Church activism during the longer period of the mid-1940s through the early 1970s. The widening and deepening of the Movement is where the primary contributions of my work will be found since critical work has begun in its lengthening.[23] I begin to "open *wide* the freedom gate"[24] by including many everyday women who made personal sacrifices to give life to a broader and more inclusive Movement, and I widen the geographical regions of activism moving beyond the South into the Northeast. My analysis of the deep moral motivations and commitments of women who are usually forced to the margins of civil rights narratives offers a critical addition to the field. I do this by mining the experiences and adding the narratives of women who were not the well-known media darlings of the Movement, yet their lives continue to expand the legacy of social activism that has existed among Black American women for centuries. This book examines a Movement that was long temporally, wide inclusively, and deep morally. After introducing the women and the communities that helped shape them, I identify and explore the virtue ethics of freedom faith, courageous resistance, and theo-moral imagination, which are evident during the Civil Rights Movement. I conclude with illustrations of how these virtues also can help ground the activist work being led by Black women in the first quarter of the twenty-first century.

As a social ethicist, I am drawn to what people do in their actions and not simply what people think and theorize. A moral exemplar represents a person of high character who acts in ways that draw others to courageous action.[25] Throughout this book, I also incorporate five women as moral exemplars through mini-interludes at the end of the main chapters that explore an overall reflection on freedom and women's leadership, each of the three virtue ethics, and the theology of movements for liberation in what can be understood as a form of call-and-response. The five women exemplars provide additional windows into the virtue ethics that are drawn from the experiences of the over forty women that I interviewed as a part of this project. Three of the moral exemplars, Miss Ella Baker, Dr. Willa Beatrice Player, and Mrs. Eberta Lee Spinks, were older women during the civil rights era and more established as what Belinda Robnett describes as a professional bridge leader, formal local community bridge leader, and an indigenous bridge leader, respectively, as a result of Baker's formal positions and organizational influence, Player's high status at the state and local level, and Spinks's reputation as a strong and well-trusted individual.[26] Their commitment and ability to use their status to protect and support younger activists during the Civil Rights Movement provided examples for the women I interviewed and others like them who were often younger activists during the Movement. One moral exemplar, Rev. Dr. Prathia L. Hall, was a colleague and comrade to many of the young women during the Movement, and yet at times she was in a position that had characteristics of what Robnett describes as a secondary leader who as a powerful orator and fearless organizer whose praying, speaking, and preaching even influenced Martin Luther King Jr., had access to both the formal and bridge leaders. The final moral exemplar, Mrs. Bree Newsome Bass, provides a moral example in the contemporary moment as a young activist who was compared to a modern-day superhero as she inspired many to take bold stances, including some of the women religious leaders of the Movement for Black Lives.

The Processional

In the Black Church context, processionals from the back of the church to the front, whether the choir, the ministers, or denominational leaders, lets you know that an extraordinary experience will likely follow. This book enlarges the existing scholarly trajectory[27] by: (1) focusing on the lived experiences of "everyday" Black Churchwomen whose historical recollections provide living texts for analysis of the social and political environment of the mid-twentieth century; (2) excavating new understandings of women's agency and theo-moral responsibility in their daily actions within the Civil Rights Movement; (3) offering additional insight into Black women's courageous resistance; and (4) analyzing Black women's social activism in both the South and the North and their development of imaginative theo-moral foundations of social change.

In a processional-like form, I share brief overviews of the chapters that will follow, each named for a song of the Movement anchored in both historic and contemporary periods. In chapter 1, I examine the social and historical influences including the Church, racially segregated communities, and Black media, which the women I interviewed described as formative factors during the Civil Rights Movement, as well as broader societal trends and conditions, such as the murder of Emmett Till, that marked the moments and sparked a desire for change. In this chapter a brief introduction is provided for the eight women, whose oral histories provide the most insights into the lived experiences of young Black religious women during the Movement.

Chapter 2 introduces the first of three virtues that support the individual and communal liberative social ethics of the Black Churchwomen. Freedom faith originates in the language of Civil Rights activist, pastor, and professor Prathia Hall and is the foundational ethic that creates the platform on which the others are able to be expressed. Freedom faith is anchored in scriptural texts, lived experiences, and prayers that are passed through generations. As a brief interlude after the chapter, Rev. Dr. Prathia L. Hall is introduced as the first moral exemplar, whom I feature as a facilitator of freedom faith.

Chapter 3 outlines the second virtue in the liberative social ethics, courageous resistance. Courage is revealed in the actions of the women despite the realities of fear. Courageous resistance requires cultivation as courage is built one action at a time. Experiences of women in both the southern and northern United States who were young high school and college students during the Movement and grew in boldness mark this chapter. Dr. Willa Beatrice Player serves as the second moral exemplar and a cultivator of courage in the college community of Greensboro, North Carolina.

The fourth chapter develops the third and final virtue, Theo-moral imagination. This virtue is found in a liminal space where God's plans are revealed and glimpses of what is possible beyond the present begin to shape larger visions. An imaginative God-given second sight creates access to see a better world that can become a reality from the place of the world that currently is. Mrs. Eberta Lee Spinks's ability to imagine beyond the visible reality in Laurel, Mississippi, makes her a moral exemplar for Theo-moral imagination.

Chapter 5 combines the three-virtue ethics of freedom faith, courageous resistance, and Theo-moral imagination and includes an ethic of compulsion rooted in a theology of movements for liberation. This theology takes as its sources songs, scripture, sayings, and sermons/speeches which were drawn from during the historic Civil Rights Movement and identifies the aspects relied on during the more contemporary Movement for Black Lives era. In a distinct difference from the civil rights era, this chapter features Black women clergy leaders Karen Anderson, Traci Blackmon, Leslie Callahan, and Pamela Lightsey, who are actively informing the theological activism of the twenty-first century. The final moral exemplar, Bree Newsome Bass, shows what a theology of movements for liberation looks like when you choose a religion of freedom and justice.

The stories of my mother's activism, particularly her repeated statement that despite the possible risks to her safety, protesting was something she had to do, changed and challenged me as a child. Thirty years later, Nana Rosa inspired me to embrace the communal-oriented reality that individual actions are much bigger than we think. Through this book, I hope that the lived experiences of faith in the midst of struggle during the Civil Rights Movement conveyed through the stories told by Black women will offer new ideas for additional analysis and faith-filled strategies in the ongoing fight for justice and freedom.

CHAPTER 1

"We Shall Overcome"

Sociohistorical Influences on Black Women's Participation in the Civil Rights Movement

> Freedom is a constant struggle.
> —Angela Y. Davis

Local movements led by everyday people are now acknowledged as an essential aspect of the Civil Rights Movement's success rather than the more widely known campaigns associated with a smaller number of charismatic leaders who were covered in the national media.[1] The Civil Rights Movement is more than the fight for a bus seat, a hamburger at a lunch counter, or the backdrop for an inspiring song; it has roots within the ongoing legacy of Black Freedom Struggles in the United States. The Movement happened in large and small ways that, when aggregated, became one of the most important social movements in modern history.[2]

There were a lot of unknowns at its inception, but a common hope and desire for freedom motivated many Blacks to fight for the right to live their lives without socially constructed limitations. The participants in the Civil Rights Movement believed their actions would be on the right side of history whether their names were recorded in history books or not. This was not a popularity contest or a quest for the superlative designation of the most likely to succeed. Success was not promised, but as the momentum of the Movement grew individual acts of resistance found common ground with the actions of others. Change began to be felt in the air along with a belief that individual and communal sacrifices and commitments in the face of threats could make things better for persons in the future so they would not face the same stings of racism and classism, but would have the freedom to live fully. Change that led to freedom became the goal for the women in my study, not credit or media recognition.[3]

Some events, such as the brutal murder of Emmett Till, touched the entire nation and formed a significant part of the sociohistorical and political consciousness of young people who were about the same age in 1955. Till's disfigured image was permanently burned into their memories, and many of these young people took to the streets and filled the jails in protest of injustice in the mid- to late 1960s. Similarly, the church bombing that killed Addie Mae Collins, Denise McNair, Carole Robertson, and Cynthia Wesley, ages 11 to 14, while they primped and prepped in the bathroom after Sunday school one Sunday morning in Birmingham in 1963, sparked a social and moral consciousness for many, especially young women close in age. These young women, who remembered seeing the violence meted out against people who looked like them, continued to pour into churches for mass meetings to receive moral motivation, collective conviction, and imperative instructions as they joined the ongoing fight for freedom that traced roots on American soil to the 1520s.[4]

Everyday women's lived experiences help to fill a gender and class void within Civil Rights Movement narratives and provide alternative views of the challenges, successes, and remaining opportunities of the Movement. I use the term "everyday women" to describe the women who were the life-blood of the Movement and in general were not the well-known women whose actions as leaders allowed their names to be known beyond their immediate community. These were the type of women you would encounter in your everyday life as the young woman at Sunday School, the classmate on the bus, or the secretary at the business. You could have easily walked by them every day without a throng of people or media reporters trying to get to them, or seeing them as specific targets for those seeking to harm and stop the Movement. Without fanfare these women were common to those around them, yet their actions in this critical sociopolitical moment make them important agents of change. The activism of women and girls did not take shape in a vacuum. It was often a response to sociohistorical influences.

The women I interviewed in the twenty-first century were generally teenagers and young women in the 1960s who became active during the heightened student-led portions of the Movement associated with SNCC. I also interviewed a few of the women who were older during the Movement and lived into their 90s, however the majority of those whose experiences fill these pages were younger. I use the term "Churchwomen" as a marker for these women and girls who were often barred from formal church leadership and theological study, yet through their experiences with God constructed a lived theological expression of liberation during the time that a group of Black Churchmen were writing about liberation theology on behalf of

Black people generally without the involvement of Black women.[5] To gain insight into many of the women featured in the following chapters, I discuss aspects of their life stories prior to the Civil Rights Movement and significant incidents they recalled in relation to larger economic, social, and political dynamics that were impinging upon Blacks during the twentieth century.[6] As a result of their early formation and often continued involvement in the Black Church faith tradition, I refer to this group as Black Churchwomen. Beginning in this chapter and continuing throughout the book, an understanding of the history of the civil rights era is broadened through the stories and experiences shared by these Black Churchwomen.

Introducing the Black Churchwomen

Often the earliest memories and influences of social activism for the women who share their experiences in these pages originate in stories of grandparents and other relatives who stood up for themselves and spoke out for justice. Their family histories of activism recount stories of courage in the deep Jim Crow South of the early twentieth century. Given the realities of lynch mobs and other violence against Black people, the courageous acts of family members were emblazoned on the memories of their children and later passed on to their granddaughters. I conducted oral history interviews with over forty women, and will draw broadly from almost half of them. However, there are eight women whose life experiences and choices create the sources I draw from more extensively for a lived religion and liberative social ethic, who I introduce here in the context of their familial, community, and individual influences. Short introductions for most of the women I interviewed are included in the appendix.

* * *

Lillian Sue Bethel was a no-nonsense type of woman who was raised in Albany, Georgia, and Central Florida. Her Aunt Helen taught her to be independent and not be afraid of anyone—a clear distinction from what most young Blacks were taught in southwest Georgia where Whites expected to be treated as authority figures worthy of fear. Lillian Sue Bethel remembers one incident when her aunt boldly stood up for herself during a shopping trip:

> We were in the clothing store [and] she was buying me a pair of shoes. We were standing there waiting to be serviced and this white lady came and got in front of us and she looked and said, no, I was here first. And, of course, the white lady exercising what she thought was her right [said], 'but you may have been here first, but I'm white.' My aunt told her she didn't care

what she was. Now, see, those were lynching words. She didn't care what she was, and I'm sure part of her bravery came from her father, who was my grandmother's brother.[7]

Lillian's great uncle, who she refers to, was a businessman in Albany who did not rely on White people for his family's livelihood. Although they were living in the age of Jim Crow, in many ways they never accepted the mindset of inequality or inferiority. The family's economic independence allowed her aunt to not fear that her words could lead to a lack of employment, but the realities and history of lynching in southwest Georgia, where at least 122 lynchings were publicly recorded,[8] made Lillian concerned that her aunt's words could literally cost her her life.

After graduating from high school, Lillian moved to New York City to live with her mother, whose quest for more than southwest Georgia could offer took her to the North years prior. Lillian worked in New York for seven years before returning to Albany, Georgia, at the age of twenty-three to complete college following her mother's sudden death. As a student at Albany State College (now University), she was an active part of the Albany Movement from 1961 to 1964. By this time, Lillian's experiences living and working in New York strengthened a perspective her aunt modeled as she grew up—she would not be apologetic for living fully, even in the Deep South. She expressed frustration with some of the older members of her hometown who were not supportive of SNCC workers fighting to secure rights for Blacks. Lillian did not believe persons from outside of Albany should work harder for justice and freedom in southwest Georgia than those who were born and raised in the area.

Therefore, as the Albany Movement began to coalesce as a collaborative effort of the NAACP, Urban League, Criterium Club, Baptist Ministerial Alliance, and Student Nonviolent Coordinating Committee, Lillian attended mass meetings at Mt. Zion Baptist church in Albany to stay connected with what was happening in the Movement. Once back on Albany State's campus, she would often encourage other young women to leave classes to march as a part of the efforts taking place. Ultimately, her protests and commitment to do something to prevent the perpetuation of injustice led to her arrest. Lillian's feistiness and commitment to seeing justice for everyone continued in jail, where she refused the personal bail her aunt attempted to provide, instead choosing to remain in the overcrowded cells with non-edible food for a week until everyone was released on Christmas Eve. Lillian's actions also resulted in her being among the nearly thirty college students expelled from Albany State in 1961 for their movement participation and arrest.

Reflecting almost fifty years later, she believed that God took care of her even in the expulsion, because unlike many students who were arrested at the same time, she had already completed all of her final exams before being jailed. Therefore, although she was forced to sit out of school until the next academic year, she did not lose credit for the term during which she was arrested. This along with her family's relative financial security enabled her to more clearly see a way forward to complete her degree and not have to count the expulsion as a complete loss.

Following her college graduation in 1964, Lillian moved back to New York City to work. She started a family, raised her daughter, and became an active member of First A.M.E. Bethel Church in Harlem where she founded and directed the community food pantry and worked with the Sunday school for many years until her death.

* * *

Doris Virginia Brunson's mother asked her husband if it would be okay to leave New York City and return home to Manning, South Carolina, for the "lying in" just before giving birth so their only child could be born in the South like they had been. He agreed, so Doris Brunson was born in Manning, but she was raised by her parents in New York City. She believes that a personal commitment to activism was ingrained in her from grandfather and father—who both pushed her to stand up for herself and others whenever the chance presents itself. Her mother taught her the color of a person's skin did not matter and her father's words "every White person isn't your enemy and every Black person isn't your friend—take people as they come," reminded her that support could come from various sources.

Doris recalls a story told in South Carolina about her grandfather who stood up for himself after a White man backhanded him for expressing his disapproval for the way his friend was being treated. Doris's grandfather grabbed the White man and held him with one hand while he pulled out his pocketknife and used it efficiently to defend himself. Doris recounts the repercussions this act of courage and defiance of racialized social norms had for him and his immediate family:

> When he finally realized that he had done it, he just let him go, and this guy fell back. So, he went home, and he told my grandmother what had happened and what he had done. He said, "I'm going to have to leave. Will you go with me?" She said, "I will go with you and the children wherever you want to go." So that night, he took my grandmother and my dad and his sisters . . . and they went to the train line. They didn't go to the train

station because they knew that the Klan would be out there and would get him. He flagged the train down with a lantern. When the train stopped, the conductor said, "What are you doing flagging this train down? We have a schedule! What's the matter with you? You crazy?" My grandfather told him what happened, and it turned out that they were both Masons, and he gave him this hand signal. He said, "C'mon, c'mon get on. Get your wife . . . go get her." They got on the train, and they went to a town that was miles away.[9]

The complicated racial dynamics of the South not only resulted in her family understanding her grandfather's actions toward the White man as courageous rather than violent, but these dynamics also facilitated the family's escape thanks to a fraternal bond, between the grandfather and White train conductor, that seemingly transcended race.

The train did not originate in Manning, so the conductor was not aware of the altercation that had taken place earlier that day. Yet because of the reality of racialized domestic terrorism in the South, the White conductor understood the need for a way of escape to be made for this family. The man her grandfather cut did not have to utter a threat to say that "he would be sorry for what he had done"; it was understood that as night fell, Klan vigilantes would deal with this Black man who had stepped out of his designated place. The disruption caused by the threat of retaliation forced not only Doris's grandfather but also his wife and children to flee their home. Memory of this flight in the middle of the night, and especially the actions that necessitated it, was permanently etched in their minds, and the story was passed onto future generations, including Doris. She was told of her grandfather's act and was taught to remain proud of the way in which her family stood up for themselves and others, and also banded together for survival even if it meant leaving all that they had. Fear was real, but the ability to resist with courage was honored. It was an early lesson that Doris continued to apply later when she began to participate in marches and activities within the Civil Rights Movement on behalf of her students for whom she wanted a better future.

Doris's parents had an expansive vision of Blackness. Her father taught her at a young age that throughout the world people of color were the majority, which mitigated any feelings of inferiority as she grew up. Her mother cast a womanist vision comparable to Alice Walker, teaching Doris that "our race is like a garden of flowers from ivory to ebony" and where people fell on that spectrum did not make a difference. Doris's mother and grandmother made their careers as teachers, so she followed in their path. Beginning in the late 1950s, as a young high school teacher at Wadleigh High School in New York City, Doris worked to use education as a door to justice and

equality for her students. It was in Harlem that she was inspired to participate in local and national marches, including the March on Washington.
As a committed teacher, who never married or had children, she considered
her students her children and she wanted more opportunities for them, so
she did what she could to help make a difference. Doris often stood up for
her students in ways that she did not for herself, including when she did
the work of an Assistant Principal for years at Wadleigh High, while only
being paid as a teacher.

Doris wanted to be a part of the swelling number of supporters at the
March on Washington, and although not a part of a group, she traveled
to DC by train determined to be "one of the bodies they had to count" as
they quantified the attendance at the historic event. Doris's decision to do
what she could when she could, at times caused her to drop everything to
join protests on the streets of Harlem in the 1950s and 1960s, even if it was
an unplanned march that she stumbled upon. An educator through and
through, she remained active with the Wadleigh High Alumni, and serves as
a board member for both the Goddard Riverside Community Center, and
the Alumni Association of Hunter College. Doris V. Brunson continues to
do community organizing in Harlem and is an active member of Abyssinian
Baptist Church where she sings in the choir.

* * *

Peggy Lucas grew up in Dolomite, Alabama, about twelve miles southwest
of the city of Birmingham. Her mother, who was a singer and a natural en-
courager, died in 1955 when Peggy was eleven years old and left an unfillable
void in her life. Peggy, who was the middle child, and her four siblings were
raised by their father with help from an aunt who lived near them. As a young
girl, Peggy was told a story which predated her birth about her grandfather
who was working in a small town in Alabama. He demanded money for the
work that he had completed, and ultimately pistol-whipped the White man
who would not pay him. When Peggy's grandfather returned home that
evening, he told his family to gather everything they could and they left town
by horse and buggy that night to avoid what likely could have been deadly
retaliation.[10] This story offered Peggy a formative model for bold stances
against injustice that she took with her during the Civil Rights Movement.

Peggy wondered if she would have been permitted to participate in the
Movement if her mother was still living.[11] She was the only one of her siblings who attended Mass meetings on Monday nights and conducted voter
education and registration door-to-door with her father Louis Lucas Jr., who
had been active in the Birmingham community for many years.

My father and I would go door-to-door asking our neighbors to become registered voters. He had been attending, the mass meetings, the Monday night meetings and, of course, he would bring that information home and that's what we would do. We had a script and it was teaching our neighbors how to read the Preamble to the Constitution. Some people were really afraid . . . and we had to convince them.[12]

Complicated voter registration processes put in place by White leaders to limit the Black community's access to the ballot resulted in the creation of citizenship schools to counter the suppressive efforts. The fact that they had to teach their neighbors to read the Preamble reflects the vestiges of systems that did not create equal opportunities for education for many Blacks who were forced to leave school, often without learning to read or write, in order to work and financially support their families.

Peggy's father modeled activism for her as they diligently worked to help other Blacks around Birmingham learn how to register to vote and how to make their political voices heard.[13] Her father taught her that exercising the right to vote was more important than any fear of retaliation. He taught that power and respect were gained through the ability to participate in the political process and elect persons you believed would best represent you at each level of government.

Peggy graduated from Westfield High School in 1962 and became a student at the local Miles College. She took the moral lessons she was taught at home and in her home church—St. John Baptist Church in Dolomite, Alabama—with her. While in college, Peggy increased her weekly involvement in the Movement when she was asked by Carlton Reese, the director of the Alabama Christian Movement for Human Rights (ACMHR) choir, to become a member and eventually record a fundraising album with them. In late April 1963, Peggy decided that she needed to do more than sing in the ACMHR choir and work one-on-one with neighbors to prepare them to register to vote, so she packed a little bag and told her father she was going to get arrested that day.[14] She always remembered that her father did not say anything to stop her, and she felt he was filled with an unspoken pride. As a part of the organized sit-ins Peggy went to J. J. Newberry's in Birmingham with a group of students from Miles College to attempt to order a hamburger at the lunch counter. She was arrested and charged with trespassing after refusing to leave until she was served. Her arrest prompted her older sister Shirley to get involved and commit a similar act, so Peggy would not be in a Birmingham jail without family. Identified now as a foot soldier in Birmingham,[15] she was jailed for five days and even placed in solitary confinement as a result of her civil rights activism. Peggy believes that the only reason she was not a part of the televised public showdown with Bull Connor and the powerful fire hoses that he ordered turned on protesters in Kelly Ingram Park is because she and other young people (including her sister) were already in jail. Louis Lucas's expectations of both communal and familial responsibility are evident in both of his daughters' active engagement.

Peggy's family feared that her arrest record had the potential to limit job opportunities in Birmingham, so she moved to Atlanta in 1964 to begin working and has remained there since. Peggy Lucas became a member of Ebenezer Baptist Church in Atlanta in 1978, where she has been an active participant in the women's ministry and the choir.

* * *

Rose Davis Schofield was raised in Elizabeth, New Jersey, and it was there that her activism took place primarily as a member of Mt. Teman A.M.E. Church. Although not supported by the women in her family, Schofield's grandfather supported her participation in protests arranged by her church and the local NAACP chapter. She recalls "White Only" signs in New Jersey and the blatant discrimination in labor practices that were deeply embedded in her city. As a teenager, Rose believed what her pastor Rev. Watts taught and preached—that any exclusions or limitations based simply on race were not right and they should be actively fought against. He also stressed that they would need to do the work to help themselves.

Rose took the lessons from her pastor to heart and looked for ways to actively challenge the injustices that were brought to her attention in mass meetings at Mt. Teman. When jails in Elizabeth, New Jersey, began to fill up with adults, the local NAACP chapter turned to children as a part of their strategy to overcrowd the facilities. Rose's grandfather gave formal permission for her to participate in NAACP activities by signing a consent form because of her age. Rose was ultimately arrested in August 1963 for chaining herself together with other young people in the middle of an active street in Elizabeth to bring attention to the need for systemic changes in the racially biased city and county construction contract bidding practices. When it was time for her release from the local jail, it was her grandfather who walked to multiple locations to pick her up.

Only a couple of weeks after her arrest for civil disobedience, and despite the objections of the women in her family, Rose's grandfather arranged for his teenage granddaughter to travel to the March on Washington to continue to fight for jobs and freedom. He trusted the men at the local bar who coordinated the bus trip from Roselle, New Jersey, to Washington, DC, so he bought a ticket for her to travel with them. Rose realized the historic moment and believed her presence would make a difference, and her grandfather knew that the collective values of the community would allow the massive event to be a good experience, even if family members did not accompany her. Rose recounts discussions around her participation in the Civil Rights Movement, including a debate on whether she could attend the March on Washington:

> I was 16 and my aunt . . . said no I couldn't go; they would never let me go anywhere. And then my grandfather happened to say I think she should go. I think it would be a good experience. And they said well she's 16. She'll be down there by herself . . . somehow my grandfather dug up the money, and I wound up on the bus and he knew these people, because it was going from some bar that had gotten up a bus load of people and they told him we'll look out for her.[16]

Rose's mother was not fully present in her life at the time, and her great-grandmother and great-aunt who raised her were afraid of White retaliation and did not think it was wise for her to participate in civil rights activities. The parents of these matriarchs had been enslaved and that proximity shaped their beliefs about what they should or should not do and the potential ramifications of challenging exploitive White power structures they had become comfortable working within. As Rose described:

> It was really rough in the house because believe it or not they actually had a slave mentality, because my great grandmother's parents were slaves, so they grew up with a slave mentality. They didn't believe in sending us to school. They told us that the only reason why they even sent us to school was because it was the law. Otherwise, they said they would have had us out there doing housework in the white man's house. I barely got through school. I had no idea. I was just going through the motion of going to school, because they didn't believe in education, so it was very fortunate that I even graduated from high school.[17]

Rose reflected that her grandfather did not take on the "slave mentality," which she described as the reason the older women in the home did not want to rock the boat and challenge White people. Instead, he believed in his granddaughter's passion for justice and freedom so he provided the critical support necessary for Rose to live out her purpose as a young woman willing to fight for equality.

The protection that her grandfather normally provided was taken on by other men from the community who gave their word that they would look out for Rose during the March on Washington. The communal orientation of northern and southern segregated communities reinforced the shared values and shared goals for progress, even when there was not full communal participation in the events that would provide the uplift.[18]

Rose's activism in the North reflected both the continuities and distinctions between southern and northern resistance. In one example, she was the only woman who mentioned the active alliances and involvement of members of the Jewish community in New Jersey. Today, Rose Schofield is an active member of Big Bethel A.M.E. Church in Atlanta, where she serves as a stewardess, usher, and member of the sign language ministry.

* * *

When I checked my voicemail one evening, I had a message saying, "This is Bessie Smith Sellaway . . . I'm just an old jail bird," and I knew she was definitely a woman I needed to interview. She was born in Round Oak, Georgia, near Macon, and lived there with her grandmother until it was time for her to start school. Direct activism was not something Bessie saw modeled in her home; however, she was acutely aware of the inequities between Blacks and Whites in her small town when she had to walk seven miles each way to kindergarten while White students passed her by on a school bus. Her father died before she was three years old, so her mother left Round Oak to seek better job opportunities about eighty miles north in Atlanta. Bessie's grandmother wanted her to have better educational opportunities than those available in Round Oak so Bessie also moved to Atlanta at age six and spent her formative years with her mother. Her first school was at Our Lady of Lourdes—A Black Catholic Church in Atlanta's Fourth Ward.

After graduating from David T. Howard High School, Bessie attended Spelman College, where she majored in Home Economics and was also certified in Early Childhood Education. She married her husband Joe while in college and soon became active in the Atlanta Movement. Her grandmother taught her to know God within herself, and encouraged her to always tell the truth, and Bessie marks these lessons from her grandmother as the genesis of her activism. Bessie grew spiritually in Lindsey Street Baptist Church under the leadership of Rev. H. W. Alexander, but she often attended meetings at Ebenezer Baptist, where Martin and A. D. King would provide strategies to test the laws of segregation by targeting actions at businesses they were seeking to integrate in downtown Atlanta. She remembers Martin Luther King Jr. stressing that if people could not refrain from violence, they needed to find another way to participate—by praying, raising money, comforting people, or something else.

While at a sit-in at a Woolworth department store, hecklers pulled Bessie's hair and sprayed bug spray at her and other protesters before police were called in and she was arrested for the first time. Throughout her many protests with other college students primarily from the Atlanta University Center, Bessie was arrested twice, spending multiple days in both the Atlanta Prison Farm and the Atlanta Fulton Jail. She still has the light blue receipts from the money that her mother and pastor put in her account at the jail allowing her to purchase toiletries and other items. Bessie explains that each time she was arrested she served multiple days in jail but was let out before the completion of the full sentence. They were told it was for "good behavior," but she notes the influence of the media attention that was spreading their actions and the overly aggressive White response around the world.

Bessie's mother, like many other adults in her all-Black neighborhood, thought she was setting herself up to be hurt, so she could not understand why her daughter felt so compelled to be active on the front lines of the Movement. Joe was supportive of her involvement with the exception of the time Bessie wanted to go to Mississippi with King for additional direct action. In that instance he was afraid she would be brought back in a coffin, so she did not go. Bessie continued to test laws in Atlanta with the hope of seeing them change so everyone would enjoy equal rights. She understood that equality would require more than protests because removing signs and unjust laws did not mean much until people changed their hearts.

After graduating from Spelman in 1963, Bessie and Joe, who was in the military, lived in Europe and various places in the United States for many years. After Joe's retirement, the Sellaways returned to Atlanta's Fourth Ward and remodeled the home she grew up in. It was at that time Bessie joined Ebenezer Baptist Church where she now participates in the Seniors Ministry and Women's Ministry of Ebenezer. She also remains committed to struggles for justice, and actively participated in multiple protests with the Occupy Atlanta, Black Lives Matter, and other movements.

* * *

Marjorie Wallace Smyth grew up in the Collegeville area of Birmingham, Alabama, one street over from the city's charismatic Movement leader, Reverend Fred Shuttlesworth. Each day she met Shuttlesworth's children at the corner and they walked to school together. For years she heard Shuttlesworth's messages of equal rights and the lessons he passed on to his children. As the youngest of eight, Marjorie describes herself as the feisty one, who would run and drink from the "Whites Only" water fountain while shopping at Parisian's department store just to see how the water tasted, much to the fear and dismay of her older sister. She grew up with the common knowledge of which days the Klan met, and she was made aware at an early age that there were certain things that Black people did not do. This knowledge did not sit well with her. Marjorie's mother died when she was seven years old, but at a young age her mother taught her the Twenty-Third Psalm and to serve a God she knew in her heart. This was a lesson that would later allow her to put other God-talk that did not align with a God-like walk into perspective.

After her mother died, Marjorie's older sister, Ruth, stayed and helped care for the younger siblings. Her mother's sister lived down the street and she stepped in to inspect their attire and hair to make sure they were presentable before they went out. It was instilled in Marjorie at an early age that she was representing her family when she did things outside of the home. Marjorie's father, who conducted Bible Study while also teaching men to read the Bible at the steel mill where he worked, taught her to pray and emphasized the importance of education so his children would not be relegated to cleaning the homes of White women in Birmingham. Marjorie began resisting the systems of segregation as a young child, asking questions about how Whites could worship God but act in ways that she believed to be ungodly.

Her civil rights activism began as a teenager in Birmingham, where she often left school to participate in mass meetings and marches. In one such march during Birmingham's children's movement, Marjorie went to the 16th Street Baptist Church with her niece Linda, who was three years younger. As they left the church and lined up to march, the police stormed in and snatched young Linda, who Marjorie had positioned directly in front of her so she could keep an eye on her. Marjorie then had to not only tell her family that she took Linda with her and they skipped school to go to the protest, but since her niece was arrested on a Friday, Linda would be kept in jail over the weekend.

Opting to not join SNCC, which was becoming too radical for her under Stokely Carmichael's leadership, Marjorie maintained her focus on grassroots activism while a student at Tuskegee Institute (now University), at times traveling deep into rural areas, including Union Springs, Alabama, where she recalled homes without running water and people who signed their names with an "X." She focused her time in those communities in order to teach them to write so they could register to vote. She believed educating them to vote would make a lasting difference, so Marjorie made letters to teach them the alphabet and taught them to write in block print. After college graduation, she went to visit her sister in New York City as a graduation gift and she has remained in the city ever since.

Marjorie is an active member of First A.M.E. Bethel Church in Harlem, where she serves as a steward and coordinator of many of the church's community outreach missions, including distributing over 600 backpacks each year with back-to-school items for neighborhood youth. She also participates in other social and political action activities as a member of Delta Sigma Theta Sorority, Inc.

* * *

Beatrice Perry Soublet comes from a family of activists, who were leaders in the New Orleans, Louisiana, community where she was raised. Her great-grandfather, Pierre Landry, became the first Black mayor in Donaldsonville, Louisiana, and served as a legislator in both the Louisiana House and Senate. Her grandfather, Henderson Dunn, founded the Hume Child Center in New Orleans as one of the oldest preschools for Black children in the South, and actively fought for equal pay and opportunities for Black teachers in Louisiana. Beatrice's father was active in citizenship work, and both of her parents were involved in the NAACP. She understood the inequities that were prominent in the South even as she saw her parents actively asserting their rights as citizens.

In one instance, Beatrice recalls when her father went to register to vote wearing his Boy Scout leader uniform as a cloak of respectability and had to have a White male to vouch for him. This was what Black people faced and worked to challenge at the ballot box once the goal of becoming a registered voter was obtained. At another time, during a shopping trip as a child, her mother defiantly placed her hand in a pair of stockings to see if the color would work for her skin tone, much to the dismay of the White saleswoman. Beatrice recalls,

> I don't care when you came down to the store. Everybody who came after you was getting waited on, and my mom used to say, "my daughter and I were here first" and this was long before integration [or] anything . . . this was when you used to buy stockings, and the salesclerk would put her hand in there to show my mama . . . , the shade—my mama said your hand is not the color of mine, let me put it on. I said, oh, oh God. But it was just the sense that you deserve better.[19]

Growing up in Louisiana, Beatrice described her mother as having a very fair complexion that actually may have been similar to the saleswoman's; however, her mother's race consciousness was such that she taught her daughter by example to always expect better treatment, even when it was not given. Beatrice's response of "oh, oh God," appears to have been an expression of embarrassment for the scene her mother might potentially create in the store, rather than a response of concern that the White woman might perceive her defiance as a challenge punishable by some form of direct retaliation.

Beatrice was shaped by the stories of her grandfathers and the boldness of her mother and father. Her willingness to challenge segregation laws and customs was evident as a teenager when she sat on the White side of the waiting room at the ophthalmologist office because they had magazines and other things that the Black side did not have.

With a legacy of activism and the support of her family, Beatrice's formal civil rights activism began when she was a student at Bennett College in Greensboro, North Carolina. The first time she was arrested, she said she did not want to have to look at the hateful stares she assumed she and other students would encounter as they sat-in, so she took Plato's *Republic* with her to read and keep her distracted while they intentionally broke the Jim Crow laws in Greensboro's S&W Cafeteria. After another one of Beatrice's arrests, her fiancé Tony Stanley asked her why she did what she did, and although she was only about nineteen years old and not married yet, her immediate response was that she did it for their children. Beatrice understood that she had opportunities as a result of the sacrifices her parents and grandparents made fighting for equality, and she believed it was up to her to do the same for her unborn children. She was a firm believer that each generation should not suffer the same indignities as the previous ones.

After the Movement, Beatrice continued to join fights for freedom and justice, including being arrested in Washington, DC, while protesting South African apartheid in the 1980s. In 2005, following her evacuation from New Orleans because of Hurricane Katrina, she moved to Atlanta where her daughter lives. Today, Beatrice is a member of Our Lady of Lourdes Catholic Church in Atlanta where she is a leader with the Social Action Ministry, and often leads the Eucharist and liturgy. Beatrice is a published poet, and an active member of Delta Sigma Theta Sorority. She participated in this study as a part of the Big Bethel A.M.E. Church in Atlanta, where her daughter Kathryn Stanley was a member.

* * *

A. Lenora Taitt-Magubane is a native of New York City, and was raised between New York and Trinidad because her Trinidadian father wanted her to receive a quality education, so she attended junior high school in her father's home country. Lenora's parents taught her to have a strong sense of self and equality, and she expected to be able to engage society without limitations ascribed to her race or gender. She was a leader who sought ways to make a difference. While a student at Spelman College in Atlanta, Georgia, Lenora was the president of the YWCA, and active in the Glee Club, Drama Club, and Canterbury Association. As a northerner, steeped in a West Indian sense of self, Atlanta was the place Lenora experienced blatant segregation for the first time on a city bus, prompting her involvement in the Civil Rights Movement. In March 1960, under the direction of her history professor Howard Zinn, Lenora's efforts to integrate a downtown theater in Atlanta by attending a production of "My Fair Lady" with Zinn, Professor J. P. Cochran, and other Black students were captured in local and national media including a featured article in *Jet* magazine and the *Atlanta Journal Constitution*.

As a leader, organizer, and strategist with the Committee on the Appeal for Human Rights (the Atlanta Student Movement), Lenora was arrested a few times and worked to create organizational systems within the jail that enabled students to receive financial support to make necessary purchases from the canteen, and to also maintain their schoolwork. Lenora graduated from Spelman in 1961 and began graduate school in Social Work at Atlanta University after encouragement from Whitney Young, who was the dean of the well-respected school of Social Work at the time and soon after became the Executive Director of the National Urban League.

Lenora later worked with the Student Nonviolent Coordinating Committee (SNCC) in southwest Georgia. Her father was ill during the height of her involvement, and even when he died, she went to the SNCC office first to make sure Freedom Riders safely reached their destination first. After leaving Georgia, she continued her activism in New York City. While she believes her father was supportive, Lenora's mother was concerned she would have an arrest record that would prevent her from getting a prized job as a civil servant, but she did not stop her. Although no one else in her family participated directly in the Movement, Fannie Lou Hamer and Ella Baker adopted her as a "daughter" and "niece." She participated in this study as a member of the Abyssinian Baptist Church in Harlem. Today, she continues to work for justice in New York City and South Africa.

In summary, all of these Black Churchwomen openly shared the stories of their upbringing as well as their experiences during the Civil Rights Movement. Some of the women, including Gwendolyn Zoharah Simmons and A. Lenora Taitt-Magubane, became what Belinda Robnett describes as community bridge leaders, and secondary formal leaders[20] as they organized and led particular aspects of the Movement with SNCC and the Atlanta Movement.

Sociohistorical Context of Black Churchwomen's Activism

Realities of a Racist Society

The fear of brutal retaliation from Whites if a Black person did not fall in line with racialized social norms was a daily reality, particularly in the Jim Crow South. Afraid of losing the power, position, and property they inherited in the womb,[21] Whites used whatever forms of repression and oppression they could to maintain their possessions and status. Beginning in the 1890s and accelerated by the 1915 release of the film *The Birth of a Nation*, Whites' perception of Black progress, and romanticized notions of an antebellum South, led to the implementation of Jim Crow laws that severely limited equal political and civil rights.[22] The corresponding resurgence of White supremacist organizations including the Ku Klux Klan (KKK) and the White Citizens' Council (WCC) began to strike fear in the lives of Blacks through physical violence and intimidation.[23] Concealing themselves with white hoods and robes, White men, women, and children paraded through cities and Black neighborhoods to project numerical strength and often to announce that they would return later to enact more destructive measures unless Blacks halted whatever actions Whites opposed. Klan members left their notorious calling card—burning crosses on lawns in Black communities—as a reminder that they would set fire to homes and churches of Black leaders whom they perceived as agitators or representatives of Black advancement.[24]

The infraction that prompted the violence was often something as minor as looking a White person in the eye, "getting too big for their own good" by working to achieve a life beyond the limited expectations many Whites had for Blacks, or standing up for the rights of themselves and their families. As domestic terrorists, the KKK and similar White supremacist organizations responded violently to actions they deemed as dishonoring Whites' assumed superiority. Klan members often lynched Black men who were accused, often without any basis, of bringing dishonor on White womanhood by looking at, speaking to, or even consensually having sex with a White woman.[25] After exacting their own form of vigilante justice, Klansmen often further terrorized Black neighborhoods by parading maimed bodies through the streets.[26] The Klan's activities surged again during the 1950s and 1960s when the fight for civil rights by Blacks threatened the social, political, and economic entitlement that racist Whites felt they alone deserved. This period also saw the rise of the White Citizens' Council, whose middle- and upper-class membership of doctors, lawyers, and business owners led some to refer to them as the "White Collar Klan" as they responded to the 1954 Supreme Court ruling of *Brown v. Board of Education* with forms of social and economic oppression.

Socioeconomic Dynamics and Migration

After the period of enslavement, 3.9 million Black people were emancipated but offered no property or resources with which to take care of their families and make a living. As the nation's economy shifted from the free labor society and natural calamity struck southern fields, the work, even at extremely low wages, dried up. Triggered by increased job opportunities as European immigration slowed and World War I began, America's first great migration took place from 1910 to 1940, when nearly 1.6 million Blacks fled the fields and shacks in the South to factories and ghettos in the North.[27] It was during this time of the first great migration that various families including those of Doris Brunson, Rose Davis Schofield, and Patricia Pates Eaton left the Deep South for the North.

During the second great migration, nearly five million more Black people left the South between 1940 and 1970, looking for greater economic freedom and opportunity. White Citizens' Councils anchored in beliefs of White supremacy linked to their interpretation of Christianity arose in the mid-1950s with a belief "there can be no compromise on segregation." The chairman of the Dallas County, Alabama, Council was lawyer Alston Keith, who said the White Citizens' Council must "make if difficult, if not impossible, for any Negro who advocates desegregation to find and hold a job, get credit, or renew a mortgage."[28] As White people's retaliation through the KKK and WCC increased in response to Blacks' pursuit of freedom and independence, including at the ballot box, Black men and women left the sweat- and blood-filled fields, along with the harsh and often violent realities of lynching, economic exploitation, and de facto and de jure segregation of the South, for the deceptively appealing bright lights and "good paying" factory jobs that still relegated them to subservient spaces of existence in the North.

Factories in the Northeast and Midwest actively recruited Black workers to the most menial and dangerous jobs, but the pay was often significantly more than working as a sharecropper in the South so they took both the opportunity for economic advancement and potential social risk associated with substandard working and living environments. Advertisements were placed in Black newspapers with national distribution such as the *Chicago*

Defender, outlining the socioeconomic benefits that awaited Blacks in the North.[29] One benefit that was not overtly advertised but was inherently understood was the ability to escape the increasing physical and economic violence in the South. Lynching, intimidation through burning homes, poisoning livestock, and more, pushed some men to often leave first to find employment and some form of stability before sending for other family members. Women also made the journey north at times as the first in their families in an effort to escape the domestic work at extremely low pay that placed them in constant proximity to White men's sexual advances and at times rape.[30] Through state-centered clubs and groups such as First A.M.E. Bethel's South Carolina Club or Georgia Club, some Black churches also played a role in helping to encourage newly arriving northern workers to embrace factory work. These religious and communal groups also created a transition space when the extended family members of southerners made their way to large bustling cities, providing places to stay, connections to jobs, and a small feeling of home through church experiences that held vestiges of the south.[31] Churches also created spaces for social events and educational opportunities from fashion shows and tea parties to night classes to enhance literacy with partial ambitions of communal-empowerment and social advancement.

Many of the young women active in the Civil Rights Movement in the North and Midwest had parents and grandparents who escaped the South by any means possible. Some started out on foot from small towns and most finished by train, taking paths from Alabama to Ohio, Michigan, and Indiana; from Mississippi and Louisiana to St. Louis, Chicago, and Detroit; from Florida, Georgia, and South and North Carolina to Washington, DC, Philadelphia, and New York; or from Arkansas, Texas, and Louisiana to California.[32]

Redlining and restrictive housing covenants regulated where Blacks could live throughout the North, South, and West. Prior to the Fair Housing Act of 1968, the federal government enacted laws that enabled insurance companies, homebuilders, and others to force Blacks into segregated communities often without a consistent level of infrastructural investment through Whites-only covenants.[33] Racial segregation was structurally built one brick at a time with the support of the government through unjust laws and policies that were developed by Whites without the ability for Blacks to vote and elect persons at local, state, or federal levels who would represent their best interest. These socioeconomic dynamics reinforced segregated living, which created both benefits and limitations.

Benefits within Segregation

Restrictions from living in integrated communities created both advantages and disadvantages. In segregated communities, Black parents were able to shelter their children from some of the painful experiences and daily indignities associated with racism and hatred as they navigated sensitive interactions with White people. Some of the women in this study, such as Marjorie Wallace Smyth, thought their parents were mean or too strict because they would not allow children to leave their community's corner stores run by familiar men and women and go downtown where the White people shopped. Marjorie and others later realized that their parents' prohibition was actually a form of protection meant to shield them from painful encounters with Whites on buses or in stores that could shatter their understanding of the loving world their own Black community provided.[34]

Many Black parents tried to limit their children's exposure to the harshness of Whites by doing the shopping without children in tow or strategically using mail order services like the Sears and Roebuck catalog to browse options and make selections from the comfort of their homes.[35] Retail environments provided prime testing grounds for respectable and equal treatment since Black shoppers were expected to pay the same price as Whites but were not given the same quality of customer service. Consequently, these spaces became hotbeds of social protests and individual acts of speaking out transformed into collective campaigns of economic boycotts with the desired goal of equal service as current customers and equal opportunities as future employees. Segregation enabled parents to shield and protect their children from many potentially negative social encounters. The love experienced in the Black community was strong among neighbors and found even greater concentration in churches and all-Black schools.

There were benefits to the segregated Black schools, which functioned as sources for systemic change that would likely not have taken place in integrated schools.[36] These were far from the good old days, yet despite limited resources, subpar physical buildings, and more, Black school teachers and administrators taught students to be proud of who they were and prepared them to achieve academically and socially at the highest possible level. As the Civil Rights Movement continued to expand, young high school and college students possessed the perfect combination of being naively fearless and optimistically hopeful, which enabled them to take greater risks than they may have realized in order to gain more than their parents and grandparents could have imagined.

The influence of Historically Black Colleges and Universities (HBCUs) as incubators for activism was experienced throughout the South. Birmingham native Peggy Lucas was already involved in the Movement with her father as a teenager, but after young leaders spoke to students attending Miles College she made a commitment to do more than sing with the ACMHR choir. Marjorie Wallace Smyth became involved in the Movement in Birmingham also thanks to students from Miles College who regularly visited her high school to plant ideas of freedom and rights in the minds of young students who were often excited to join in the fight. Marjorie's involvement continued when she became a student at Tuskegee Institute where she joined a local civil rights group of likeminded students. Beatrice Soublet's exposure to and influence by CORE happened as a result of their collegiate targeting while she was a student at Bennett College, where she along with students at North Carolina A&T were taught about nonviolence as a tool for activism.

Lillian Sue Bethel, Bessie Sellaway, and A. Lenora Taitt-Magubane found out when protests, mass meetings, and other movement events were going to happen through informal communication channels at Albany State and Spelman Colleges. While historic images might lead you to believe that the streets and jails were constantly filled with freedom-loving coeds, in reality, many Black colleges' official support for student activism varied greatly. Pearlie Craft Dove explained that sometimes the variation was based on pressure presidents received from state legislators as state-funded institutions. At other times it had to do with fear of losing financial support from White donors, or it was as a result of the president's own conservatism and worry about the safety of students and the potential long-term impact such activities could have on the uplift of the Black community if they were arrested.[37]

Beatrice recalled that Dr. Willa Beatrice Player, the first woman president of the all-women's Bennett College, was concerned about students' safety, but she was proud and supportive of her students' participation in the Movement in Greensboro, at times meeting with students in her office to tell them so. Johnsie Williams Thomas, who was also a student at Bennett, recalls activist activities being mentioned during the vespers service on campus.[38] Conversely, Dr. Albert Manley, the first Black and first male president of Spelman College, was not very supportive. Lenora met with Manley to try to gain support for the stances she and other students took or to at least help him have a better understanding of their goals.[39] Following a student sit-in in March 1960, Manley commended Spelman students for their courage, but he also chided them to focus on obtaining their education since that was the reason they were in college.[40] At the neighboring Clark College (now Clark Atlanta

University), Dr. Pearlie Clark Dove was a professor who gave students active in the Movement extra assignments so that they would not fall behind while in jail. She also held the hands of parents to offer comfort to those who did not understand why their children would risk the investment their families were making in them to attend college.[41] Lillian believed that Dr. William H. Dennis, the President of Albany State, was forced to suspend her and other students who were arrested for their participation in the Freedom Ride protest in 1961. She justified his actions explaining, "He didn't have a choice. This came down from the State, because it was a State School."[42] Despite the mixed responses from school administrators, the teaching from professors committed to advancement inside and outside of the classroom as well as the positive pressure to join in with others made the all-Black high schools and colleges critical spaces for the cultivation of activism.

Segregated schools enabled ideas of radical change to be birthed among many young people who later reflected on being too naïve to realize the full extent of the possible ramifications of their choices. While all the students at these schools were Black, they were not monolithic socially, economically, or politically. Some believed in and felt compelled to participate in the Movement, despite the risk to their education, while others did not. Beatrice Soublet and Lillian Sue Bethel described some of their classmates and even roommates who decided not to participate because they did not want to risk losing scholarships or being expelled from school, saying that their parents sent them to college to get an education and not to join a movement, likely repeating the words that had been drilled into them. Others simply did not believe in the goals or methods of the Civil Rights Movement. Although not every student at a Black college participated, those who did, like the women in this study, recognized the urgency of the moment. While in an Atlanta jail, A. Lenora Taitt organized a schedule to keep her and the other young women focused. The schedule included two study periods each day so they could maintain their schoolwork.[43] These women took precautions to maintain their academic standings to the best of their ability, but their actions also showed a willingness to sacrifice their formal education and future careers for the Movement if necessary.[44]

Black-Owned Media

From newspapers to magazines and radio, Black-owned media facilitated the spreading of images, thoughts, and ideas between the North, South, and West, and as a result helped to influence activism and garner support for the Civil Rights Movement. Women I interviewed in both the US North and

South recalled family discussions about articles in primarily northern newspapers such as the *Pittsburgh Courier*, the *New York Amsterdam News*, or the *Afro-American*, that showcased the activist stances being taken to continue the struggle for freedom. One of the main groups in the North that women remembered hearing about were members of Abyssinian Baptist Church in Harlem and the Reverend Adam Clayton Powell Jr. who pastored the church from 1937 to 1971. Beginning in the late 1930s Powell led protests and marches in places where Blacks shopped or paid for services but were not given equal opportunities for employment and advancement. In one such effort, Local No. 338 of the Retail, Wholesale and Food Employees' Union in New York began "Don't Buy Where You Can't Work" economic campaigns in 1937. By 1961, as other civil rights organizations began to look at economic factors, they drew from the wisdom of earlier efforts. In the 24 years since their efforts began, the Union experienced success "bargaining with the employer for improving working conditions and a greater share of America's worth," which enabled them to boast in the *Amsterdam News* that more than 500 members in the Harlem section took home almost $3 million in salaries a year in addition to medical services for themselves and their families as well as sick and retirement benefits.[45] Newspaper reports on such events inspired a sense of activism and respect throughout the nation.

Mamie Till-Mobley's bold decision to publicize the raw images of her 14-year-old son Emmett Till's brutal murder in *Jet* magazine in 1955 exposed the deadly realities Blacks faced in the South. Till's murder marked a coming-of-age moment for many young people whose parents could no longer shelter them from the painful race realities that could lead to their death. Black-owned media provided coverage and critiques that White media did not.[46] In North Carolina and New York, Pat Smalls and Rose Fofana both recalled sitting around the dinner table as their families discussed images of lynching, including the brutal murder of Till as reported in *Jet*,[47] and reports about sit-ins in Black newspapers like the *Norfolk Journal and Guide*.[48] The Black-owned media outlets covered the full spectrum of realities of Black existence throughout the United States, from high society international travel, to church announcements, social events, protest activities, and violence against Blacks. Newspapers like the *Pittsburgh Courier* also helped start and promote campaigns such as the Double V (victory at home and abroad) campaign during World War II.

Black radio stations, such as Atlanta's WERD, played a significant role in connecting the community and communicating messages without a White filter. DJs not only played protest music but also helped announce when mass meetings would happen and provide a platform for organizers, including

Lenora Taitt, to speak to more than those who attended formal mass meetings.[49] The DJs knew the community and used the language of the people which could move listeners to direct action and other forms of support, in ways that were often leveraged as a strategic tool. Black media planted seeds that often took root when young women later became associated with activist churches or colleges or when they created individual acts of protest because they were inspired and emboldened by the media coverage of others.

There were many sociohistorical factors that influenced the activism of young Black women during the Civil Rights Movement, all who lived at the intersections of race, gender, and socioeconomic class. Black women relocated to northern and urban cities in search of better job opportunities and economic advancement. All-Black schools provided environments that became kindling for the activism that sparked all over the nation, and Black-owned media helped to promote and support campaigns.

The Influence of the Black Church

Since its beginning, socioreligious activism has been a part of the core reason for the existence of the Black Church.[50] Socioreligious activism reflects a belief that religious practitioners have social responsibilities to act in ways that reflect and reinforce the love and justice modeled by their God. For many Movement participants, the "religious" aspect of activism is a part of the spiritual ethos at the very heart of their being. This spiritual sense is central to African-centered notions of religion, and as a result socioreligious activism that permeates areas of health, politics, and more are not always limited to a particular denomination or faith tradition. Such activism indicates a conscious commitment to action, not passivity or blind agreement; socioreligious activism means acting in a way that challenges injustice deliberately and forthrightly.

Since the days of enslavement, the Black Church has served as a place for sharing information and supporting strategies of survival and resistance.[51] This ranged from teaching methods of working efficiently so that tasks would be completed with minimal brutality from overseers, to plans for insurrections such as those organized by Denmark Vesey and Nat Turner, to Harriet Tubman facilitating stops on the Underground Railroad and orchestrating military strategies during the Civil War. Historian C. Eric Lincoln argues that the very existence of the Black Church was the "concrete evidence of the determination of Black Christians to separate themselves from the White Christians, whose cultural style and spiritual understanding made no provision for racial inclusiveness at a level acceptable to Black People."[52]

The fight for freedom and justice through socioreligious activism was a central aspect of the Civil Rights Movement in the Black Church community. From the use of churches as the primary location for weekly mass meetings, to the reappropriation of religious songs into Movement songs, and the generous sprinkling of well-known scriptures in speeches designed to motivate action, religion permeated and undergirded the Movement. The Black Church as a place for dignity and self-determination has a unique role in Black Freedom Struggles.

Migration shifted the geographical locations but not the deep faith connections of Black people who left the South for the North and West. Patricia Pates Eaton was an active member of Abyssinian Baptist Church in Harlem when I interviewed her, but she grew up in Chicago. Her parents made the journey to the Midwest from Mound Bayou and Macon, Mississippi, and stayed closely connected to the South through family members, including Patricia's aunt and uncle, Sadie and Fulton Ford, the owners of White Rose Cleaners in Mississippi. Her uncle Fulton Ford's brother Louis, was Mamie Till-Mobley's pastor in Chicago, so Till-Mobley stayed with Patricia's aunt and uncle during the trial of her son Emmett Till, and had a designated driver to take her back and forth from their house to the courthouse.[53] The connections to a safe place to live and transportation during what was the most trying time of Mamie's life were made through the Black church and the corresponding close familial and communal networks.

Many older activists eagerly adopted religious language, acknowledging religion as the most powerful vehicle by which to generate long-lasting support across generations of primarily southern Blacks, and persons "Up South" in the North who faced different struggles but also supported southern efforts to fund organizations including the Southern Christian Leadership Conference (SCLC) and Student Nonviolent Coordinating Committee (SNCC). A few northern churches including Abyssinian Baptist and Mt. Teman A.M.E. had pastors who took active roles in preaching and modeling direct engagement. Without the social stability of the Black Church, and the empowering beliefs of an expansive religious understanding of love, the nonviolent activism of the Movement may not have succeeded in its long fight for freedom and justice. The Black Church is certainly not without its flaws, and it was not the only Black institution creating physical space for the expansion of the work, but it was the most central and longstanding.[54]

Religious activism was not limited to the traditional church. One of the most clearly identified socioreligious activist organizations was the SCLC, which grew out of the marches and protests in Montgomery, Alabama, and other southern cities in the late 1950s. The organization was the brainchild of a diverse group, many of whom were without the same explicit religious leanings, yet were steeped in the same socioreligious ethos as the communities their work would serve. In 1957, three strategists, Ella Baker, a Black Christian woman, Bayard Rustin, a Black Quaker man, and Stanley Levinson, a White Jewish man, organized what would come to be known as the SCLC at Levinson's kitchen table, where the working papers that established the organization were drafted by Rustin and edited by Baker.[55] The SCLC, and its affiliates such as the Nashville Christian Leadership Council and the Virginia Christian Leadership Council, had a goal of promoting love and justice through direct action in nonviolent ways.

In the fifth working paper presented at the initial gathering during the founding of the SCLC, a method for training and dispatching nonviolent shock troops and offering recognition for their risk was considered. "It has been suggested that the protest movement gives a public award to each person who suffers physical or loss of property in the campaign. It is further suggested that an appropriate award might be a Bible inscribed by the protest chairman."[56] The reward for the risk was the reinforcement of the religious foundation that was a part of the bedrock of the community's socioreligious activism.

Similarly, at the founding of SNCC in April of 1960, charter members developed a statement of purpose, drafted by James Lawson, which also reflected the socioreligious activism from which the organization was born.[57] The statement read in part:

> We affirm the philosophical or *religious ideal of nonviolence as the foundation of our purpose, the pre-supposition of our faith, and the manner of our action.* Nonviolence as it *grows from Judaic-Christian traditions seeks a social order of justice permeated by love.* Integration of human endeavor represents the crucial first step towards such a society. . . . By appealing to conscience and standing on the moral nature of human existence, nonviolence nurtures the atmosphere in which reconciliation and justice become actual possibilities.[58]

SNCC's overt emphasis on nonviolence as a presupposition of their faith and a social order of justice permeated by love, expresses a socioreligious ethos that existed within the Black community and was expanded on through this movement work.

However, even while religion and faith were vital to the Movement, not all Black churches were willing to participate. C. Eric Lincoln explains that the Civil Rights Movement affirmed and challenged the Black Church's understanding of its responsibility as an agent of social change. Lincoln criticizes

Black Church leaders who professed involvement through the SCLC, but really only offered financial support, preferring to not visually associate with activists. Amelia Boynton Robinson, Wyatt T. Walker, and others noted that many Black pastors were afraid to open their own churches for meetings.[59]

Lincoln's observation of the limited participation of many Black churches in the Movement reinforces what has been known anecdotally for years. While the faces captured by the media were often those of Black clergymen, within individual communities, a minority of the Black clergy were actually activists.[60] Optimistic figures report that 43 percent of all Black churches participated in the Civil Rights Movement in at least some small way, most of them southern rural churches in which the inequalities that Blacks faced were more pronounced than in some of the urban environments.[61] Civil rights veteran Wyatt T. Walker observed that up to 90 percent of the ministers in Birmingham were *not* supportive of the efforts of the SCLC, even during the height of the Movement.[62] Whatever the percentage, it is clear that there are very few instances of even half of the Black Church community participating in the Civil Rights Movement; perhaps future research will provide more precise evidence of engagement.

There are various reasons why many of the Black churches and their pastors did not participate in the Movement. Some churches were simply too small to hold the number of people who attended the weekly mass meetings. Others became increasingly afraid of White retaliation as the bombings of churches and homes of those who were associated with the activism increased throughout the South and North. There were more than fifty bombings in Birmingham between 1947 and 1965, including the 1957 bombing of Allen Temple A.M.E. Church in Bessemer, where choir members were hit with plaster and debris when the bomb exploded,[63] and the most well-known 1963 bombing of the 16th Street Baptist Church. Growing up in Birmingham as a child, Marjorie Wallace Smyth remembers the windows of her home rattling many times by the impact of the bombs set off at Rev. Fred Shuttlesworth's nearby home.[64] Fear was real, but faith enabled them to push through it.

Amelia Boynton Robinson recalls that in Selma, Alabama, they often struggled to get ministers involved.

> Convincing the black ministers that the time to help their people was now and the place was right here was harder. Almost all ministers had to be begged to let us have meetings in their churches (we could not go to the armory, schools, courthouse, and other political places) and after we persuaded them, the church would be opened by the sexton but the ministers would conveniently disappear at the meeting time.[65]

Boynton Robinson notes that after a few years and the brutal treatment of some of the young SNCC volunteers like Bernard and Colia Lafayette who came to help Selma residents stand up for their rights, a few churches and ministers began to offer help, but many remained largely uncommitted to the full struggle for Black freedom. Some ministers would not stand up and push for changes out of fear of repercussions from White persons who had originally given the land for churches, or who provided resources that assisted the church on annual days and in times of financial difficulty. In yet other cases, ministers who enjoyed some level of status within the White community did not want to jeopardize their privileges and perks, so they did not openly challenge the status quo. These ministers sold their silence for small trinkets of personal benefit that did not help their church members or the wider community they served. Not all the women in my study attended activist churches; some of them attended churches on Sundays with their family where both their ministers and members were silent on civil rights issues, so on Monday evenings they joined mass meetings at different churches which were committed to standing up and speaking out. As young women, they approached their community as a dynamic space that did not require a firm allegiance to a passive form of faith, but rather active freedom faith.

Peggy Lucas, Alicia Roberts, and Marjorie Wallace Smyth recall going to churches to attend Mass meetings on Monday nights to find out the information regarding the local movement in Birmingham, as well as to participate in a transformative communal religious experience that inspired them to continue fighting for justice. These women did not always have the support of their home church or pastor, but they did not allow that to thwart their participation, instead embracing the support of other churches and pastors within the broader Birmingham community.[66]

Socioreligious activism has been a part of the Black Church in America since its creation, but only a minority of Black churches actively participated in the Civil Rights Movement. The low numbers of actual participants disrupt the popular narrative but reinforces social movement theory that suggests that activist participation is rarely over 20 percent. Although the number of churches participating was small, the faith of the people who crammed into the churches that were not afraid to open their doors for the Movement was very large.

The sociohistorical underpinnings of Black Churchwomen's activism presented here are socioeconomic factors in the larger society: segregated neighborhoods that created communities where love and care armed Blacks to face indignities from Whites on the outside; media outlets that covered news of importance to the social and political well-being of the Black community; and a heritage of socioreligious activism in the Black Church. Molded by these influences, many Black people, including the women in this study, mobilized a struggle for all. Through their ongoing activism they practiced a lived religion of justice and freedom that, while a part of a legacy within Black liberation, found unique expression for women in the Civil Rights Movement. An aspect of this expression can be understood through three virtue ethics—freedom faith, courageous resistance, and Theo-moral imagination—that I identify through the lived experiences of Black Church-women whose beliefs about God and influence from the community led them to be active during the US Civil Rights Movement.

Ella Baker

A Believer in Freedom and Black Women's Leadership

Born in Norfolk, Virginia, on December 13, 1903, to Georgianna (Anna) Ross Baker and Blake Baker, Ella Josephine Baker was forged for the fight for freedom at a very young age. Raised in a religious and at times rebellious family, her formerly enslaved maternal grandfather, Mitchell Ross, was determined to create opportunities for his family and others and expand their realities of freedom. Ross was a well-known Baptist pastor who focused on teaching and serving the people and communities in four churches on his circuit compared to what he seemed to deem as more shallow charismatic communication from the pulpit that did not change the substance of a person's life.[1] As the founder of Roanoke Chapel Baptist Church, Baker's grandfather allowed her to sit next to him in the pulpit as a child in the seat normally reserved for a visiting minister (much to the dismay of her mother) and travel with him as he ministered to the churches on his circuit.[2] Her mother, Anna, was active with Baptist women's missionary gatherings locally, throughout the state of North Carolina, and the broader region. She often involved her daughter in missionary activities. By the age of seven, Baker was a leader in the Sunshine Club, which was a missionary adjunct, and after joining the church at age nine, she noted reading the full Bible two or three times by the age of ten.[3]

Her mother, and women like her in the community, were important influences who sought familial and communal uplift through both Christian virtues and education. Baker was taught by her mother the virtues of humility and service to others, especially since her relatively middle-class upbringing came with an obligation to other women and children without access to education and other privileges her family enjoyed.[4] Historian Barbara

Ella Baker, Atlantic City, NJ, August 10, 1964. Ella Baker speaking at a private meeting of MFDP delegates at Union Temple Baptist Church. She argued against accepting the Credentials Committee compromise. Source: 1976 George Ballis/Take Stock/TopFoto

Ransby describes the activist and woman-centered faith of Baker's mother and the other women as akin to the Social Gospel popularized by Walter Rauschenbusch and others, but with an even greater connection to the points of pain and the solutions the women provided by creating orphanages, aiding the sick and elderly, raising funds and providing scholarships to Black students at Historically Black Colleges and Universities, and other church-sponsored educational institutions.[5] As Ransby notes, the religion of Ella Baker's mother and the Black Baptist women Baker was shaped by was "an activist religion that urged women to act as positive agents for change in the world."[6]

As a trained teacher, Anna Baker made sure that education and opportunities for advancement were fundamental in the Baker household. Ella Baker and her siblings were taught to read by their mother before they reached formal school age. Baker excelled in school and began attending boarding school at Shaw Academy in Raleigh, North Carolina, in 1918 and continued her studies at Shaw through her collegiate days. During this time, her critical thinking around the Bible and the role of the Black church appear to expand in ways that enabled her to make independent choices regarding how faith would operate in her life. She was deeply influenced by the intellectual rigor of her mentor Benjamin Brawley, who was her professor, debate coach, and adviser for the campus newspaper Baker wrote for. Baker's skills as a public speaker, which were developed in the Baptist church of her youth, and a debater sharpened as a member of Shaw's debate team enabled her to advocate for what she saw as more just conditions on campus in the areas of student attire, curriculum, and more, even if the issues were not of personal concern for her. Ella Baker graduated from Shaw University in April 1927 as the valedictorian. She spoke at commencement encouraging her classmates to "Awake youth of the land and accept this noble challenge of salvaging the strong ship of civilization by the anchors of right, justice and love."[7] Unable to afford to begin graduate study in sociology at the University of Chicago, Baker moved to New York in June and lived on W 152nd Street in Harlem with her cousin Martha, who had been raised with her as a sister, and Martha's husband. Baker was not sure of what her next steps would be, but she was determined to not be limited by the seemingly only career choice available to educated women, a schoolteacher, so she explored what New York had to offer.

The transition to New York City opened an exciting and stimulating world for Baker as she deepened and sharpened her social and political awareness, even as the timing of her arrival two years prior to the Great Depression, would create unexpected challenges. The impact of the Depression on the Black community was even more detrimental than for many who were in the White community as Blacks were often the last hired and first fired with jobs, so Baker did what she could to help others pull resources together in ways to support each other. One of her earliest efforts in this area was as one of the founders and national director of the Young Negroes' Cooperative League in the early 1930s where they bought collectively through consumer cooperatives. Baker served in editorial roles with *American West Indian News* from 1929–1930, and the *Negro National News* in 1932, where she used the journalism skills that she had been developing since her days at Shaw University to compellingly tell the stories of the people in Harlem. In association with her work helping create better opportunities for Black workers, she and Marvel Cooke conducted ethnographic research to expose what was described as "The Bronx Slave Market" in their article by the same name published in the NAACP's *The Crisis* magazine in November 1935. The two women watched and interviewed Black women who were being exploited as domestic workers in the homes of White women, who often paid $1/day for back-breaking labor, and the women were often exposed to the sexual advances of the husbands and sons in those White homes.[8] Ethicist Rosetta Ross notes three perspectives on human dignity that characterize Baker during this era, asserting that "human dignity entails . . . liberty and control of one's body, . . . human liberty consists of opportunity and responsibility for its exercise, and . . . organizing is a powerful weapon against injustice."[9] Baker's journalistic and investigative work led to her employment with the Works Progress Administration (WPA), and by the late 1930s she began organizing with the National Association for the Advancement of Colored People (NAACP) as an assistant Field Secretary.

Her involvement and influence with the NAACP quickly grew, elevating Baker to the NAACP National Director of Branches from 1943–1946. This important and highly involved work was often unappreciated by the national office. By this time she was married to Thomas J. Roberts, yet ignoring the gendered expectations of the times she described leaving New York alone around the middle of February to work in the South and staying until June or July and returning south again between September and November, often traveling to towns and cities in Alabama, Georgia, Mississippi, Virginia, and other areas, meeting with the Black community to understand their needs locally and helping them identify solutions to their challenges by building networks with people in neighboring areas throughout their state and region.[10] Baker's schedule was often very grueling, speaking at times up to sixty times within a week before traveling to the next city. As a critic of the NAACP's elitist structure and constant focus on increasing the number of members, whose membership dues funded the legal arm, while not actually involving the people at grassroots levels, Baker worked to increase the leadership capacity at the local level by developing a series of regional leadership conferences between 1944 and 1946 in New York City, Shreveport, Tulsa, Atlanta, Jacksonville, Chicago, Easton, and Indianapolis. The leadership conferences convened under the title, "Give People the Light and They Will Find the Way," reiterated one of her foundational beliefs that with the right information, skills, and opportunities, people did not need external leaders to come in as saviors; the people could learn to lead the change they needed themselves. Baker pushed field secretaries to know the issues and culture of each location and customize their approach to meet the needs of the community when developing programs.[11] Building on her earlier experience with Black women's exploitation in areas of work made available to them, Baker worked alongside labor organizations in the south in the fight for equality and seemed to always keep the needs of the people in the most vulnerable positions at the front of her priorities.

Ella Baker left her role as national director in 1946 after conflicts with Walter White and becoming guardian for her niece Jackie, who was nine years old at the time. Baker later returned to the NAACP when she was elected president of the New York City chapter in 1952. She moved the chapter headquarters from downtown to an area of Harlem where they could be in closer proximity to hear and address the concerns of all Black people, those considered everyday working class as well as professionals. In the first year under her leadership, the New York chapter focused on school reform, desegregation, and police reform and built coalitions with other organizations, including those with Puerto Ricans, who comprised the second largest group of persons of color throughout the city, in an effort to increase their impact. Her work on behalf of the New York chapter often caught the attention of New York City newspapers, which covered many of her public demonstrations and other strategies.

Despite her early Christian formation through her family's Baptist roots and Shaw University, Baker pushed away from her earlier desires to be a medical missionary and, as biographer Barbara Ransby describes, began living the life of a different type of missionary, "traveling from one town to another preaching the 'Gospel' of racial justice, and at times attempting, as she herself put it, to 'pass a miracle.'"[12] Biographer Joanne Grant also notes Baker's membership at Friendship Baptist Church on 131st Street in Harlem, where she attended Sunday worship services and continued to support the church financially when she worked in the south, including mailing a check for $160 to her pastor, Rev. Thomas Kilgore Jr. "to cover church contributions for 17 Sundays" while in Atlanta with the SCLC. Her pastor also allowed Baker to share with the congregation when she returned to Harlem.[13] Kilgore supervised the New York SCLC office from 1959–1963 and was one of the organizers of the 1963 March on Washington. By the standards of some of the larger churches in Harlem at the time including Abyssinian Baptist Church where some of the women whose stories fill pages in this book attended, Friendship Baptist was smaller. Rev. Kilgore was originally from South Carolina and after graduating from Morehouse College, he spent a decade pastoring in North Carolina.[14] So, although he was ten years younger than Baker, considering the communal-oriented religious influences of her grandfather and mother, and his southern roots, Baker's connection to a church with an activist pastor who seemed focused on tangible change for Blacks in New York and beyond is not surprising.

By the mid-1950s, Baker was a well-seasoned and well-connected social justice activist whose networks throughout the North and South would prove beneficial as she began to share her inclusive form of leadership with new civil rights centered organizations. Inspired by the Montgomery Bus Boycott, Baker co-founded the organization In Friendship on January 5, 1956, with Bayard Rustin and Stanley Levinson to direct economic support to the burgeoning southern movement. More than twenty-five religious, political, and labor groups joined together to raise funds used to support the Montgomery Improvement Association, NAACP, Southern Christian Leadership Conference (SCLC), and others.[15]

The SCLC was founded as the bus boycott in Montgomery began to come to an end. As a group of ministers in the South, it is surprising that in 1957, Ella Baker moved to Atlanta and served as the first director; but her ability to organize within communities allowed her to stand out from others and lead despite gendered limitations. By 1958, she was spearheading the SCLC Crusade for Citizenship voter registration campaign, which began to develop a strategy for communal empowerment through the ballot, and reinforced many of the things she had previously worked on as Director of Branches for the NAACP. Baker ran the SCLC's Atlanta headquarters for the first two years and stepped in as Executive Director when John Tilley resigned in April 1959.[16]

Baker was known to have some conflicts and critiques of the Black male preachers who in her experience did not value the intellectual and political contributions of women, and whose patriarchy-drenched actions did not always reflect the morals they proclaimed.[17] In April 1960, two months after the sit-ins in Greensboro, North Carolina, sparked similar stances by young college and high school students throughout the South, Miss Baker, as the young people called her, organized a meeting of the young activists at her alma mater, Shaw University. The leaders of the NAACP and SCLC each wanted the energetic activists to become youth arms of their national organizations, but Baker encouraged them to remain independent. It was during this gathering that the Student Nonviolent Coordinating Committee (SNCC) was born, with Ella Baker as their wise sage and guide in the struggle for Black freedom.

Through the influence of Baker, the work of SNCC focused on the needs of local people and sought to empower them to become stronger leaders within their own communities. In 1964, Mississippi Freedom Summer created the opportunity for many of the changes Baker envisioned when she traveled through the South with the NAACP thirty years earlier to become realized as Black men, women, and children were educated in ways that enabled them to vote and run for political office to reclaim their power and overcome the White supremacist systems that sought to relegate them to a place of inferiority. That summer, when the SNCC leaders focused their efforts on Mississippi, they were able to leverage the relationships and networks of activists Baker developed in the region decades earlier and help take significant steps forward by educating and empowering those who needed it most. The work in Mississippi opened the pathway for the Mississippi Freedom Democratic Party (MFDP) where local leaders influenced by the SNCC challenged voter intimidation and suppression and pushed the Democratic Party and the nation to face the duplicitous reality of a single race-centered democracy that left Blacks outside of the halls of power.

From the 1930s through 1980s, Ella Baker's desire to see Black people fully live out the freedom their citizenship entitled them to led to her active involvement as a leader, organizer, and strategist for some of the most impactful civil rights organizations of the twentieth century—the NAACP, SCLC, SNCC, MFDP, and others. Baker broadly shaped young people and grassroots leaders who were often overlooked by Black male ministers, who embraced their position as what Belinda Robnett categorizes as formal leaders in contrast to Baker, who is categorized as a professional bridge leader.[18] Young women leaders, including A. Lenora Taitt-Magubane whose lived experiences are partially captured in this book, were able to look to Miss Baker as a mentor and role model for Black women's leadership in ways that fundamentally shaped the Black freedom movement.

Ella Baker was a woman of her time and a woman ahead of her time. Her family's legacy of resistance, resilience, and religious convictions that influenced how they interacted with and tried to make conditions better for God's children deeply shaped her and as a result those she impacted. The arch of Baker's influence is long as a movement ancestor whose leadership strategies and models continue to provide insights for many activists in the twenty-first century as her legacy remains anchored to the quest for Black freedom.

CHAPTER 2

"Woke Up This Morning with My Mind Stayed on Freedom"

Forming Freedom Faith

Freedom faith grounds the first component of the liberative social ethics I uncovered in the lived experiences of Black Churchwomen during the Civil Rights Movement. It is central to the underlying desire many women felt for a way of life that was significantly better than any that was possible under Jim and Jane Crow segregation. In the documentary *This Far by Faith*, civil rights activist, pastor, and professor Prathia Hall uses the term "Freedom Faith," a "faith in freedom and a faith for freedom,"[1] to describe a reality and way of being that many of the women I interviewed also experienced. As Hall shared in the film:

> The local people had wisdom of the ages. They had lived in this system of brutal racial injustice all of their lives, and for their generations past. How had they done that? They had done that because each generation had passed on to the next generation this thing that I call *freedom faith*. This sense that I'm not a nigger, I'm not a gal, I'm not a boy. I am God's child. And as God's child, that means that I am everything that I'm supposed to be.
>
> It may cost my job, it may cost my life, but I want to be free, and I want my children to be free. So, I'm going down to the courthouse, and I'm going to sign my name. And I'm going to trust God to take me there and I'm going to trust God to bring me back. That's courage. That's faith. That's freedom faith.[2]

Courage, faith, and freedom are virtues that run throughout published accounts of civil rights activists as well as my own interviews. These virtues, passed down from generation to generation, were often reflected in women's memories of their grandparents or older family members whose commitment to the struggle for freedom inspired the young activists to continue the fight when opportunities presented themselves during the Movement. Very often, in the stories they shared with me, overlapping themes worked together to illuminate a freedom faith that was rooted simultaneously in the women's understanding of a God of justice and their desire to work with God—and God through them—to bring about change.

Freedom faith was evident among Black women, men, and children during the period of enslavement in the United States. Drawing on Apocalyptic and Exodus biblical narratives—with liberators such as Denmark Vesey and Nat Turner, and even Harriet Tubman, a new Moses who safely delivered hundreds of God's people from bondage—a focused and collective boldness to confront oppression was made tangible as more Blacks began to desire, envision, and take risks to embrace physical freedom. This freedom faith was an enduring virtue that was passed down in songs such as "Oh Freedom," with lyrics that included "Oh, freedom, Oh, freedom, Oh, freedom over me. And before I be a slave I'll be buried in my grave and go home to my Lord and be free," as well as prayers cried out in the midnight hour, and through stories of God's previous deliverance, provision, and protection.

Freedom faith has had a particular expression for Black women in America in the mid-twentieth century that is rooted in two elements: first an inborn desire for not only physical but also emotional and social freedom, and second an inherited legacy of faith that staked claims on God's promise of freedom. However, nearly one hundred years after the physical emancipation of Black bodies in the United States, there was still a lack of social and political freedom and flourishing that Black women, men, and children could fully enjoy. Whether expressed in the songs, prayers, scriptures, or the general experiences of Black women, as the traditional civil rights era began to emerge, a desire to be free was linked to a firm belief and understanding that the time for change, the time for justice, and the time for freedom is always *now*!

By the mid-twentieth century, *chronos* time was giving way to *kairos* time. It was something many felt within their bodies, even though they could not name it until they had the opportunity to get involved in the Black freedom struggle that came to be known as the Civil Rights Movement. Many Black women knew intrinsically that freedom was imminent, and the time had come to join with like-minded individuals to act on the intrinsic knowledge that they were God's children and should be treated as such. In a system of foundational beliefs maintained through long periods of Black struggles and separations, freedom faith is an active and critical faith that draws on a unifying vision of humanity received from God which challenges personal and structural inequalities based on the social construction of race.[3]

Since the beginning of humanity, African people have been people of the Spirit and people of faith, therefore faith remained foundational to the struggles for freedom in the Black community in the United States. This ancient freedom faith was grounded in the prayers and pleas, the songs and scriptures, and the visions and visitations of the Holy Spirit. This transgenerational freedom faith was passed down in the clapping of hands, the amen of affirmation, the power of praise, and the repetition of prayers which were believed to reach the ears of God as they had for their ancestors. Although women were often barred from formal religious leadership, they were consistent practitioners of the faith that undergirded Black survival and resistance.

Women Leaders Leveraging Faith

Ruby Hurley was an active leader in the southern Freedom Movement who tapped into the faith deeply baked within the Black community to stimulate active participation in the face of fear. Working most closely with the National Association for the Advancement of Colored People (NAACP), Hurley served as the National Youth Secretary from 1943 to 1950, and the Southeast Regional Secretary and, later, Director, working with chapters in Tennessee, Mississippi, Alabama, Georgia, and Florida, beginning in 1952 until she retired in 1978.[4] Hurley opened the first NAACP office in the Deep South, and although historic Black Churches were prominent in her hometown of Washington, DC, in the face of southern oppressors she came to rely on a particular kind of faith in God that Southern Black women and men drew on to sustain them. With a Pauline spirit, Hurley became all things to all people so that she might win some to the cause of freedom. She was once described by *Jet* magazine in a multi-page article who noted "the bravest and perhaps most militant woman in all Dixie is calm, steel-nerved, Ruby Hurley."[5]

When investigating extrajudicial executions of Black men, she broke through social barriers, often dressing as a field worker so she could easily move among sharecroppers and others to gather as well as share information. Hurley also used the language of Black churchgoers to challenge the activation of their faith in the fight for freedom. When describing her strategy for recruitment with the NAACP, she explained:

> I did use the Bible, and I found this effective in saying to our people, "You go to church on Sunday, or you go every time the church doors are open. You say 'amen' before the minister has even had the word out of his mouth. Many times you don't know what you're saying 'amen' to, but you're still saying 'amen.' Yet you tell me you're afraid. Now, how can you be afraid and be honest when you say, 'my faith looks up to thee', or when you say

that 'God's going to take care of you?' If you don't believe it, then you're not really being the Christian you say you are . . ." Then, I've also talked about—still do, as a matter of fact—the business of what Christianity really means, whether they really will walk on streets paved with gold, and how important is that when you can't walk on streets paved with concrete down here; and drinking milk and honey when your children don't have good, substantial meals on this earth. Isn't this more important? So, I used the Bible, really, as a basis in dealing with our people.[6]

Pressing the tension between belief and action and the this-worldly versus other-worldly orientation that C. Eric Lincoln and Lawrence Mamiya identify in Black religion,[7] Hurley critiqued a form of Christianity that was docile and disconnected to the lived realities of Black people. Hurley was an active Black Churchwoman who tapped into her faith as she engaged in her work, serving as an officer at Atlanta's Warren Memorial Methodist Episcopal Church Woman's Society of Christian Service (now United Methodist Women) and president of the denomination's United Methodist Women, after she retired from the NAACP.[8] She challenged the mindset of Christians who passively participated in religious activities and inactively absorbed the teachings of a radical Jesus and justice seeking God. Hurley made it clear to Black Christians that their freedom was inextricably linked to faith, and she emphasized that this had real-world relevance.

The Bible teaches in Hebrews 11 that faith is the substance of things hoped for, the evidence of things not seen. A. Lenora Taitt-Magubane called the type of faith Hurley expected of people "blind faith." It was a faith that was critical of religious rhetoric that subtly seduced followers into the acceptance of oppression. Many young women who were led by their faith to get involved in the risky and uncertain freedom struggle did so with blinders that helped limit distractions. As Lenora reflected, "when you believe in what you are doing, you don't have the fear." She continued, "being students, we were thinking about the cause and we really weren't dealing with the possible consequences, because I don't think we knew them all and we were blinded by the cause, if you will."[9]

Blind faith was sometimes referred to by other women who shared their experiences with me as a partial naiveté that allowed their focus on the reward of freedom to eclipse their fears, in spite of the potential risks involved. Unlike students, many older Black people, like those Ruby Hurley challenged in the South, had seen the deadly ramifications of challenging the deeply entrenched status quo that Whites constructed. Therefore, they could not allow themselves to be blinded by hope or even faith. They became conditioned to keep quiet and avoid confrontation. As a result, their fears were often greater than their faith. However, a blind faith and belief that all things would work out for their good as long as they focused on the righteousness of the cause, allowed students to narrow their focus and overlook many of the life-threatening interactions they faced while maintaining their goal of changing the American society.

There was a common Christian-centered religious ethos rooted firmly within the Black community of the twentieth century. While it was certainly possible to do the work of freedom without a deep religious faith, Ruby Hurley's strategy reinforced the reality that faith could be used as a tool for good when it challenged the practice of patiently praying and waiting for God to fix the failures of humanity, and instead faith was used actively as a way to partner with God to make the necessary changes. Even without articulating and ascribing a particular religious belief, a rich faith, that had been passed down through the generations, was imbued within each area of the Black communal experience and it could be tapped to stimulate engagement in the ongoing struggle for freedom.

Strategist, organizer, and Movement leader Ella Josephine Baker is often associated with her critique of Black male religious leaders whose affinity for media spotlights and social status limited their ability to be *with* the local people in ways that honored their experience and wisdom in grassroots approaches to justice. Baker, while not a professed Black Churchwoman, was born in Virginia but raised within a multigenerational communal Black Christian ethos in the enclave created by her grandparents in Littleton, North Carolina, on land where they had once been enslaved but had since purchased. Her grandfather was a Baptist preacher and his influence shaped the entire family. Baker's grandmother told her stories of slave revolts and how she had been whipped for exerting her agency and refusing to marry the man who had been selected for her by her enslaver. Her grandfather sought ways to ensure the survival of his people (biological and otherwise) and mortgaged his farm to help buy food for Black families impacted by a bad flood.[10] Believing in God also meant believing that God would provide the capacity to help others in need. Baker grew up helping her mother with missionary activities in her community and began participating in mission society meetings as a young girl. She continued to work with the North Carolina Baptist Women's Union State Convention into her early young adult years.[11] Baker explained that growing up she took religion seriously and felt that to believe in God meant to change the way that you lived and acted. She also followed the example set by her family of placing a very high value on humanity, and making sure that those who were in need could be provided for.[12]

Ella Baker began actively working for justice in the 1930s when she built a critical network throughout the south as a Field Secretary, and later Director of Branches with the NAACP. Miss Baker, as most of the student activists she mentored through the SNCC called her, was an important strategist whose decades of experience and non-ego-driven ethos was deeply respected by younger activists. In 1960, writing in the *Southern Patriot*, a few months after SNCC's founding, Baker, age 57 at this time and aware of generational batons being passed, described the determination of the young people she worked with and the impetus of their struggle. "By and large, this feeling that they have a destined date with freedom, was not limited to a drive for personal freedom, or even freedom for the Negro in the South. Repeatedly it was emphasized that the movement was concerned with the moral implications of racial discrimination for the 'whole world' and the 'Human Race.'"[13] Baker recognized that freedom does not have individual origins and it should not be held as the possession of select individuals. Freedom is the God-given birthright of everyone. Freedom is transcendent and universal. It is inclusive and disruptive of structures and systems that enforce limitations. So even while addressing the Freedom Rally in Hattiesburg, Mississippi, on January 21, 1964, Baker explained, "I always like to think that the very God who gave us life, gave us liberty."[14] She did not quote a sermon or a scripture, but a belief that had been passed down and she embraced as a core value. This God-centered belief of life's inextricable link to liberty undergirded the fight as Baker and others worked to fully inhabit what had been freely and equally given by God.

When multiple Black bodies were found while dredging Mississippi rivers and swamps looking for missing civil rights workers James Chaney, Andrew Goodman, and Michael Schwerner in June 1964, Baker made a statement that has since been well-quoted: "until the killing of Black men, Black mother's sons, becomes as important to the rest of the country as the killing of a White mother's son—we who believe in freedom cannot rest until this happens." These words make the respect of human life central and forward a James 2:14–26, "faith without works is dead," form of freedom faith.

The message of God creating all of humanity in God's image found regular refrains in the rhetoric of Black preachers even if older church members did not fully believe they would experience the implications of that equality in their lifetime. In their homes, churches, and schools, the Movement activists who shared their stories with me learned at a very young age that despite the de facto and de jure segregation that shaped their lives they were equal to White people in the eyes of God. Not satisfied with accepting things as they were, many young women such as Prathia Hall did not believe that discrimination and oppression were designed or destined by God. So, when the opportunity presented itself, they actively resisted and did what they believed to be God's work of establishing equality by challenging social and political structures that deemed Black people and especially Black women unequal.

A Foundational Faith Built on Scriptures

The young activists were confident in their beliefs about belonging to the family of God because they knew there were no caveats or footnotes establishing phenotypical exceptions to God's creation offered in the Biblical texts from which they drew their assurance. How could a God who created ALL in God's image say that some people should be free to flourish with the best support and resources available, while others should be given inadequate leftovers and provided intentionally lower quality materials with which to build their lives, and be expected to accept positions of inferiority in perpetuity? If anything, young women who were exposed to more inclusive Biblical teachings looked at Revelation 1:14–15 that described the son of God as one with hair like wool and feet the color of burnished bronze, and geographical clues such as Jesus's flight into Egypt where he lived in exile as a young child and was seemingly not out of place (as the blond-haired, blue-eyed European portrayed in White churches would have been). This made them feel certain that Blacks were made in God's image perhaps more than others. Even as young people, Black women and girls constructed an understanding of God as a God of justice and freedom who often did not reflect the same God White Christians seemed to know.

Scripture plays a significant role in the religious underpinnings of the Civil Rights Movement because Biblical texts point to past experiences with God and God's people, while also giving guidance and hope for the present and future. A common aphorism in the Black Christian ethos is that God is the same yesterday, today, and forever. Without the aid of a Bible, I asked women I interviewed to identify a favorite scripture from the Movement and write it on an index card. Historically, the Biblical texts of Black freedom struggles have centered on Exodus narratives or those highlighting eschatological battles and hopes.[15] However, these were not the scriptures that the women I interviewed recalled. Instead, they relied on a variety of texts during their involvement in the Movement that raised themes of God's love, trustworthy guidance, strength, endurance, joy, provision, justice, and forgiveness. Despite the antiquated language, formality, and omissions, the rhythm of the King James Version (KJV) of the Bible allowed for easier memorization and recitation and it was the most widely used translation during the civil rights era, so it is the version I use here for reference.

Bringing to life the example David sets in Psalm 119:11, "Thy word have I hid in my heart that I might not sin against thee," Peggy Lucas's older sister encouraged her to quote "her scripture" when she faced challenges while protesting in Birmingham. One of the scriptures Lucas quoted was the Twenty-Third Psalm, which was the Biblical text most often referenced by the women I interviewed. This of course made sense because during the civil rights era it was often learned in early childhood and regularly recited at home, church, and even during morning devotionals in school. This Psalm was part of the cultural and spiritual ethos, and as a result it was one of the best-known and therefore most portable biblical texts in the Movement.

Peggy felt that this scripture covered all situations during the Movement, including God providing shelter in stormy times and providing everything for activists to keep calm amid hard life choices. Lillian Sue Bethel also shared this scripture, explaining that she believed her life reflected the Twenty-Third Psalm as God provided everything she needed during the Movement and throughout all aspects of her life. This well-known poetic Biblical text was often committed to memory and could be easily tapped for the strength to continue to face challenges and the faith to keep fighting for freedom. These young women activists were not looking for God to provide a way of escape *from* oppression as Exodus narratives sought, but provision and leadership *in the midst of* oppression while they partnered with God to work to bring about change. This understanding of God within the Civil Rights Movement reflects a different central scripture interpreted in a way that enabled them to see a God in the mid-twentieth century who might not "deliver them" through removal, but would be with them as they took up the fight where they were. God was a present help and provider in all of life's situations, and the experiential nature of Psalm 23 reminded the women of this.

Peggy and Lillian, as well as many women like them, understood that the path toward freedom and justice required that they walk through some of the deepest valley experiences the United States would undergo in the one hundred years since the emancipation of enslaved Blacks. White hatred was spewed at them and they were the targets of pure evil simply for wanting to change the imbalances and inequities of daily life. Although they believed they were being led down paths of righteousness, each day young women led efforts to integrate schools, restaurants, interstate transit waiting rooms, and other public spaces, they faced manifestations of evil in what might be characterized as various valleys.

Verses four through six of the Psalm were especially important. The media captured the experiences of young women and girls like Autherine Lucy at the University of Alabama; Elizabeth Eckford, Minnijean Brown, Thelma Mothershed, Melba Patillo, Gloria Ray, and Carlotta Walls at Central High School in Little Rock, Arkansas; Ruby Bridges at William Frantz Elementary School in New Orleans, Louisiana; and Charlayne Hunter at the University of Georgia, walking through the shadow of death as they braved narrow paths to integrate schools in the mid-1950s and early 1960s while throngs of White protestors yelled and physically threatened harm against them. While a shadow is a projected reflection, the fears generated in the hate-filled shadows were tangible.

In the face of evil, activists who simply wanted to live freely summoned strength by singing (out loud or to themselves) the verse "We are not afraid," from the unofficial movement anthem "We Shall Overcome." They could also recall the fourth verse of the Twenty-Third Psalm to remind them that despite the reality of evil, God was there, protecting, shielding, and comforting them like a shepherd does for sheep. When young college women like Bessie Sellaway chose to go to restaurants where local and state laws and customs prohibited them from sitting and eating with White people, they recalled the fifth verse of the Psalm, which said God would prepare a table before them in the presence of their enemies. This bolstered them as they sat at lunch counters and endured being assaulted, spat upon, having their hair pulled, and sprayed with insecticide.

These young women literally sat at tables waiting to be served coffee or a hamburger in the presence of their enemies. As they recalled the verse which described that God would anoint their head with oil, the ketchup, sugar, and salt that was poured on their heads by angry Whites at downtown lunch counters took on different meanings and interpretations for these women. It is God who prepares the table of daily bread in the presence of those who desire to do harm, and despite the discomfort likely on both sides, God ensures a reserved seat at the table. God's protection does not mean that the presence of evil and potential harm is absent, but that God is also present in the situation.[16] The promise in the sixth verse, that goodness and mercy would follow them, reinforced the women's belief that they were doing God's work, and gave an assurance that God's emissaries would remain close with them. Faith that drew from Biblical texts such as Psalm 23 gave women the ability to endure when physical violence, even death, was a real possibility.

Marjorie Wallace Smyth listed both the Twenty-Third Psalm and Proverbs 3:5–6 as inspirations for her involvement in the Movement. As part of the Biblical wisdom literature, this portion of Proverbs underscores both a need to trust in and rely on God for proper guidance of one's actions. The ability to trust the Lord and not your own thoughts, inclinations, or even fears identifies the mindset of a person anchored in their faith. During the Movement, God was believed to be a trustworthy guide who could protect grassroots activists even when the paths along which God directed them led directly into the valley of the shadow of death. Trust required a relationship which testified that even if God had not specifically guided them down these paths before, since God guided their forebears through slavery, God could be trusted to guide them through Jim and Jane Crow in the mid-twentieth century.

The experiences of many of these women revealed that the Lord did not always speak clearly to direct their paths, which sometimes caused uncertainty. Learning to wait on the Lord for guidance and strength was a skill that often needed to be acquired, especially when protests and Movement efforts extended from days to months and years. In times of trouble, Beatrice Perry Soublet, a student at Bennett College in Greensboro, drew upon Isaiah 40:31. The Prophet Isaiah's imagery provided insights into how she and other young women could endure in the long struggle for freedom. Many young activists believed what they were doing was the Lord's work, and the Lord would ultimately move on their behalf so they could achieve victory in what they understood as a moral struggle.

Isaiah 40 promised that if they did not rely solely on themselves but worked with God, their diminished human capacity would be renewed. They would soar in their quests, run victoriously in their race, and walk confidently toward justice without fainting. As a grassroots theologian, Beatrice explains the verse's significance:

> God will always lift you up with wings like eagles . . . if you put your faith in God and you can move forward no matter how difficult the test . . . we used to sing "Walk and never tire" as a part of one of our songs. . . . If I had to encapsulate the ideas of the Movement [it would be] that you just have to keep going because your strength comes not from you anyway, but that if you trust in God that you are going in the right direction and doing what is just for God's people, God will be with you and will lift you up and you can run and not tire.[17]

The God of Isaiah was one who strengthened both young and old, and provided them with endurance to keep marching on to Freedom Land, no matter how long or difficult the journey.

In 1960, while a student at Spelman College in Atlanta, Georgia, A. Lenora Taitt-Magubane was also the president of the Young Women's Christian Association (YWCA) in her area. As a part of this organization, she and others regularly attended various churches for worship as they studied religion. She recalls an encounter one Sunday morning at a White church in Atlanta not far from the Atlanta University Center:[18]

One weekend we . . . decided we would visit a church in the West End . . . all of the churches in the West End were what you would call traditionally White churches, and I don't even know whether that church is there now, but I remember we went in the church and the man said we couldn't go in. And [I'm] saying, you know, we've really come to worship, and the man said well you can't come in here. And one of the things I remembered about that was I said, what are you going to do when you get to heaven? Are you going to in fact segregate people up there? He said, if I'm there and I can, I will . . . He said I will be up there at the gates and I will make sure. And that struck me, and it was really very hurtful, you know, that one could say on the one hand one believed in the Lord, one believed in Jesus Christ, and on the other hand, that you would live and die to be a segregationist. And I guess that was the determination, that subsequent weeks following when we were planning the sit-in that there was really no turning back . . . I was more and more committed to doing that.[19]

Compared to her experiences in her hometown of New York City, Lenora was not accustomed to the blatant segregation and separation that limited interactions across races in Atlanta and throughout the American South.[20] She believed that any place where God was worshipped should be open to all believers. Though she had not traveled much more than a mile from the utopic historically Black college she attended, she and the others had walked into a very different world, a world in which God was used to sanction segregation, that would be maintained not only temporarily on earth, but also eternally in heaven.

Lenora could not understand how someone could profess a belief in Jesus Christ and take such an absolute stand for segregation's racial separation in the church. What kind of God would welcome those types of encounters? How small and narrow-minded must that God be? She envisaged Jesus Christ as one who brought different people together and spent time with them. She knew the story of the Canaanite woman who corrected Jesus's segregationist actions, pushing him to be more open, loving, and just when she said that even the dogs eat the crumbs that fall from their master's table.[21] Yet when Lenora asked the White man at the door of the church whether or not he would block Black Christians from heaven, her challenge did not convict him, as he did not see his desires of exclusive racial segregation in heaven as antithetical to Christian beliefs. He accepted and supported racial segregation and believed that the God he worshipped did too. Lenora encountered segregation on buses and in stores, but it was this interaction at the entrance of the church that strengthened her resolve and commitment to fight for justice.

A. Lenora Taitt-Magubane knew she was encountering evil at the door of the church and the man's response was not centered in love. She leaned on her faith as she challenged him and his stance as a Christian. During the Movement, Lenora drew on First Corinthians 13 to emphasize her love ethic as the foundation for her understanding not only of God, but also how those who follow God should act. Often referred to as the love chapter, this text reminded Lenora that the work she was doing to break down racial barriers would not mean anything if her motives were not centered in love. Any actions to draw attention to herself as a person who was doing a "great thing" or being the better person would do a disservice to the good that she was attempting to accomplish. She and those with whom she worked were to rejoice in the truth, as they maintained their beliefs and hope while enduring daily trials. The most important portion of the scripture for Lenora was the thirteenth verse, "And now abideth faith, hope, and charity, these three; but the greatest of these is charity." She further explained, "one of the things you realize regardless of what you have, one is duty bound to give back and if you don't, then life is pretty meaningless, especially if you've been fortunate enough to have. Even if you struggled to get it, then even more so. But once you get it, you need to help others who are in the struggle to move to that point. And if you do that, then living in fact is not in vain." The charity that grounded her actions built on her faith in God and her hope for the future, yet she knew her work would not amount to much unless everything she did was centered in love. This love from God was an action word that became a way of life requiring those who had resources to help those without. Lenora did not always accept what "De Lawd" said, as she and others jokingly referred to Martin Luther King Jr., but like King, she understood God's agape love as radical, complicated, and countercultural in many ways. It was a love she could put her faith in as she worked for freedom and justice for all.

Mississippian Fannie Lou Hamer was another grassroots theologian who regularly interpreted biblical texts through the theme of freedom. Rosetta Ross notes that although Hamer did not make the connection between social activism and what she believed it meant to be a Christian, once Hamer became active in the Civil Rights Movement, Ross describes it as the consummation of Hamer's faith.[22] This faith came alive through Luke 4:18, in the words of Jesus, which she also quoted as her personal testimony; "The Spirit of the Lord is upon me, because he hath anointed me to preach the gospel to the poor; he hath sent me to heal the brokenhearted, to preach deliverance to the captives, and recovering of sight to the blind, to set at liberty them that are bruised." Like other women, Hamer's faith compelled her to act to bring freedom to anyone who was bound and limited in many ways.[23] Karen

Crozier describes Fannie Lou Hamer's practical theology as revolutionary, anchored in her lived and embodied experiences of liberation, freedom, justice, healing, love, education, and reparations.[24] Hamer explained that as Blacks in America, "We can't separate Christ from freedom," a concept Crozier explores as Hamer's articulation of Christ's freedom.[25] Freedom was a critical aspect of Hamer's virtue ethics.

Passing Down Freedom Faith

Beatrice Perry Soublet relied on the faith passed down in her family to help her stand up to injustice during the Movement in similar ways that her parents and grandparents had done before her. Her great-grandfather, Pierre Caliste Landry, had been enslaved, freed and then resold into slavery for $1,650, a price Beatrice will never forget. Similar to Ella Baker's grandfather in North Carolina, after emancipation, Landry had a clear idea for how he wanted his family to not only live but thrive, so he promoted education and faith in both his family and the broader Louisiana community. Pierre Landry modeled faith and leadership on the path to freedom, becoming the first Black mayor in the United States when he became mayor of Donaldsonville, Louisiana, in 1868, and also serving as a member of the Louisiana House of Representatives, Senate, and School Board, all positions from which he fought daily for justice and increased freedom for Blacks.[26]

Beatrice's great-grandfather had a grand vision for the future of his family and wanted all fourteen of his children to succeed, so they all went on to receive a higher education. Beatrice was taught that her great-grandfather also wanted his children to be respected, so he gave them regal sounding names including Lord Palmerston Landry, Lillian "Lady" Burdette Landry, and Lord Beaconsfield Landry, who went on to become a doctor in the Algiers neighborhood of New Orleans and operated a free clinic for poor residents.[27] As Beatrice grew up, she learned about her family's history from the enslavement of her great-grandfather through the work that her aunts, uncles, and her parents continued to do in the twentieth century on behalf of the Black community. When asked why she thought her family was active in social change and uplift, Beatrice shared:

> I think that my family's faith in the church . . . faith in God, faith in—if you're on the right side, eventually if you're on the side of justice and goodness, eventually it comes through. I think that would have to have sustained them . . . Where [does] that desire to do and to feel that things could get better [come from]? I just think it's faith. I really do, . . . and then what else

are you going to do? Just what else are you going to do? ... You can't just give up, so I guess that might have been what pushed them on.[28]

The commitment to not give up and to rely on faith in God to sustain you while you do the work to enhance the lived experiences of others, is Freedom Faith in action.

Beatrice recounted her family's conversations around the dinner table regarding the difficulties Blacks faced in a segregated southern society. Her great-grandfather was a pastor and later presiding elder in the Methodist Episcopal Church. Both her maternal and paternal grandfathers were ministers, one an Episcopal priest and the other a Congregational minister, and they, along with the women in the family, instilled a legacy of faith that was connected to the work of justice. Beatrice's family legacy of relying on faith to fight for freedom, led her to conclude, "You know we can do better, we can be better, and we can make society better."[29] Beatrice says she remembers that her great-grandfather was free but sold into slavery, and each time she makes a purchase for something near the amount assessed as the value of his life she is reminded of both the literal and figurative cost of freedom. This causes her to fight even more to maintain it for herself and others. She took risks during the Civil Rights Movement as a student at Bennett College and believed that what she did through student sit-ins and other nonviolent direct actions to draw attention to the injustices Blacks faced, was a part of living out the active faith that had been passed down by her family.

An educator, retired principal, and member of the NAACP and N'COBRA, Beatrice continued to engage in ongoing fights for freedom from the anti-war movement and anti-apartheid activism during the late twentieth century including publishing poetry with critiques of race relations, displacement after Hurricane Katrina, and ongoing wars in the early twenty-first century.[30] An active member of Our Lady of Lourdes Catholic Church in Atlanta, she relies on her faith in God to sustain and guide her actions. Beatrice also made sure to pass on the freedom faith she inherited to her daughter and son who have continued the fight for justice as attorneys, educators, and religious leaders.

Mass Meetings as Sites of Freedom Faith Formation

Albany, Georgia, native Janie Culbreath Rambeau joined the Movement along with her friend Annette, who encouraged her to get in line with those who had already gathered on Jackson Street singing their conviction that

"We Shall Overcome." She soon became committed to the struggle and acknowledged the role that believing in God played in their desire for freedom. For Rambeau and others, a belief in God was central during mass meetings throughout the week and even shaped those for whom church attendance was not a regular practice on Sunday mornings. It was in church that they were reminded and encouraged to hold on to the undeniable fact that everyone was created equal by God. As Rambeau describes it, the meetings reinforced the belief that "God meant for us to be free, totally free, not just out of slavery, but free."[31] Faith created the foundation from which the work of freedom was launched. In later years, Rambeau became the first Baptist woman ordained in her area, and founded the House of Refuge Baptist Church where she continued to connect her faith to justice in her local community and beyond.

Prathia Hall understood that both individuals and churches were often afraid to open their doors to Movement leaders from outside of the community. "It took all the freedom-faith that one could gather to open those churches for the movement classes and meetings, where we affirmed each other in the struggle."[32] For those that did open their doors, in addition to sermons and songs which created an emotional buoy of support, prayers created space for direct intercession with the God who was believed to be near those who call on God in truth.[33]

Power in Prayer

Prayer is how we open our hearts to God, how we make that vital connection that empowers us to overcome overwhelming obstacles and become instruments of God's will . . . prayer gives us strength and hope, a sense of divine companionship, as we struggle for justice and righteousness.[34]
—Coretta Scott King

I believe that through the prayers of the people, you can hear the hopes of the people. In their pleas for God to move on their behalf and provide freedom, a theology featuring a God who steps in the midst of human situations and is attentive to the cries of oppressed people becomes apparent. The prayers that were uttered to God silently in moments of fear and anxiety and those offered publicly in mass meetings, pray-ins, on the steps of local and state government buildings, and jails were generally extemporaneous prayers within the Black Church tradition and therefore were not written down or otherwise recorded. Marjorie Wallace Smyth remembers general themes of the prayers at mass meetings in Birmingham, "You know when you're fourteen, fifteen, that age, you think about all of them as . . . , Lord have mercy on us and guide us and protect us, cover us with the blood of Jesus Christ, I can remember that."[35] The blood of Jesus represented salvific power and the covering noted God's promise in Exodus 12 that the blood of the lamb placed over the doorpost would be a visible signal for death to pass over that home. Jesus's blood as the sacrificial lamb could symbolically cover those who invoked it in prayer for similar protection, and it also meant his blood would suffice in place of their own.[36] This ritual covering through prayer strengthened their faith to keep fighting *within* and not necessarily to be delivered *from* the struggle for freedom. Women's Political Council leader Jo Ann Gibson Robinson recalls spirited devotions of prayers and hymns during the mass meetings in Montgomery during the bus boycott. She notes, "Prayers were offered for 'endurance, tolerance, faith in God.' There were prayers for city commissioners; for 'misguided whites'; for the weak, and for all races and nations."[37] Prayers were also the vehicle to articulate what womanist ethicist Katie Geneva Cannon explains as "biblical faith grounded in the prophetic tradition that helped Black women devise strategies and tactics to make Black people less susceptible to the indignities and proscriptions of an oppressive White social order."[38] This womanist act ensured prayers were not only for those participating in the activism, but also for Whites who were opposing the change Blacks sought.

When young people arrived in Mississippi en masse in 1964, they were seen as an answer to prayers and the manifestation of the faith of Black women such as Fannie Lou Hamer and Eberta Spinks who saw the young SNCC workers as the substance of things hoped for and the evidence of things not seen.[39] Freedom would come at a cost that faith would help them pay. Freedom faith is an inherited virtue that was forged in the context of oppression which sought to limit or completely deny freedom. This virtue had origins in Africa and was strengthened in Black struggles on American soil, and then passed down to both young and old determined to live and fully flourish. As Prathia Hall notes, "These sons and daughters of those enslaved ancestors continued to hold on to that freedom faith. That freedom faith fired and fueled the fight. By that faith and in that faith, they finally stood up in the [mass] meetings and announced, 'I am afraid . . . But I want to be free.'"[40] Like Hall, many of the young women who traveled south to help the Movement were inspired and encouraged by women, men, and children who fought daily to make decent lives for themselves in the deeply divided South in spite of the regular occurrences of domestic terrorism. Hall notes, "everyone was impacted by the faith that the people had, their courage was so much a product of that faith and what makes people able to face death as a fact of life."[41]

Bernice Johnson Reagon described a transformation that took place when she started to hear the songs and prayers she had heard all of her life with new ears that were tuned by her experiences in the Albany Movement. As she described,

> It felt as if they were saying exactly what we were going through. "Lord you know me, you know my condition, and I'm asking you to come by here and see about me" was prayed every second Sunday at Mt. Olive Baptist Church, No. 2 by the mother of the church. But when she did it in a mass meeting just before a march, those words named our situation . . . That prayer, which had sounded old, was new and immediate; it was about us, pressed down by racism and wanting the power of the universe to be with us as we marched.[42]

Reagon's epistemological stance deepened through the power of the prayers offered by the mothers of the church as activists prepared to face oppressive forces.

Prayers had transformative power in mass meetings; not only in the way you thought but in the environment you encountered. During the Movement, one study of the membership in the Alabama Christian Movement for Human Rights (ACMHR), which replaced the NAACP when the organization was banned in the state, found 98 percent of those polled to be members of a church.[43] As a result of the teachings at church and direct experiences while protesting in the streets of Birmingham, Marjorie Wallace Smyth believed that she and others were working on the side of God, and the character of a God of justice was strengthened by walking with God in the struggle.

As a teenager, after participating in a mass meeting at a Baptist Church in downtown Birmingham, Marjorie walked out of the church with others to begin their nonviolent, direct-action demonstration. Across the street they saw the Commissioner of Public Safety, Eugene "Bull" Connor, directing the firemen to turn the fire hoses on them, saying "Get those niggers there," but as Marjorie explains, "They turn on—there were long hoses and not a drop of water, but we were prayed up, I don't care what nobody say, we were just prayed up."[44] For her, being "prayed up" meant that the words of prayer lifted during the mass meeting before walking out of the church resulted in physical protection by God who heard their prayers and interceded on their behalf. Marjorie described herself along with other young people and leaders participating in nonviolent direct action as spiritual people whose prayers were powerful enough to temporarily stop the violence perpetrated against them, and prove to the White men seeking to do them harm that these young Black Churchwomen were on God's side. Experiences like this encouraged Movement participants to tap into freedom faith that connected them to a God who heard their prayers and responded directly in the midst of their struggles.

As Marjorie and others walked in the authority of God, even when professed White Christians such as Birmingham's Eugene "Bull" Connor sought to do them harm, they believed that their God, this God who heard the prayers of Black women and girls, broke through time and space to shield them. They understood the impotence of the water hoses to be a display of God's power protecting them from evil. Such incidents shaped Marjorie's understanding of God as a God of protection and justice. This also supports Rosetta Ross's descriptions of attributions of divine intervention as reflective of Black religious women viewing themselves as "partner to divine work with responsibility to participate in changing social life."[45] Communication with God through prayer was real and immediate for Marjorie, and her faith led her to expect results from the effectual and fervent prayers of women, men, and children who braved Birmingham streets. In general, this expectation did not lead to a belief that God would always respond in such a spectacular way as to always stop water hoses from functioning, but it did sustain their hope that God would ultimately show up and support them in their fight.

Public prayers as vocalized freedom faith occurred not only within the walls of the church, but also often in the street or even in jail. A. Lenora Taitt-Magubane explained how young women jailed for protesting were sometimes asked to pray for those who had been arrested for other reasons before they would go to their court hearings. Students such as Lenora were often referred to as Freedom Fighters, and women prisoners in jail at times for much more serious offenses, including murder, welcomed the prayers of Lenora and other students because they believed young women like her were imprisoned for righteous reasons and consequently had God on their side.

Young women like Lenora took on roles as spiritual leaders in non-traditional ways and operationalized their faith in their pursuit of freedom. One such righteous leader and organizer in the Southwest Georgia movement was Prathia Hall. Her prayers and preaching encouraged and influenced many within the Movement. Albany, Georgia, native Bernice Johnson Reagon notes that generally women did not pray publicly in church with the exception of Saturdays, at times, or for an annual Women's Day service. So, when Reagon heard Prathia Hall and Kathleen Conwell pray, these young Black women, who made the journey from the north to help in the southern freedom struggle, had a lasting impact on her.[46] Reagon shared that both

Prathia Hall and Kathleen Conwell's public prayers included the phrase "I have a dream" while they were active in Southwest Georgia, and Martin Luther King Jr. is said to have been present to hear these young women pray in that way. This included one night at Mt. Olive Baptist Church in Terrell County, Georgia, in October 1962 where Hall powerfully described her dream with a repeated refrain of "I have a dream," a phrase which King later incorporated into his famous speeches in Detroit and Washington, DC.[47]

Prathia Hall understood the power of prayer as both a transformative element for individuals and a way to receive communal support. In 1962, she described how the fears of southern residents led them to help young activists like herself in the only way they knew how—through prayer. Hall recalled their experiences during voting drives, sharing "It's fear that slams the doors in our faces and hope that makes those same people whisper about us and get down on their knees and pray for us."[48] The hopes of the people in Southwest Georgia were seen in their silent prayers for the students who were risking their lives to obtain the freedom and justice that many of these older people desired but were too afraid to fight for themselves. On the other hand, there were other women such as Eberta Spinks in Laurel, Mississippi, Carolyn Daniels in Terrell County, Georgia, and "Mama" Dolly Raines in Lee County, Georgia, who served as Movement Mamas for SNCC. Raines not only opened her home and the resources of her farm to the students, but she also sat up and held a protective watch over them at night with her twelve-gauge shotgun. She was willing to fight for those who were putting their lives on the line working for the freedom of the Black community. Mama Dolly was a midwife in that rural area and she told SNCC organizer Charles Sherrod, "Baby, I brought a lot of these white folks into this world, and I'll take 'em out of this world if I have to."[49] Her beliefs and commitment made it possible for SNCC workers to have freedom from fear at night as they rested so that they would be ready to continue to fight another day.

Prayer has a unique place as an expression of the virtue of freedom faith through a very personal form of two-way communication with God. As Marjorie expressed in the example above, she believed the prayers she and others lifted requesting protection were responded to by God in the form of water hoses that would not turn on. This increased her courage when she prayed because she believed God not only heard her, but also could make a change in her experience by revealing a Divine presence in her acts of resistance. The Lord's Prayer often brought a sense of peace when Margie Davis heard it sung by a fellow protester in a way that pierced through the heavy fear-inducing moment of being arrested and held in a large outdoor space in the rain not knowing when help would come. The Lord's Prayer calmed Margie as she felt God's peace. Prayer is a place where people who sought to join the work for freedom could be vulnerable with God about their experiences and needs, and it is also a way that God provided direct interaction with those who were praying. Whether done silently as a part of personal devotion and dedication, or publicly as a part of communal support and strengthening, prayer is a creative and often charismatic way for scripture to be invoked, Godly promises to be remembered, stories of past victories to be recalled, and messages of hope to be expressed. One method of passing down freedom faith took place in public prayers. There is both an intimacy and a vulnerability to prayer when all hopes, fears, concerns, and needs are placed on the physical or metaphorical altar before God. There is also liberative power in releasing concerns to God, who has proven to be more than able to handle all things big and small in past freedom struggles, and is expected to do no less in present struggles. Prayer was a method of personal and communal empowerment as a result of a relationship with God.

As with so many aspects of the Civil Rights Movement, public prayers were often focused on the communal needs of the people and not the individual praying. Prayers were offered for the transformation of the oppressor as well as endurance for the oppressed as they fought for a better future. As Coretta Scott King put it, "Throughout the movement, we prayed for greater human understanding. We prayed for the safety of our compatriots in the freedom struggle. We prayed for victory in our nonviolent protests, for brotherhood and sisterhood among people of all races, for reconciliation and the fulfillment of the Beloved Community."[50] Prayers were an important conduit for the transference and passing down of Freedom Faith. The prayers of the people revealed the hopes, desires, and faith of the people, and their expectations that God would both hear them and respond.

Faith in Humanity

Freedom faith did not only mean placing faith in God; it also meant having faith in oneself—an important, even necessary component of freedom faith. In their youth, many of the women I interviewed said they actually did not always reference God as the source of their action, whereas as adults they believed it was the hand and will of God that had been with them throughout their civil rights involvement. Some women, like Lillian Sue Bethel, retained a belief that God was with her and other students as they protested. While she was active in the Albany movement, she regularly attended Bethel A.M.E., which was her family's church. However, she walked away from the church after the Movement. When the urgency of freedom was no longer immediately in front of her in such a way that it required reinforcement through faith, she also realized she was still mad at God for her mother's sudden death when she was a young adult. She reflects, "it's interesting how God plans things when you don't know what's happening."[51] Years later, when she returned to the faith tradition in which she had been raised, she joined First A.M.E. Bethel Church in Harlem, New York, making a commitment to live out her faith in a way that helped others. As a result, she worked as the leader of the food pantry that helped fill the gaps for those in need, providing a stopgap for food insecurity in the face of economic uncertainty.

Historian Charles Payne notes that, "those [who] joined the movement in its early days would not have known that things would work out as they did . . . Faith in the Lord made it easier to have faith in the possibility of social change."[52] As Black Churchwomen continued fighting for freedom it was the inherited faith of their foreparents that kept them going even when their own faith was not as certain. This was a critical faith rooted in liberation that questioned restrictive White notions of freedom and justice for all of God's creation. These women believed that oppressive situations would not remain the way they were. They had faith that if they stepped out on behalf of God to change policies and practices, even at the risk of their lives, God would remain with them. Freedom faith enabled young women in the Movement to resist deeply embedded injustices by courageously acting in imaginative ways that were rooted in the faith they inherited.

Rev. Dr. Prathia L. Hall
A Facilitator of Freedom Faith

After multiple church burnings in 1962, Bernice Johnson (Reagon) and others were gathered in a mass meeting in a Black Baptist church in Albany, Georgia. It was there she heard a young Black woman who had come from the North praying with the power to call down the spirit of God to protect protesters. At that moment, Johnson knew she was experiencing something that would shape her life.

Born in Philadelphia, Pennsylvania, on January 1, 1940, to Reverend Berkley Lucas Hall Sr., a "race man" and founding pastor of Mount Sharon Baptist Church, and Ruby Johnson Hall, a missionary who instilled in her children a deep love for God and God's people, Prathia LauraAnn Hall became a powerful voice of the southern freedom movement in the 1960s. Her parents "lived within the tradition of racial uplift as service to Christ" and believed "the struggle for freedom was a holy and sacred struggle."[1] They raised Prathia and her siblings to embrace an African worldview wherein "the religious and the political were profoundly integrated," thus setting a foundation for faith and freedom to be woven tightly together in her life.[2]

The Halls founded Mount Sharon Baptist in 1953 and through the church worked to meet the needs within their predominantly Black North Philadelphia community by helping young people increase their literacy and providing food for local families. Rev. Berkley Hall was committed to embracing full freedom for Black people as a reflection of God's justice on earth. He exposed Prathia to the top minds of the day as he shaped her spiritual and intellectual life. "My father never let the fact that I was a woman be an excuse for not being the very best I could be, whatever it was I was doing." Hall noted, when describing her upbringing, "When I was a child he took

Prathia Hall, a spokeswoman for demonstrators in Atlanta, GA, reads a statement demanding an end to discrimination and segregation to Mayor Ivan Allen Jr., Jan. 29, 1964. Source: AP Images

me to hear preachers he thought were the best. He took me to hear Paul Robeson and Mordecai Johnson and Nannie Helen Burroughs."[3] Her mother regularly involved her in missionary society programs and community work.[4] Raised in a deeply religious family where she says there was "an intense passion for justice," and there was "an understanding that justice was a Divine agenda."[5]

Prathia Hall was encouraged by her parents at an early age to challenge systems of racial and economic injustice that sought to limit the flourishing of Black people. In 1958, she won top honors in an Elks oratorical contest with her ten-minute speech on the merits of the Constitution.[6] Always trying to find a way to do what she could for others, she became active in local and regional civil rights efforts as a teenager. As a pre-law student at Temple University, she wanted to go to Tuskegee in Alabama during the summer to gain richer experiences in Black history and culture, but her father stopped short of letting her get involved in Movement work in the Deep South, which he felt could be too dangerous. For the next year she insisted to her father, "You are going to have to release me to the struggle."[7] When Berkley Hall died the week of February 1, 1960, the student movement was exploding in the South and Prathia felt free to join the action. Her mother felt comfortable with her desire to become a civil rights lawyer, but was fearful of the direct-action work Prathia sought. Hall reflected, "But finally, a few months after my father's death in 1960, she understood I *had* to go. 'Well, then, God keep you,' she said," and from then on her mother became one of Hall's biggest supporters.[8]

In addition to the example set by her parents, Hall was also shaped by a peace tradition in high school and college through her involvement with Fellowship House in Philadelphia (an interracial, multifaith organization founded by Marjorie Penney in 1931) where Mordecai Wyatt Johnson and Howard Thurman often spoke in the late 1940s and early 1950s.[9] It was through her work with Fellowship House that in 1961, during her junior year at Temple University, she participated in a northern section of the Freedom Rides. In response to a call from Juanita Jackson Mitchell of the Baltimore NAACP, the first Black woman to practice law in Maryland,[10] Hall and others challenged the intrastate accommodations in the bus terminals on the Maryland Eastern Shore to test the December 1960 *Boynton v. Virginia* Supreme Court decision. A segregated bus station in Annapolis, Maryland, became the location of the first of what would ultimately become at least ten arrests during Hall's civil rights activism.[11] Her first encounter with jail was for a period of what she described as two or three weeks as she and others committed to the increasingly popular jail-no-bail strategy started in February 1960 by students at Florida A&M University to help draw attention to the injustices throughout the nation. Hall considered this intentional act and the corresponding consequence of her baptism and initiation into the Movement. Years later when reflecting on her activism, she shared, "I believe I was born in, and born for, the freedom struggle."[12]

The call to help those in the South who lived under the restrictive and dehumanizing weight of Jim and Jane Crow continued to draw Prathia Hall deeper. Leaving Temple University with one course in dispute, having been educated in the fields of political science and religion in the classroom, and about the birth right of freedom in her church and community, she headed to Georgia and enlisted in the war that was already raging on the southern front.

Prathia Hall visited family members in Virginia as a child, and it was during one of those trips at the age of five that she felt a distinct and dehumanizing sting of racial segregation on a train that stayed with her. In describing her father who left the South forty years before she began doing her work there,

Hall noted, "I feel that he left the South to somehow redeem me. And it's my job to come back and redeem somebody else."[13] Entering the South as a young adult, Hall watched women, men, and children risk their lives for the cause of freedom in ways that she had never witnessed before. They marched, she said, in the "spirit of Jesus and in the spirit and faith of their ancestors."[14] She recognized that southern Blacks had often been protesting in silent ways for centuries, including the women working in kitchens during slavery who spit in food, or intentionally broke items in small acts of resistance.

As a facilitator of freedom faith, Hall explained, "Our job was to draw out and liberate those aspirations" to protest injustice.[15] This faith ushered in a belief that God enabled those actively involved in the struggle for freedom to be alive in that particular time and space to confront and challenge segregation and racial injustice in all of the places it had taken root including in the hearts of people. From the start of focused direct actions in Albany, Georgia, in December 1961 until the time Hall arrived in 1962, seven hundred people had been imprisoned for pushing back against the racist system. She joined Charles Sherrod, the SNCC Project Director for southwest Georgia, and quickly became involved in the work. In doing so, Hall lived out the type of active and socially engaged faith that had been modeled by her parents and intensified by the fearlessness of some southern Blacks she encountered who understood the potentially dangerous consequences but tapped into something within to take action nonetheless as a manifestation of their freedom faith.

Hall faced death multiple times while working in southwest Georgia. As a result, she did not have to wonder, imagine, or take someone else's word for it; she knew that standing up could literally cost your life and yet she stepped boldly into the "river of Black protest" that continued to flow towards justice.[16] "[L]iving in the face of death, this constant, perpetual encounter with death in order to live the struggle, is, I think, the most powerful expression of freedom faith."[17] She described the "long, cautious, and caring educational exchange" that took place between the SNCC students and the Black women and men in rural communities whose very existence revealed lessons on how to live "without surrendering humanity or dignity to those who sought to crush them."[18] It was the lesson of faith in the struggle for freedom that Hall took with her in the work she dedicated her life to during and after the Movement.[19]

Freedom came at a cost that faith helped the activists pay. When Hall was working on voter registration and education in southwest Georgia's "Terrible" Terrell County, she and other SNCC students stayed in the home of Mrs. Carolyn Daniels and her son Roy Patterson. As a beautician, Daniels owned her home and business in Dawson, Georgia, so she was not reliant on an income from Whites. This gave her independence that most, outside of Black medical doctors, non bi-vocational ministers, morticians, and men "protected" by labor unions, did not have. Daniels opened her home to the young activists fully knowing the potential risks. One night, while talking, Prathia Hall, Jack Chatfield, and Christopher Allen dropped to the floor when shots rang out and bullets penetrated Daniels's home from the outside. Hall's hand was grazed by a bullet and two other young men were struck more directly.[20] During the Movement, Daniels's home was shot into at least twice, and it was bombed.[21] The presence of Prathia Hall and the other activists and their desire to help the community break free of the stronghold of segregation generated a potentially deadly response from Whites who vehemently rejected change that could empower Blacks. Hall's faith and determination was strengthened by Daniels whose desire for freedom for others compelled her to resist in the face of personal risk, and vice versa.

A gifted orator, Prathia Hall became known for the power of her prayers and her preaching, which she had been nurturing since the age of three when she began giving speeches in church. She used her God-given gifts to pass on the virtue of freedom faith to others through her words and deeds. SNCC organizer Judy Richardson describes being moved to tears when transcribing one of Hall's speeches because the words were so powerful.[22] Hall's words not only influenced Martin Luther King's best known "I Have a Dream" speech, but King, even with his patriarchal practices, acknowledged that Prathia Hall was the one person who he would prefer not to follow on the podium during their many interactions, especially during the Albany Movement.[23]

In late December 1963, Prathia Hall was arrested on a state trespassing law as part of the Toodle House sit-ins in Atlanta. By that time, Hall was twenty-two years old and a clear leader in the Movement.[24] As one of SNCC's strategies, Hall was a stockholder in the Toodle and Dobbs House Corporation before her arrest which made her jailing even more impactful and allowed her access to shareholder meetings to challenge their discriminatory practices directly. She had been taught by her parents to work creatively on the divine agenda of justice and she knew that direct engagement with systems of power was a requirement for justice in that moment. In early 1964, after Hall's leadership in southwest Georgia, Selma, Alabama, and Greenwood, Mississippi, she moved to Atlanta to become SNCC's Coordinator of Atlanta Activities.[25] She continued to inspire others to face their fears and tap into their faith as they offered their lives in the service of the struggle for freedom.

When describing her life in 1995, Hall explained, "The central commitment of my life can be summarized in two words: faith and freedom. I have been formed by that sector of African American religious tradition which understands the religious and political to be integrated in faith and practice. It is from within that stream of the tradition that leadership for the African American freedom struggle has emerged. I believe that contemporary African American liberationists continue to be impacted by that tradition. Since childhood, my academic and community work have been motivated by an intrinsic dynamic relation between faith and freedom."[26] Hall later reflected, "Many contemporary people, not just young people, today do not understand the role of the African American church and faith. We still have much of the notion of the African American church as a pacifier of faith, as something which kept people from protesting instead of fueled and fired for freedom."[27] She was raised to draw from the fire of the church and be motivated to act on the virtue of freedom faith, and she used her life to help facilitate this dynamic engagement by others who committed to fight for freedom and justice.

As the focus of SNCC began to move away from a nonviolent, direct-action model, Hall redeployed her leadership roles in the organization and increased her leadership in the Black church. She returned to her native Philadelphia and pastored her late father's church for nearly twenty-five years, in 1977 becoming one of the first African American women ordained in the American Baptist Churches USA. She also earned a Master of Divinity and PhD from Princeton Theological Seminary in Christian Social Ethics, defending her dissertation, "The Religious and Social Consciousness of African American Baptist Women" in 1997. Hall served as Associate Dean of Spiritual and Community Life, Director of the Women's Center, and Dean of African American Ministries at United Theological Seminary in Dayton, Ohio, and held the Martin Luther King Jr. chair in Social Ethics at Boston University School of Theology before her death in 2002.

CHAPTER 3

"We Shall Not Be Moved"
Cultivating Courageous Resistance

Doing the work of freedom during the Civil Rights Movement meant believing that something different was possible and worth working for, even if it might require audacious and courageous acts to achieve. Maya Angelou served as director for the SCLC's New York office and was active in struggles for Black freedom from the early 1960s until her death. She described courage as "the most important of the virtues, because without it, no other virtues can be practiced consistently."[1] Angelou understood the need to cultivate courage in the ongoing work of resistance.

> I realized that one isn't born with courage. One develops it. And you develop it by doing small, courageous things, in the same way that one wouldn't set out to pick up [a] 100 pound bag of rice. If that was one's aim, the person would be advised to pick up a five pound bag, and then a ten pound, and then a 20 pound, and so forth, until one builds up enough muscle to actually pick up 100 pounds. And that's the same way with courage. You develop courage by doing courageous things, small things, but things that cost you some exertion—mental and, I suppose, spiritual exertion.[2]

Angelou's assertion that courage is the preeminent virtue through which other virtuous acts are possible makes courage foundational for a moral life.[3] Faith can ground the conviction necessary to tap into the courage to accomplish worthy goals. During the Civil Rights Movement, the need for resistance in the face of oppression was constant, and therefore opportunities to develop and cultivate courage were plentiful.

Courage is revealed in actions. Courage is different from confidence in that it is associated with a potential cost or risk for the acts that are willingly undertaken. When activists sang the Movement anthem *We Shall Overcome*, they added the verse "We are not afraid" as a declaration of courage in the face of threats to acknowledge that there were real reasons to be afraid but they chose to stand up against systems of injustice regardless. In their courageous fight for justice and freedom Black Churchwomen and girls, uncloaked and unmasked, were often resisting White people in their small towns who knew them by name, knew where their families worked and lived, and knew the schools and colleges they attended. Often the simple act of speaking up when unfair treatment was encountered—whether attempting to register to vote, protesting unfair practices in front of a store, or marching to show collective strength—could result in physical violence and arrest. Many of the collegiate women who were active in the Movement were first-generation college students with great expectations placed on them by their communities to honor the sacrifices and investments that were being made by their families so they could pursue their dreams. Many of their biological and church families prayed for them as they went off to school with the belief that after learning and being exposed to new things they would in the words of the unknown poet, "Bring dat college home." However, it was the expanded vision of those communal dreams that enabled many of the young women to take risks to join the Movement, absolutely convinced that the time had come for change. Boldly resisting oppression and intentionally committing acts that could bring shame and retaliation on a family was a serious and courageous choice in the mid-twentieth century. A choice not entered into lightly, but with hope-filled intention that through their actions change would come.

Defining Courageous Resistance

Courage can be understood as an action of the heart and core of one's being. Courage begins inwardly and is performed outwardly. Courage is a response to something that could be dangerous or fear inducing. Courage requires acting despite fear and it is a conduit through which bold and brave actions become possible. Courage is the one consistent virtue enacted by Black women identified in my research as well as that of womanist ethicists Katie Geneva Cannon and Melanie L. Harris.[4] Resistance is the creative act of withstanding and opposing individuals, groups, institutions, or systems. Active resistance requires courage. History testifies that, while our awareness about their resistance or the "success" of the acts may vary, courageous resisters always exist when injustice is present. Resistance does not have to be a dramatic spectacle to be impactful, nor does it have to take place through large organized and mobilized groups. It can be one five-year-old Black girl making the choice to use the same restroom facilities as White adults, or it can be hundreds of students violating an injunction and marching down public streets threatened by police and White citizens to draw attention to the need for equity in public spaces.

From the bold stands of Indigenous women and men to the creative escapes, acts of sabotage, and revolts of enslaved women and men, oppressed persons have courageously resisted on American soil and elsewhere for centuries. The Civil Rights Movement marked a particular time within a long tradition of freedom struggles in which individuals and communities joined together to resist injustices within society. While masses benefited from the commitments of those who actively fought for justice, the risk takers during the Civil Rights Movement often comprised less than a quarter of the community.

Many of the women who were drawn to direct action during the Movement had been independently challenging the social injustices and inequities they discerned during childhood. In the 1950s, these individual actions looked like Bessie Sellaway sitting on the front seat of a city bus on her way to Spelman College and daring to speak back to the elderly White woman who tried to make her move; Marjorie Wallace Smyth drinking from the "Whites Only" water fountain in the Parisian's department store in Birmingham as a self-described feisty child to her older sister's fear and dismay; and Lillian Sue Bethel confronting a White man who tried to sell pornography in the Black communities in Albany and telling him to take it and peddle it in his own neighborhood.

In one well-known example, with full knowledge of the possible response because of her previous run-in with James Blake, the Montgomery bus driver who exercised what he described as his "police powers,"[5] Rosa Parks made the choice to refuse to move and stand in the back of the bus when a White man did not have a place to sit in the White section. Parks, who was a long-standing active leader in the NAACP in Alabama, had been trained in school desegregation methods during a two-week workshop at the Highlander Folk School four months prior to her public stance. Septima Clark taught Parks at Highlander and noted that after participating in the training Parks "gained enough courage, enough strength to feel that she could stand firm and decide not to move when that man asked for her seat."[6] Although a nonreligious institution, Highlander played an important role in the cultivation of courage by training and equipping grassroots leaders, enabling them to be ready to act whenever the opportunity presented itself. Parks describes thinking of the recently murdered Emmett Till in the moment when she was approached by the bus driver and decided in the manner of the old spiritual that she would not be moved. Parks shows us through her initial stance and subsequent legal pursuit that courage is a choice and resistance is an intentional act.

Courage Involves Potential Risks to Self and Community

On the night of January 30, 1956, one month into the Montgomery Bus Boycott, Martin Luther King Jr. was speaking at First Baptist Church and Coretta Scott King was home with their first child, Yolanda, when their home was bombed. Coretta and Yolanda were not physically harmed, but the community was literally up in arms. Rosa Parks wrote about that moment, reflecting the power of faith in the face of fear, noting, "we do not know what else is to follow these previous events, but we are trusting in God and praying for courage and determination to withstand all attempts of intimidation."[7] Parks's prayer for courage to withstand the attempts of Whites to intimidate and therefore silence Blacks was rooted in her experiences working with the NAACP in the 1940s as an investigator of violence enacted against Black women and others. She knew that the attempt to kill the King family was only the beginning, and she wanted Montgomery's Black community to tap into their faith as the foundation of the courage it would take to stand up and resist long enough to produce substantive change. Rosa Parks became a nationally known heroine of the Movement, but she was also an everyday Black Churchwoman and active member of her local A.M.E. Church and NAACP chapter where she led the Youth Council. She had a personal commitment to justice and a love for the respect and dignity of all people.

The King family home was targeted because the young preacher was identified in the media as the formal leader of the burgeoning Montgomery Bus Boycott. Even when civil rights protest activities consisted of large groups, anonymity was rarely possible for many Blacks since photographs, names, and sometimes home addresses and employers—particularly information obtained during arrests and attempts to register to vote—were often published in local White-owned newspapers and magazines. Therefore, the risks entailed with openly challenging deeply entrenched oppressive structures could potentially result in retaliation against the community and not simply the individual protestor.

As high school and college students, the actions of Rose Davis Schofield and A. Lenora Taitt-Magubane were photographed and published in the *Daily Journal* newspaper of Elizabeth, New Jersey, and the nationally distributed *Jet* magazine respectively, and Gwendolyn Robinson Simmons's arrest became known to the Spelman College community before she could say anything in her defense because of coverage in the *Atlanta Constitution*.[8] The publicity surrounding these women as well as the arrests of Lillian Sue Bethel in Albany, GA; Peggy Lucas in Birmingham, AL; Rose Davis Schofield in Elizabeth, NJ; Bessie Smith Sellaway in Atlanta, GA; Margie Davis in Birmingham, AL; Beatrice Perry Soublet in Greensboro, NC; and A. Lenora Taitt-Magubane in Albany, GA, meant that their information was known and could possibly be used for physical or economic retaliation against them and their families or the state-funded schools they attended.

Margie Davis described some of the questions she was asked when being processed by Birmingham police.

> They took us one by one and they fingerprinted us. And they asked us a whole lot of questions—"What's your name?" and you told them your name. And they wanted to know your parents, and we were told not to tell them that. We told them we didn't know. So, they would ask you stuff like, "nigger, you don't know your parents name?" and we would go "no." The questions continued, "Now, where your daddy work? You got a daddy?" No. That's all we would tell. We couldn't say. Because we were told—my mother and my father worked—my father worked at US Steel, and they said they'd get him fired. So, we were told don't disclose nothing but your name.[9]

The United States Steel Corporation and its Fairfield plant was one of the largest employers in Birmingham. In the 1960s the employment peaked at more than 4,000 workers in the Birmingham area.[10] The relative security of union jobs such as those at US Steel enabled some Black fathers to support their daughter's resistance although in general these men would not risk actively protesting themselves. Margie said unlike many adults, as teenagers they did not have enough sense to be scared or allow any fears that did arise to stop them. Each act gave them courage to continue to direct their actions in ways that would draw attention to the injustices Blacks faced even if it meant jail or other forms of retaliation.

Some family members saw the arrests as badges of honor, but in other cases, the "criminal" records of the young women brought concerns regarding the types of future career opportunities that would be available to them with an arrest record, no matter how just the cause. Others knew that their children's arrests had potential ramifications for the entire family if jobs were lost, credit was stopped, insurance was canceled, evictions were issued, and more. Not only were families at risk, but so were institutions of learning and advancement that benefited the broader Black community. For example, Albany State and other state-funded colleges were put in precarious situations when state legislatures threatened to withdraw critical funding if students actively protested.[11] Yet despite familial and societal apprehension, many young women at state-funded colleges including Lillian Sue Bethel, Bernice Johnson (Reagon), and Annette Jones (White) protested and courageously resisted, boldly serving their time in jail for what they believed in, nevertheless.

"I Ain't Afraid of Your Jails"

As a high school senior at Fairfield Industrial High School, just a few miles outside of Birmingham, Margie Davis describes her upbringing in the all-Black community as a sheltered and loving one in which parents and other community elders did their best to protect young people from the painful experiences of segregation. Birmingham was a city formally established after the Civil War. Rich in natural resources, it was a major industrial city with high mineral deposits leading to robust steel production. The new town grew quickly and as it became a city it reinforced racial segregation practices and limitations dominant throughout the Deep South. As a child, everything Margie needed was within her Fairfield community. "We had very nice homes. We had our own high school, we had our own elementary school, we had our own parks. We were very secure. There were little corner stores up in there. We didn't come out of that community. So, coming up as a child, I didn't know anything about Birmingham."[12]

Although Margie's parents, like other adults, did business with Whites in Birmingham, she and other children had very limited interactions with White people. She recalls, "there were rare times that my parents took me downtown. But I saw the "For Colored" drinking signs and "For Whites" drinking signs. She [her mother] didn't take us down there too often so we wouldn't be exposed to it. But we knew about it. We lived in fear, like everybody else, of Whites coming to the neighborhood and bothering us."[13] The external threat to her self-contained and peaceful area seemed probable since by this time Birmingham had earned the moniker "Bombingham" because there had been more than forty bombings, primarily in all-Black communities, between the late 1940s and mid-1960s. Despite her community's desire to protect and limit children's exposure to hatred and violence, Margie knew that it existed and even as a child she knew that it was wrong.

Margie's high school principal, Professor Edmond Jefferson "E.J." Oliver, was one of the extended community elders who not only tried to protect students, but also prepare them to be productive citizens in integrated spaces as a form of respectability politics of survival within the segregated system.[14] One of Professor Oliver's (he was referred to as professor and not principal) well-known aphorisms was, "It is better to be prepared and have the doors of opportunity closed in front of you, than to be unprepared and have them wide open! Segregation and Jim Crow will ultimately end, so the question is 'What will you do?'"[15] As the Civil Rights Movement continued to grow in Birmingham, SNCC's James Bevel and other young leaders heavily recruited students from Miles College, a historically Black college founded in 1898 by the Christian Methodist Episcopal Church, and from the neighboring Fairfield Industrial High School which was only a few blocks away. Professor Oliver did his best to prevent students from leaving school to join in with civil rights efforts, but he was not always successful. One day, when students were changing classes, they took advantage of the movement outside of the classrooms and a mass exodus ensued.[16] Margie Davis describes it this way:

> So, when the demonstrators were standing outside trying to get us to come out, they were out there talking about Dr. King needed us, and well, you know, at that time it was the thing of everybody was kind of fired up and ready. So, we were too. And when they kept going, Professor Oliver locked the doors and said ... don't nobody leave. Well, we start going out. We start pushing the doors open and he just—we jammed up in the door so bad he had to let us down. We were pushing. And everybody was out.
>
> The leaders ... were working with Dr. King. They were saying they need us. They need us. If you want to do it, come to Miles College on the campus. So, kids started scattering. So, I decided, I'm gonna go. So, nobody knows where I am ... one of the girls who lived not too far from me, her name is Regina Smith, I told Regina, I said are you going? She said, "no I'm scared, I'm going home." So, I said tell my mama I went. So, I did.[17]

Disobeying their principal or any other person in authority took courage. It meant going against sociocultural norms of obedience and respect deeply rooted in southern Black communities. The possibility of retaliatory violence and arrest for participating in the nonviolent marches in Birmingham could not be minimized. Regina's rational fear reinforces the power of Margie's courage as a teenager in the face of the unknown. Although it may have seemed effortless and somewhat spontaneous to participants outside of the core organizers, in general, significant research, strategy development, and preparation took place before acts of resistance like the one Margie described.

The SNCC leaders who assembled at Miles explained the path the young people would take as they walked through the Vining and Vinewood areas of Birmingham, noting what would likely happen when they reached the main thoroughfare of 3rd Avenue. It was at that intersection they predicted the police would be waiting. Margie describes singing and holding hands as the large group of high school and college students walked along the designated route. She continues,

> Sure enough, as we got down on 3rd Avenue, here comes all these police cars and these school buses . . . So as we start running, cops are behind us in cars. Some have gotten out running behind. And they had those dogs. They had those big black dogs and they were running behind us too. And it was very scary because the traffic is running, we're running, police running, the buses are running . . . So, the cars going one way . . . and I ran up on the median and I fell. And when I fell I looked up and there was this police car coming right at me. And he was going to run over me. But little old Helen [a very petite classmate] yanked my arm and pulled me out of the way.[18]

Accounts support Margie's estimates that thousands of kids were arrested along with her and there were too many to place inside the jail, so they were held in the open courtyard area.[19] There were so many young people they barely had room to move around.

That evening, the police brought Martin Luther King Jr. over on the back of a flatbed truck with his hands cuffed behind him. He was allowed to approach the wire fence and speak to the young people being held in custody. Margie recalls King saying, "be strong and do what our leaders had told us to do." King prayed with them and then he was taken away. King was not only a sociopolitical leader of the Movement, but also a spiritual one. His prayers and admonishment to be strong reinforced Margie's courage in the midst of potential terror.

That first night, a storm rolled in and the young students were left outside in the rain until around 3 a.m. One of Margie's clearest memories of that dark, cold, and scary time was the peace that came over her from a girl who sang "The Lord's Prayer." In the face of fear, it allowed Margie to return to the faith she was taught in Sunday School at Galilee Baptist Church in Fairfield. It was crowded and the darkness prevented Margie from seeing whose voice was so beautiful that it silenced her fears as the melodic notes were carried by the wind to every corner of the courtyard.[20]

Margie described how she and the other students were transferred from their first holding place to another location under the cover of darkness. As they were loaded into police vehicles, "they rode us around Birmingham for hours, just back and forth, fast, turning, we're falling on each other. So, we finally got to Fair Park Arena. That's where we were housed for three days."[21] Nearly fifty years later, she recalled being afraid of what could happen at night and the terror of hearing girls being taken from their holding area the first

Young female protesters in detention in Birmingham May 1963. Source:
©Bob Adelman

and second night they were in custody and raped by police or guards. As
her thoughts traveled back to those days, she realized she never knew what
became of the teenage girls who were screaming as they were abducted by
the police and then silenced by the trauma their bodies held. The horrible
conditions at the makeshift jail included repulsive food such as grits with
roaches sticking out, overcrowded sleeping areas where you were lucky if
your head could make it on a mattress while your body remained on the
cold concrete, and limited bathrooms that did not work—conditions made
even more untenable as many of the young women were on their menstrual
cycles.[22] Margie realized that her parents did not know if she was dead or
alive and the stress of her mother's potential angst began to affect her physically. Unbeknownst to Margie, her mother began praying for her from the
moment Regina reported that she was part of the protest. After three days
in custody, her mother finally found out where Margie was located and went
to the makeshift jail with Rev. Boykin, one of the pastors in the neighborhood, to get her out. This praying mother was determined to retrieve her
daughter before anything bad happened to her, and after "cutting up" as

Margie describes it, her mother's dramatic scene compelled the officers to let Margie out after-hours without going through a more official release process.

Despite the horrors of being arrested and held for three days Margie's commitment to the freedom struggle remained. She drew on lessons she was taught in Sunday School at Galilee Baptist Church as she found the courage to act. As she described it, there was support and agency within the community that shaped her, where friends or family members were free to actively protest at points of battle drawn by White segregation practices or stay in the comfort of the all-Black areas and pray and give funds to support bails. While everyone in the Fairfield community may not have been supportive, there is a sense of agency that Margie, her friend Regina, and her mother illustrate which did not ostracize Black women and girls on either side of the struggle. In reflecting on her choices, Margie remarked, "I was always one of those kind of militant type girls . . . If they said, let's go. Okay. I'll go. So I guess with doing that and being from Fairfield and in that era, if you asked me if I had to do it again I'd say yeah. I'd do it again."[23] Even with the knowledge that she gained as an adult regarding the depth of the danger that they were in as young people, Margie believed she would once again tap into the courage to resist injustice so that life could be better for others.

Janice Wesley Kelsey was also arrested as a part of what is known as Birmingham's Children's Crusade in May of 1963. She was not concerned as much about any fall-out from marching with protestors as she was about messing up her grade point average that she had worked hard to maintain as a high school student. After James Bevel awakened her to the inequities she experienced in Birmingham, the awareness prompted her to go through nonviolence training where she and other students watched films from various southern cities and were encouraged to respond, "to violence by singing a freedom song, bowing on our knees, covering our head for protection or saying a prayer." Janice decided she would participate when the opportunity presented itself.[24] The morning of the designated D-day, she packed some additional personal items in her bag as she went to school. Along with her school supplies she included the family's shared tube of toothpaste, soap, a change of underwear, and a jacket because she was warned that it would be cold in jail. Janice and her friends were excited as they checked in with each other that morning to make sure that everyone was committed to walking out.[25] They were still planning to march, however, the potential of not doing well in school, the one thing that had been ingrained in Janice as the way forward for her community, made her pause. So that morning, as she prepared to resist the systems which held her people back regardless of their educational standing, Janice asked her first period teacher at Ullman High

School what she describes as a hypothetical question. "If some kids walked out of class, are they going to fail?," to which her young teacher responded, "if everyone walks, there's no one to fail." With that, Janice felt confident that the school officials would not do anything to stop them, so she spread the word to other students. Courage, which is often a result of actions chosen in the face of fear, was strengthened by the assumed support of the school and community that shaped them.

That day, the agreed upon signal was the school bell indicating the change of classes. The ringing of the bell that day marked the change in the trajectory of many young lives as they summoned the courage to resist expectations of passive acceptance of the status quo. In a scene not quite as dramatic as Margie's experience at Fairfield Industrial High, students at Ullman started yelling "It's time! It's time!" and began walking out and the teachers did not stop them. One teacher's strategy was to turn her back and start writing on the blackboard so she would not see them leave. This simple act of resistance enabled the teacher to subversively support the students without verbally saying that it was okay to leave school and join the march.[26]

Janice left school, marched, and was arrested along with other classmates. They were taken to family court and then transported by school buses to the county courthouse in downtown Birmingham. She recalls the excitement of riding the yellow buses as she and others cheered their arrival. Their puzzling reaction exposed yet another inequity in the southern city because despite the tax dollars their families paid, Black students were not allowed to ride a school bus like White students but were instead forced to walk to their segregated schools regardless of the distance. As Janice sat down on the front seat of the bus, it was an experience to remember for many reasons.

The Board of Education of the City of Birmingham issued an order on May 20, 1963, directing principals to suspend or expel students who participated in the demonstrations, and Professor Oliver of Fairfield High threatened to enforce the decision, but the Black community rallied to support the students.[27] Despite the community support, some students in Birmingham were suspended, in some cases for being arrested during a Saturday march which was not a violation of school attendance policies. Rev. Calvin Woods, whose daughter Linda Cal Woods was suspended from Washington School only days before the end of the academic year, brought a suit against Theo R. Wright, Superintendent of Schools of the City of Birmingham, Alabama. When the lower court ruled in favor of the Board of Education, Woods appealed to the Fifth Circuit Court of Appeals.[28] Stirred by the courage and convictions of young people, many in the community began to work to cultivate and strengthen their efforts to resist the injustice that had seemingly always been.

Protestors loaded on a bus and taken to a detention center. Birmingham, 1963. Source: ©Bob Adelman

Cultivating Courageous Resistance

Courageous resistance is cultivated among both individuals and groups; it marks a move beyond the space of naïveté that can take place during a liminal assessment of dual realities as self and collective and forces an encounter with real conflicts. Courage to resist inherently requires an openness to take risks. On the surface, many acts of resistance during the Civil Rights Movement might seem benign, however, even the seemingly small acts of sitting in a particular seat on a bus, walking into the front door of a business, requesting to purchase a cup of coffee, or praying at the altar in a church could and often did result in emotional, physical, and spiritual harm. It has been argued that courageous resistance to injustice nurtures communal forces and builds social capital when the resisters refuse to turn away if they or others are victimized.[29] Young activists like Margie, Beatrice, Janice, and others who engaged in the struggle comprised a minority within the Black community, so they often relied on each other for support.

Not unlike the mob mentality that fueled racist opposition, the presence of other activists resisting oppression often strengthened an individual's resolve to continue to fight. Beatrice participated in training sessions led by CORE where through simulations of being heckled and pushed by aggressors, she and others learned to clear their minds and not react by saying or doing anything. They trained and prepared as best as they could. Yet, Beatrice reflects that the simulations and real situations differed, noting, "you have this information and you're told how you can react and how you should react and how you should not, but you really don't know until you go through it . . . we were prepared for whatever."[30] The preparation was a part of the cultivation of courage as unknown terrors were anticipated and strategies of safe nonviolent resistance were shared. Beatrice recalls her first arrest when she was a student at Bennett College in Greensboro, North Carolina.

> [I]t was a Thanksgiving weekend or something and they had had this big ad in the paper. 'Bring your family to dinner at S&W Cafeteria,' so we had with us a young man who was a Quaker. He was a European American guy, and so . . . there were 50 of us in all that were arrested, . . . So, we all came and we sat down at the seats in these people's cafeteria, and I'm reading my book and he said . . . 'I brought my family. You advertised. I brought my family for Thanksgiving dinner.' 'Oh no. We don't serve colored,' [*mimicking the voice of a southern White woman*] so we just sat and we sat and we knew we'd be arrested.
>
> We just sat and we sat until the police came and people were eating around us and people were looking at us like we were inhuman. What are you doing here, you must be crazy kind of thing, but again, I didn't make eye contact with anybody. My little face was right in my book [she took Plato's *Republic* with her], and then the police came and took us away and there were other people who . . . must have been outside while we were inside because they were singing. They were outside. I remember the singing, and so some people were not ever to have come in . . . It was very, very planned.[31]

The organization and planning of the sit-in ensured that there would be audible support as well as visual witnesses for the fifty students and at least one Bennett faculty member sitting inside the cafeteria. The supporters stood in harm's way on the outside of the cafeteria as a mob gathered and police were called for those participating in the peaceful direct action on the inside. In a mutual exchange, the courage of those sitting inside reinforced the courage of students who remained standing outside singing freedom songs including "Ain't Gonna Let Nobody Turn Me Around" and vice versa. Beatrice described the options that they were given in their training to go limp and be carried away as a refusal to cooperate or to walk out on their own when arrested. Beatrice chose to walk out of the restaurant with her head up and her nice dress undisturbed. Despite mental and physical preparation, along with the training and support of those who stood outside in solidarity and to counter negative responses, there came a moment when Beatrice felt her courage falter momentarily when she realized that she was being taken to jail for her actions.

> You're aware of what's going on with you, that the police are taking you, but the song is still resonating . . . you hear them singing and you feel the song and then bam, that door closed . . . it was a sound—the sound of the door closing, that combination, that door closing, which was a literal separation from these other people and emotional separation in a sense from your support, the music. It was just overwhelming . . . for that moment, and I do think that that professor was there. Her name was Elizabeth Laizner I think, because she saw in my eyes for just that moment a kind of shock. Bam! [*Mimics the sound of the vehicle door slamming*] And I remember her reaching her hand out or something and we were both saying to each other "it's going to be alright." It was kind of like, now do you realize what you have really done.
>
> You know, it's one thing to decide you're going to stand out and sing somewhere or hold a picket sign even if you're standing up to people that are saying unpleasant things. That's one thing, but now you have separated yourself and you don't know where you're going and what's going to happen to you.[32]

Singing was a strategic tool utilized to build courage.[33] Another song Elizabeth Laizner recalled singing during protests in downtown Greensboro was "We Shall Not be Moved."[34] As long as Beatrice was with the larger group and could hear the singing of those supporting them outside, she remained courageous and committed. It was when the doors of the police vehicle slammed and muted the reassuring singing, that Beatrice began to realize her intentional communal act of resistance could have unknown individual consequences, especially in the South. She paused to face her reality, but she did not stop and break down. Although her worst fears of being taken somewhere that others would not know about and having something terrible done to her were not realized, she understood how the powerful and strategic support of others, particularly in this case the professor and those singing, reinforced her own courage to resist.

After Beatrice's first arrest, she continued to participate in Movement efforts in Greensboro. She was arrested the second time at the end of her sophomore year. This time she waited until after she completed her final

Paddy wagon behind Loveman's department store. Birmingham 1963.
Source: ©Bob Adelman

exams to participate in the sit-in so that she would not lose credit for the academic year in the way that some others who were arrested before finishing the term had. Beatrice walked out of her last final and back to her dorm room where she packed an overnight bag and told her roommate, who did not take part in the Movement, that she was going to jail. Drawing on the faith and desire to fight for freedom that her family raised her with, there was no hesitation or expectation that her actions would not trigger an arrest. She was doing what she felt she had to do, and her courage continued to build with each act of resistance.

The all-women's Bennett College (a United Methodist Church-related institution) that Beatrice attended had a history of activism including leading protests against the Carolina Theater in 1938 over its practice of editing Black people out of films.[35] In the 1960s, she and other Bennett students were able to cultivate their courageous resistance with the supportive leadership and protective guidance of Bennett's President, Dr. Willa B. Player. Dr. Player advised the Bennett Belles (as the students are known) as they planned and strategically organized the Greensboro sit-ins months prior to the famous February 1, 1960, act by four male students from North Carolina A&T. After the initial enthusiasm of the sit-ins the Belles continued to protest and be arrested regularly. When Movement efforts began to wane in Greensboro it was often the women from Bennett who stepped up and kept the pressure and attention on dismantling the Jim and Jane Crow policies and practices. Their president, Dr. Player, believed in their activism so much that she decided missing classes while arrested would not count as absences and made sure that teachers took class materials to students while they were in jail. Dr. Player courageously resisted the expectations of Black college leadership by not bowing to White pressure at the city or state level. A 1964 Bennett graduate recalls Player saying she would give out diplomas in jail if she had to. In the face of uncertainties and potential violence, her consistent support and leadership cultivated courageous resistance and undergirded the actions that allowed Bennett students, faculty, and staff to play significant roles in the development and executions of strategies in the fight for freedom and justice.

The courage to resist racist segregationist practices was also seen in the actions of Evelyn Jones Frazier, who opened Frazier's Café Society on West Hunter Street (now Martin Luther King Jr. Drive) in Atlanta's West End. Frazier's Café became one of the main locations on the west side where civil rights leaders would gather to strategically plan Movement activities prior to meetings being held at Paschal's restaurant (owned by brothers James and Robert Paschal) which often receives most of the recognition as an Atlanta civil rights planning site. Meetings that were held at Frazier's Cafe included several of the early SNCC sessions, and some of the only multi-racial planning and strategy meetings held on Atlanta's west side since it was illegal at the time for Blacks and Whites to come together in that way. Frazier had a room in the back of her restaurant where she allowed Movement leaders to meet without being seen by those driving by. She decided early in her career as a restaurateur that she would serve anyone. "I made my unofficial policy ... whoever wanted to dine at my place could do so without regard to color. Afterall, we were all God's people."[36]

As a Black woman business owner and active leader at Big Bethel A.M.E. Church, Frazier made the decision to not cower in the face of threats she regularly received for allowing Blacks and Whites to meet and eat together in her restaurant.[37] One regular patron told me about times when Frazier would occasionally walk around the restaurant greeting customers and pausing to look in corners.[38] He initially thought that she was looking for rodents, but later found out that a bomb threat had been called in and as a woman of class and courage she calmly maintained control as she made sure that her customers were safe without triggering alarm. Each time that a threat came, she trusted in God to protect her and courageously resisted while her restaurant continued to be a racially diverse gathering place. Her courage in the face of fire enabled leaders, including John Lewis, to feel confident and comfortable planning direct actions for SNCC from Frazier's Café.

During the Movement there was a reciprocal and contagious nature to courageous resistance. Much like a hot coal that grows in a fire when in proximity to other coals but quickly dies out when alone, courage sparked courage, and resistance sparked resistance.

Building Courage

As a young woman in New York City, Lillian Sue Bethel showed up on 42nd Street to support the northern efforts of Freedom Riders in 1961, before moving back to Albany, Georgia, for college. Having lived and worked in New York City for seven years before returning to the South, Lillian was older than many students at Albany State, and her "real life" experiences meant she was often viewed as a trusted source. Lillian describes encouraging others on campus to get involved in the Movement and not sit back. Her lived experiences solidified her understanding that there were persons across the nation engaged in actions to fight against the injustices and inequalities Blacks faced.[39] At the time, she found that fear limited many of the older people in her hometown of Albany who did not want to become involved in the freedom struggles despite the oppressive conditions in which they lived. In the beginning, this included Lillian's family, as well as some of the younger local people who initially did not see anything wrong with the inequitable situations that had always existed.

However, eventually many of them came around to see the need for change. Describing the general environment in Albany's Black community she shared, "you were taught in a sense to be fearful of authority. The only authority was White. I wasn't taught to be afraid of anything."[40] In a counter to what she saw as the norm, Lillian's courage was the result of her upbringing with a strong and independent aunt, Helen Burke Johnson, who would not accept White southerners' assumed superiority.[41] She modeled and cultivated resistance daily in small ways for Lillian.

As a college student Lillian felt she should be an active part of the change that was taking place because she knew the limiting systems of segregation should not exist, and as she described, her mind was already there in this space of future equitable existence. She saw students coming from the North to help in the southern freedom struggle, and she did not want others to fight more for those she knew and loved in the South than she did. She knew people looked up to her, and she utilized her closeness with younger students to convince them to get involved:

> There was a young lady in school, Tootie, we always called her Tootie . . . She, and a couple of others who were younger than me, we had developed a relationship and I could talk to them, and if they knew I was going I could get them to go and would ask them to get other folks to try to go . . . because we had a relationship it was easier to talk to them and get them to go and say . . . you know we need to do this we ought not to be doing this and blah, blah, blah. And they joined me in going to whatever marches we had and to the meetings. In fact, when I left school, I think they were still involved.[42]

Lillian understood the power she possessed to influence other students. She also knew that the younger students would have more courage to fight for justice if they did their resistance work as a part of a group, with other young women they trusted, so she recruited them to join her.

The first SNCC meeting with the Albany community took place in October 1961 in the basement of Bethel A.M.E. Church, under the pastorate of Reverend Ben Gay, where Lillian and her family attended.[43] The first mass meeting took place at Mt. Zion Baptist Church, which became one of the key locations for the transmission of information and motivation. Lillian says she got swept up into what was going on and the life lessons taught in the Albany Movement were as, if not more, important as what she and others were learning in their college classrooms.

Lillian's actions were not without risk for herself or the other young women she encouraged to participate. Vernon E. Jordan Jr., who served as the Georgia NAACP Field Director at that time, let the Albany State students know that the Georgia Board of Regents would immediately suspend students who had pending federal or state litigations against them.[44] Despite the warning, Lillian was determined to not let what happened to Freedom Riders in Alabama happen to the ones who rode into Albany. So, she and others went to city hall near the bus station to make their presence known as a counter to any negative actions that might have been planned. As she explained, "The whole idea was those people that were coming, we were not going to allow them [White segregationists] to beat them up without some support."[45] As a result of Lillian's commitment to resist the segregation practices of the Deep South, she and nearly forty other students were arrested and held in jail for a week, and Martin Luther King came to support them. Their arrests led Albany State President William H. Dennis Jr. to support the state mandate and suspend all of the college students who were arrested, including Lillian Sue Bethel, Annette Marie Jones (White), and Bernice Johnson (Reagon).

Annette Marie Jones (White) was not only expelled, but she also lost her crown as Miss Albany State College, 1961–1962. She felt the support of her actions from other students, and in the words of their undefeated football coach, Obie W. O'Neal, who said to Annette on behalf of the team, "You will always be our golden queen."[46] However, she expected official support from the college as she and the other students were acting based on what they were being taught at Albany State, "to solve problems, to challenge injustices, and to stand up for our beliefs."[47] Instead, after a large demonstration at city hall that she, Lillian, and hundreds of other Albany State students participated in, Annette said, "the college put an end to such action through threats of job loss, loss of scholarships, full and immediate repayment of loans, and dismissal."[48] In spite of the college's threats, about one hundred students continued to resist and were subsequently arrested.

Annette's response mirrored that of Lillian and others. Annette explained, "I never felt that my choices or actions were wrong because I made them based on what my conscience and sense of justice compelled me to do."[49] She believed she had been born into the Movement by virtue of her place as a young Black woman in segregated Albany and her family's commitment to justice and the nurturing she received from her church community that reinforced love and the dignity of all people. "All the years of my life I was searching for some way to make things better, like I had been taught around the fireplace since I was four years old."[50] SNCC gave form to the rage that built up within her in the segregated South and she knew that even if it cost her something in the short-term, her courageous actions would make a difference for future generations. Annette was forced to repay part of the scholarship she received as Miss Albany State and she lost the graduate fellowship that the queen always received after graduation. Resistance required courage and courage involved risk and potential sacrifice.

In protest of the expulsion of the students, Albany State's Dean of Students, Irene Ashbury Wright, resigned and continued to support the students. Although the male administrative leaders on campuses including North Carolina A&T, Spelman, and Albany State acquiesced to White and elite Black expectations of compliance to racist practices, women administrators including Dean Irene A. Wright and President Willa B. Player helped to cultivate courageous resistance among students. Unfortunately, many, who were first-generation college students, were not able to recover after their suspension and they paid a deep and long-lasting cost for their courageous resistance.

Northern Cultivation of Courageous Resistance

Unlike Beatrice and Lillian, college students who could make choices to join the Civil Rights Movement without notifying their parents, the experience of Rose Davis Schofield differed because of her young age and the structure and policies of the local NAACP chapter in Elizabeth, New Jersey, for minors. Francis Kennedy served as the president of the Elizabeth NAACP from 1959 to 1963; he explained that the consent forms "were used to protect the kids and the organization. It proved no coercion; the kids were volunteering to participate and even be arrested."[51] Before Rose could participate in activities that might result in her arrest, a consent form had to be signed by an adult guardian. Her southern-raised mother, aunt, and grandmother feared retaliation by Whites in New Jersey who they relied on for jobs as domestic workers, so they did not support her participation. These women's fears were based on their lived experiences growing up in a deeply segregated South and their proximity to Whites in whose homes they worked. White-owned newspapers often included addresses of persons arrested or otherwise detained for involvement in acts of resistance, making the protesting actions not simply dangerous for the activist but also their families.[52] However, Rose's grandfather encouraged her and signed the consent form so she could actively participate in protests and gatherings throughout the city.

One of the daily protests Rose participated in during the summer of 1963 was organized by the Elizabeth NAACP and her pastor, Rev. Lasalle Marshall Watts, was one of the coordinators. This was a time when Elizabeth's Black community was anchored with multiple churches, a dentist, an undertaker, and other Black-owned businesses. Following the leadership of the NAACP, they fought for Black contractors to have the opportunity to submit bids and be fairly considered for construction jobs in the city of Elizabeth and Union County more broadly. Kennedy describes multiple efforts to challenge local injustices that he helped organize and lead, with the effort to generate bids for the expansion of the county courthouse annex and jail as the largest collective action in the northern New Jersey area. The annex expansion was built at a cost of $5 million taxpayer dollars, yet no Blacks had access to benefit from that form of work.[53]

Rose recalls that they would often meet at her church as a staging place, and each day a certain number of children were assigned to be arrested, especially since the adults needed to work and the students were out of school for the summer. They made sure the young people were teenagers but not old enough to be considered an adult in which case an arrest would have a greater impact on their future.[54] After protesting for multiple days, the younger protestors including Rose decided to make a larger statement because the White construction companies were continuing to move forward with their plans. It was a very hot summer that year, and many young people might have easily used that as a reason to stay home. Yet, with courage and conviction Rose made a stand by taking a seat along with other teenagers in the middle of the street between Caldwell Place and Rahway Avenue that led to an active construction zone in downtown Elizabeth. Kennedy explained that he and Henry Brown purchased the locks from a storage agency (the adult leaders had a way to release them if necessary) which were used on the chains connecting the young people to the dump trucks as anchors and they used their bodies to block the construction entrance.[55] Rose describes the experience this way,

> I wasn't just on the sidewalk or somebody's house or at the church. We were in the street. We were blocking the street. So, traffic could not come up and down that street that's for sure. We made sure of that. And we were up early in the morning, . . . it had to be during the summer that we were doing this, because we were up in the morning and up late at night, because sometimes we didn't leave church 'till 10–11 o'clock at night, 12 o'clock at night because they would do their planning, and we would be there with the adults.
>
> We were chained and there was this big Mack Truck and it was coming to unload something in that area where they were building, and we were all sitting there chained together. I mean it was something that they could unlock because we were all children, . . . I guess I had to be about 15 or 16 years old, something like that in that age group. The truck just kept coming and coming and then I'm like oh no is he really going to hit us? They took a picture and I'm just like this [*shows expression of shock on her face*] looking at the truck and you could see the dog and the emblem.[56]

Rose's disruption of the construction company's business and courageous resistance to unjust policies and practices as a teenager reflected the significant and consistent support from her grandfather, godmother, and the courage that was cultivated by her pastor at Mt. Teman A.M.E. Church.

> Our pastor, Pastor Watts at that time, during the Civil Rights movements pertaining to Martin Luther King, he decided that this is something that we needed to do as our church, and we would be the headquarters for it even though we were a little tiny church. I don't even think we were as big as the bottom part of this church [*Big Bethel A.M.E.*], but he decided that this is something that he had to do and wanted to do. So a lot of times we would meet at our church and then we would meet at other churches in town, but our church was the spearhead of the project.[57]

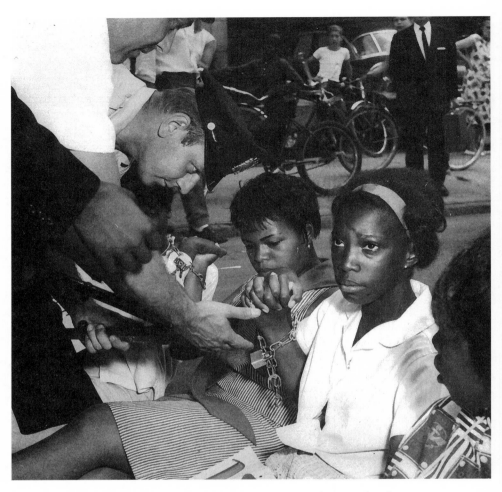

Rose Davis Schofield far right and other teens as police cut the chains in Elizabeth, New Jersey. August 9, 1963. Source: Image courtesy of Francis Kennedy.

Rose recalls Pastor Watts explaining to the congregation that despite their relatively small size, they were going to make space available. He exposed Rose and others to structures for activism that were in-line with their Christian principles. He, like many justice-focused Black pastors, made sure that all church members belonged to the NAACP. "On Sunday mornings when Reverend Watts got up there, he talked about God, but he talked about what we had to do for ourselves, too. We had to help ourselves, and in order

Young people protesting in Elizabeth, New Jersey, blocking large construction trucks. August 7, 1963. Source: Image courtesy of Francis Kennedy.

to help ourselves these are some of the things we had to do. We had to have demonstrations. We had to have the marches, you know, and so forth and so on—and the money. And people didn't mind giving money."[58] Rose was taught the idea of sacrifice and socioreligious responsibility from her pastor, and she felt compelled to do whatever she could to help fight the injustices she saw around her.

Rose participated in daily protests but did not see any changes on the part of White city leaders or the construction company, so she moved from a five-pound to twenty-pound bag of rice/courage. She and other teenagers decided to take the level of disruption up and create a bigger awareness within the community and region as the police stepped in and arrested them for blocking the construction site. When she was arrested, her grandfather walked all over Elizabeth to find the police station where she was being held so that she could be released into his custody.[59] Rose knew she did not have support from the women in her family, but knowing that her grandfather was fully behind her and her pastor constantly preaching that it was the right thing to do, cultivated the courage to stay in the fight for justice as she and others resisted the White establishment that maintained racially segregated practices in New Jersey.

Strengthening the Virtue of Courage

Gwendolyn Robinson (later Zoharah Simmons) was raised by her grandmother in Memphis, Tennessee.[60] She, like so many other young Black people growing up in the South, was protected by her grandparents and father from the harsh realities of the deeply racist society that existed outside of her all-Black community. During the summer between her junior and senior year of high school Zoharah wanted to work and earn money for college. As she applied for jobs advertised in the local newspaper, she was constantly rebuked and told that the office and department store jobs she sought were not for a "colored girl." After one such dismissal she found herself stuck in a storm and drenched by rain as thunder and lightning surrounded her. When she noticed White adults inside the downtown stores looking at her through the window and not offering shelter, feelings of fear, anger, and hatred toward Whites arose in her for what she believed was the first time.

As she boarded a city bus to go back to the safety of her Black community, she sat dripping wet on the front seat and dared anyone from the White bus driver who had issued the verbal directive, "Gal, I don't want no trouble; you better git on to the back, where you belong," to the Black patrons who were afraid for her and themselves and beckoned her to come to the back, to try to physically move her. In that moment as the White driver spoke the teenage Zoharah found the courage to hold her ground and her resistance began. "I looked away from them, unmoved, and stared straight ahead. I had no plans, no rational thoughts. I did not know what I was going to do. All I knew was that I was not going to give up my seat without a struggle. I didn't know how far I was prepared to go. I thought, *I am a human being, not a dog. I am a person just as good as they are.*"[61] Zoharah later realized that what she had done on that rainy afternoon was potentially more dangerous than she knew, yet her courage in that moment awakened something in her and she subsequently joined the NAACP youth organization. She began singing in the NAACP choir and was shaped by their messages of justice and the call for freedom. In Maya Angelou's analogy, she was picking up a five-pound bag of rice and cultivating courageous resistance.

Zoharah earned a scholarship to Spelman College, a private women's college in Atlanta, and although she had promised her grandmother that she would not do anything that distracted from her schoolwork, she was exposed to teaching and preaching in Atlanta that continued to pull her toward the Movement. Zoharah was raised in Gospel Temple Baptist Church in Memphis and she wanted to stay true to her roots, so when a classmate invited her to West Hunter Street Baptist Church only a few blocks from Spelman, she agreed to go and continued to attend each Sunday and became active in the choir. She also met the pastor, Movement leader Rev. Ralph David Abernathy. Although she tried to heed her grandmother's admonitions, Zoharah cultivated her resistance not only in the classrooms of Spelman College, but also in the pews of West Hunter on Sunday mornings and during Mass Meetings on weekday evenings.[62]

Zoharah describes her move toward resistance as gradual, but the changes in the way she thought, believed, and acted were clear and began to define her life. Her involvement began by helping out behind the scenes at the SNCC headquarters which was within walking distance of her campus. Under the leadership of James Forman and Ruby Doris Smith Robinson, Zoharah initially worked in support capacities typing press releases, stuffing envelopes, and mimeographing in an effort to ensure her actions would not be found out by administrators at Spelman or her family back in Memphis. She committed to staying away from the more public and dangerous activities and worked hard to maintain her grades so that she would not put her scholarship at risk. As the first person in her family to go to college she did not want anything to come in the way of her goal of graduating. She was able to balance her backroom activism with academics during her first year, but shortly before the start of her second year, a new spark was started with the 1963 March on Washington for Jobs and Freedom. Although her grandmother prevented her from boarding the buses that traveled from Memphis to DC, she devoured everything she could about the event, and as the community gathered in the living room to watch the coverage on her family's television, she selectively shared that she had met Martin Luther King Jr. and Coretta Scott King, and had been to Ebenezer Baptist Church in Atlanta to the amazement of her

Memphis neighbors, without revealing that her connection to the Movement went deeper than casual encounters at church.[63]

As the new school year began her involvement catapulted from behind the scenes to a leadership position when she was elected by the Committee on Appeal for Human Rights (COAHR) to serve on SNCC's board as a part of the coordinating committee from the Atlanta University Center (AUC).[64] Much like Lillian did at Albany State, Zoharah also began recruiting other young women from Spelman to join her at the SNCC headquarters. She began participating in targeted demonstrations along with other Spelman students and initially she was able to strategically leave before police stepped in. However, in the spring of 1964, while protesting in front of the Pickrick Restaurant in Atlanta owned by staunch segregationist Lester Maddox, Zoharah was arrested for her first time along with other students. The students sang loudly to strengthen their courage as they were apprehended by police. As if picking up the thoughts she had during her first act of resistance as a teenager in Memphis, Zoharah recalls thinking to herself as she looked through the bars of the paddy wagon on her way to jail, "sometimes a woman has got to take a stand and do what she's got to do."[65] She summoned courage to resist the segregationist practices of local businesses and when the time came she drew strength from the other young college women who were arrested with her as they all faced the realities of jail together.

Zoharah was justifiably afraid that she would be kicked out of school for her actions. Spelman professors taught classes that mapped the history of Black freedom struggles and encouraged students to take their place within them, however the male dominant administration was not supportive of those actions. When she and the other students were released from jail, Zoharah had to face the Dean, who made her call home and explain to her grandmother what she had done. She was then placed on probation for lying about where she was and bringing dishonor to Spelman by being arrested. Her classmates, however, were encouraged by her courageous acts and eagerly cheered her return from jail when she entered the dining hall. Despite the fear of losing her scholarship, which was the only reason she was able to attend Spelman, Zoharah describes being "bitten by the bug of resistance" and her actions to stand for justice and freedom would not stop.[66]

Zoharah and other young women at Spelman built up their courage with each act. They decided to create a strategic sit-in campaign targeting a national fast-food chain, which had multiple locations in Atlanta. Over the course of three days, they sat-in from the morning through the lunch hour with the goal of disrupting business in a way that took its profits in order to prompt a change in its segregation practices. The first two days were without much incident as the managers would close the doors so no one else could enter after the Black students arrived. By the third day, however, the White resistance had elevated from passive closure to active violence.

Zoharah describes how the windows had been coated so it was impossible to see in or out. When the manager announced the closure of the restaurant as had been done on the previous days, Zoharah noticed something different in the facial expression of the White waitresses who knew what was about to happen next. Zoharah and the other students were attacked by young White men who had been hiding in the back of the restaurant with sticks and clubs. The restaurant manager and waitresses also joined in the melee with the White women grabbing and scratching the students who were sitting in. The nonviolence training that the young women participated in took a back seat to their desire to protect themselves in the face of the ambush. Zoharah punched and pushed the waitress who attacked her, and she began throwing plates and cups at other White aggressors to keep them away.

This kind of predictability of Whites' violent responses to Blacks' assertions of equality led James Forman to assign three men from SNCC to accompany the Spelman women at a distance in case something like this happened.[67] The men broke through the glass door and began to beat the White men who were attacking the women. When Atlanta's police arrived, they charged Zoharah and the other students with crimes including "inciting to riot, rioting, disorderly conduct, assault and battery, and destruction of private property."[68] This arrest would mark Zoharah's second time in jail, and this time she and the others would stay for three days. She was now carrying a twenty-pound bag of rice.

When the bug of resistance bit Zoharah, it also pushed her to begin to actively resist some of the restrictive practices and policies at Spelman. She helped promote rallies on campus to obtain more freedom for young women who were extremely limited in the places they were permitted to go during the evenings. These patriarchal limitations of in loco parentis were often viewed by the administration as necessary for the physical and psychological protection of the students who understood the potential dangers in the deeply segregated city of Atlanta, which despite its self-proclamation was definitely not a "city too busy to hate."[69] When President Albert Manley and the Dean of Students dismissed Gwendolyn Robinson (Simmons) and Barbara Simon from Spelman after their second arrest, the women of Spelman found the courage to stand up and stage a protest on the lawn of the President's home demanding that the two be reinstated. This act put the more than one hundred students who gathered for the rally in jeopardy of retaliation, but the bug of resistance that fueled the fight for freedom and justice had bitten others as well and they would not back down. Through the support of her Spelman sisters, Zoharah was once again allowed to stay in school but under even stricter probation than after her first arrest.

None of the women in my study admitted going to events with the intention of having the spotlight placed on them as individuals. They were not seeking to have their names featured on the nightly news as the "real" civil rights activists who were willing to take risks without the financial safety of being on Movement organization payrolls. At times their actions were collective and at other times they acted alone, without others there to support or even bear witness if something went wrong, knowing full well that their womanhood would not protect them from danger. The young women's courage was invoked in the face of physical, emotional, and spiritual risk, yet they persisted. The courage to resist required a commitment to act that grew out of a heritage of resistance that was often a continuation of the way they, and other Black women, had been living in the world for much of their lives. They found courage to act despite opposition because they believed the justice and freedom they imagined for themselves and future generations had been placed in their thoughts by God.

Dr. Willa Beatrice Player

A Cultivator of Courage in a College Community

Students at Bennett College for Women were some of the most active young people in the Greensboro movement. Greensboro believed itself to be more progressive than other southern cities, yet, at one point during the height of the nonviolent direct activism that challenged segregation practices nearly 40 percent of Bennett's student body had been arrested and jailed for their bold actions. Bennett's students found the courage to apply their Constitutional rights and resist segregation through the support of Dr. Willa Beatrice Player, the President of Bennett College.

Born in Jackson, Mississippi, on August 9, 1909, Player and her family moved to Ohio in 1917, the state in which she received the majority of her formal education from elementary school through college. Upon graduation from Ohio Wesleyan in 1929 she returned home to become the first Black woman teacher in the Akron school district. After completing her master's at Oberlin College in 1930, Player was hired to teach Latin and French at Bennett College and serve as director of religious activities. While teaching, she studied abroad in France and obtained the Certificat D'Etude from the University of Grenoble in 1935. She later earned her EdD from Teachers College, Columbia University, in 1948, where her dissertation, "Improving College Education for Women at Bennett College: A Report of a Type A Project," became a template for the work she continued to undertake as she emphasized student engagement with complex social problems in the broader community.[1] Player began to take on administrative leadership roles serving as Director of Admissions and Acting Dean, Coordinator of Instruction, Vice President, and ultimately the first female President of Bennett College from 1956 to 1966.[2]

Dr. Willa B. Player, Bennett College Yearbook. Source: Image courtesy of the Bennett College Archives at Thomas F. Holgate Library.

Two years into her presidency, as the Civil Rights Movement and the fight for freedom and justice continued to grow, Player created space for the cultivation of courageous resistance in Greensboro when other Black leaders were afraid.[3] After local Black schools and churches closed their doors for fear of White retaliation, on February 11, 1958, from the pulpit at Bennett's Annie Merner Pfeiffer Chapel, Martin Luther King Jr. delivered his speech, "A Realistic Look at Race Relations," addressing the fight for school integration in Greensboro.[4] Player made sure that Bennett seniors were inside the packed chapel along with community members. All other students and guests were able to hear King's words via speakers set up in satellite areas throughout the campus. This speech was credited for helping spark flames in young people who became student leaders in the Greensboro movement including then sixteen-year-old Dudley high school student Jibreel Khazan (Ezell Blair Jr.) who listened from one of the nearby buildings and later became one of the Greensboro Four whose February 1, 1960, sit-in brought renewed energy to the Civil Rights Movement nationally.[5]

When Bennett students met with Player in the late fall of 1959 to discuss a sit-in they planned in downtown Greensboro, she agreed with their desire to challenge injustice as they experienced it, however, she recommended that they wait until the spring semester started so they would not lose momentum when students went home for winter break.[6] Students from the Agricultural and Technical College of North Carolina (later North Carolina A&T University) had also been a part of the initial planning meetings with Bennett students that fall, including some who were a part of the legendary February 1st act.[7] Caught off guard, Bennett Belles who had been waiting for a unified and organized start, joined the sit-in on February 2nd and continued to remain some of the most organized and courageous resisters over the three years that marked the primary period of the Greensboro movement. The Student Executive Committee for Justice, co-led by Gloria Brown from Bennett and Ernest Pitt from A&T, was formed and began operating by the second day of the sit-ins with goals to set strategy, keep students informed, and recruit more protesters.[8]

Dr. Player recalls finding out that Bennett students were involved in the sit-ins when she saw a couple of the young ladies on the front page of the New York Times Magazine.[9] From the very beginning she was clear that she was not going to prevent her students from participating. Player met with key faculty members including Mrs. Louise Streat and Drs. George Breathett, Chauncey Winston, J. Henry Sayles, and Francis Grandison, all of whom were long-standing members of the Bennett and broader Greensboro communities, to figure out an approach for providing support. They discussed the purpose of a liberal arts college and determined that what the Bennett students were doing was an expression of the tenets of a liberal arts education. In Player's words, this education was "freedom of expression. It was living up to your ideals, building a quality of life in the community that was acceptable to all. It was respect for human dignity and personality. And it was a recognition of values that applied to all persons as equals and all persons who deserved a chance in a democratic society to express their beliefs."[10] Distinct from most other college students, those who attended Bennett had the direct support of their president who was convinced that their actions were a part of engaged scholarship that put into practice the things she hoped they were learning in the classroom.

Often if CORE needed a place for twenty to thirty people to meet and organize, Bennett's campus, including Pfeiffer Hall's social hall, provided the perfect place.[11] Dr. Player not only supported her students' activism, but also that of the faculty and staff, including Rev. Hatchett, Rev. Bush, Mr. McMillan, Elizabeth Laizner, and others as they worked with student protesters.[12] Activist faculty members continued to teach even when they stayed out late protesting with students. The daily sit-ins during the height of the Greensboro Movement required a daily infusion of students during the lunch hour. Dr. Player made sure that Bennett students who participated did not miss out on anything. Many lunch counter protests were organized so that they would be the most disruptive for the businesses and the least disruptive for the students' schedules. Faculty member Elizabeth Laizner describes that under the direction of Player, the young women who were going to picket S&W's restaurant during the profitable lunchtime rush, were provided an earlier lunch by the college's dietitian, Mrs. Jones, during the chapel break hour. Because they were living their faith out in action, they were excused from chapel for that day and Laizner would ensure there were enough faculty members from Bennett and A&T to drive the students downtown to picket the store during the lunch hour and bring them back to campus in time for their 1:15 p.m. class.[13]

When Governor Terry Sanford highly encouraged the presidents of North Carolina A&T and Bennett to convince their students to stop protesting, Dr. Player refused to comply.[14] Later, Player was anonymously tipped that students had been placed in an old polio hospital without inspection of the facility, making it not legally sanctioned to hold them, so she researched the legal code in the library and challenged the chief of police.[15] Governor Sanford wrote a letter to the acting president of A&T, Lewis Dowdy,[16] and under the Governor's direction the A&T students were released into the custody of the college.[17] This plan was not acceptable to Player who met with a police captain and explained the code and her pursuit of legal action if her students were not removed from the polio hospital. She explained to the captain, "unless they [police] agreed to lift the charges from the Bennett girls, that they were going to stay out there and I was going to pursue this other thing." Player then went to the makeshift jail and met with her students telling them, "Now, you just stay here."[18] She further explained to the students, "Bennett College is not a jail and we will not accept [students] released into our custody until the chief of police lifts your sentences."[19] The students knew they had a consistent advocate in their president. It was Player's belief that the city should not have arrested the students if they did not have suitable places to retain them. Player's work on behalf of her Bennett Belles as they courageously stood up for justice paid off when the charges against them were withdrawn and they were able to leave the polio hospital and return to campus.

Dr. Player met with the president of Bennett's student senate and confirmed that she and the faculty intended to support them and asked that the students give her a daily report of their plans.[20] She later explained that the students did not need her "approval" because what they were struggling for was within their rights. Her support created an environment for creative and courageous resistance. When reflecting on this years later Player noted,

> the students were very cooperative, and they would always come to me first to tell me what they were going to do, or what they were planning, or what it was all about, and they would ask me if I had any suggestions. And so it was a communication and give-and-take that was so open that the students never did anything behind your back, or feeling that it was something that you did not approve of or holding back what they were going to do.[21]

Player felt comfortable with the way in which the student leaders kept her updated and this enabled her to make arrangements behind the scenes to be sure that Bennett students would be as safe as possible as they stood up against the deeply entrenched Jim and Jane Crow laws of the south.[22] As Bennett Belles filled the jails in Greensboro, and learned socio-political lessons outside of the classroom, Player ensured they did not fall behind on the education taking place inside the classroom. She met with Bennett faculty and administration each night to guarantee that students received what they needed to maintain their college courses. She described the operation they set up as something akin to an army camp where they had mail call, took extra food to the students, and faculty members delivered assignments to the jails each day so the young women did not fall behind.[23] During the first semester of the sit-ins Player's niece, Linda Brown, recalls her aunt saying, "They are acting out of their conscience. They will take their exams in jail if they have to, and we will make that possible."[24]

Unlike many other Black college presidents with active student bodies, such as the president of Spelman College in Atlanta, who called parents to warn them that their children were on the brink of suspension for their activism, Player sent telegrams to the parents of all of the Bennett students who were in jail. One such telegram in May of 1963 read, "Your daughter is among student demonstrators who refused bond and accepted arrest. The college is doing everything possible to assure her safety and well being. Shall notify you if the situation requires. Please feel free to write or call

Broadway 2–3609. Best Wishes Willa B. Player President."[25] Dr. Player also reached out to influential friends to help pay the bail of Bennett Belles.[26] While helping cultivate their resistance she made sure that they were able to maintain their schoolwork while in custody and made financial provisions for them to be released when their time came.

Player proclaimed to the Greensboro community and beyond that Bennett was "a liberal arts college where freedom rings." Her students' impact was felt throughout Greensboro with Operation Door Knock, which significantly increased the number of Black registered voters. The Bennett Belles did not stop at registering voters but also made sure it was logistically possible for Black women to vote by babysitting children so mothers could go to the polls on election day.[27] Player even marched with students and community members from Bennett's Student Union Building to Elm Street in downtown Greensboro during the spring of 1963.[28] Her actions were not without retaliation as Bennett student Johnsie Williams Thomas recalls a cross being burned on campus as a response to Player's actions.[29]

Dr. Player was a woman of faith and she lived out her faith through educational leadership. She was an active member of St. Mathews Methodist Episcopal (later United Methodist) Church in Greensboro. She spoke throughout the nation at mission schools, annual meetings, and college seminars, and served as a leader in the denomination working with the National Commission on Religion and Race of the Methodist Church and the National Commission on United Methodist Higher Education. She supported activism through education and created an environment at Bennett College where students, faculty, and staff were able to play important roles in the courageous fight for justice.

When speaking with Beverly Guy-Sheftall for an interview published in *SAGE: A Scholarly Journal on Black Women*, Player emphasized things that she wanted to be remembered for one day regarding her work during the Civil Rights Movement. "When you want to accomplish the best in your life, you not only involve other people, but you *free* other people to perform as they see best. That's why I never said to the Bennett students to go to jail, but when they went on their own beliefs, I wanted them to be sure to realize that they did so because of what *they* had learned—because of the kinds of experiences they had at Bennett which enabled them to go to jail with dignity and purposefulness."[30] Willa B. Player was a cultivator of courageous resistance, and women including Beatrice Perry Soublet and Johnsie Williams Thomas became actively involved in the Civil Rights Movement as Bennett students as a result.

CHAPTER 4

"Keep Your Eyes on the Prize, Hold On"

Testing Theo-Moral Imagination

Philosophers and theologians have long examined the concept of moral imagination. Moral imagination can be understood as "the presumed mental capacity to create or use ideas, images, and metaphors not derived from moral principles or immediate observation to discern moral truths or to develop moral responses."[1] I perceive Theo-moral imagination along a spectrum of sight, imagination, and vision, where what you see gives you the ground from which to imagine more or something different, and that imagined reality allows you to construct a vision by which to obtain it. Theo-moral imagination happens in a liminal space, where hope works in collaboration with imagination, allowing a person to deftly move beyond physical and social boundaries because from the liminal space they see possibilities of more than they were previously aware of which exists outside the limitations of the current spaces they occupy. At times it may only be a glimpse of more, but it inspires a vision that can be worked toward with greater clarity regarding what strategies may be required to make access to the new space a reality. A distinct attribute of Theo-moral imagination is that what is seen both in the present and the future from the liminal space is revealed and made known in relation to God and the Divine. The radical visions that are constructed in order to make the theo-morally imagined possible are God guided.

Catholic theologian Philip S. Keane describes imagination as "a playful judgment leading us toward a more appropriate grasp of reality."[2] In many ways it is through a freedom to hope more is possible that judgment and other forms of limitations can be at least temporarily released. Hope is often possible because of previous encounters in relationship to the Divine. Theo-moral imagination, therefore, is not simply an intellectual exercise, but one connected to Divine revelations and visions of possibility. Theo-moral imagination is the space where God's plans are revealed. It is a liminal space where glimpses of what can be become visible, and strategies are constructed to make the visions that are revealed probable.

The power of imagination is that it unfetters thoughts and opens possibilities for more beyond what is currently known. The virtue ethics I have named Theo-moral imagination opens a second sight as a result of visions God provides which align with the teachings and traditions of faith, and can be checked against the moral mandate of justice as an output of love that most religions profess. When people are able to see themselves in ways that align with how God sees them, they are no longer constrained to the limiting visions of others, and they are therefore able to make changes rooted in the moral mandates for God's creations. During the Civil Rights Movement, women's Theo-moral imagination was often associated with revelations connected to the Christian faith as articulated through their hope for a more just future. This often led them to take bold actions they believed were ordained by God and therefore understood as something they "had to do."

Philosopher David Hume views imagination as a guide where we can envision how we would *feel* if the particular circumstances we played out in our mind's eye took place. A Theo-moral imagination allows a person to visualize what they would *do* in a particular circumstance. This was most evident in the women I interviewed who believed there were certain moral actions they had to do. For many women, their lived experiences created a state of hopeful anticipation of change that was based on revelations they received from God through scriptures, songs, and personal divine encounters.

Within the field of contemporary virtue ethics, imagination and narrative are influential concepts for ethical development and assessment.[3] In Christian Social Ethics, womanist ethicists have often relied on the imaginative aspects of Black women's narrative through literature to move beyond well ingrained forms of limitations in White male-dominated academic epistemologies.[4] Katie Geneva Cannon notes that within literature, imagination can be used by Black women to "crack the invidiousness of worn-out stereotypes."[5] Ethicist Thelathia "Nikki" Young describes imagining in communal familial structures explaining that "the process of imagining might be understood as simultaneously *survivalist*, in that it allows an individual or community to hold a consciousness about ideological and material circumstances that may be distinct from the reality in which we find ourselves; and *prophetic*, by making room for a vision that not only replaces the experience of current realities but also evokes action that makes new possibilities real."[6] Imagining therefore opens pathways that create future options that are not limited by present conditions.

John Paul Lederach insists on the centrality of imagination in the work of conflict transformation. Lederach suggests that: (1) "moral imagination develops a capacity to perceive things beyond and at a deeper level than what initially meets the eye"; (2) imagination emphasizes the creative act that takes place as "art makes moral reasoning possible"; and (3) "moral imagination has a quality of transcendence" causing it to break free from structural dead-ends.[7] Lederach sees moral imagination as the ability to see things rooted in real world challenges and imagine the creation of a solution that does not yet exist.[8] This reinforces my belief that moral imagination works from a liminal position, where new realities are believed to be possible but are not yet tangibly attainable.

As Lederach asserts, art is a conduit of moral reasoning. While Lederach looked to visual art for inspiration, art in all forms can be a vessel to facilitate change. During the Civil Rights Movement, Theo-moral imagination was expressed in song lyrics such as "Up above my head I see Freedom in the air, there must be a God somewhere," and in the creation of plays, poems, and other influential artistic works of the Black Arts Movement including Lorraine Hansberry's Broadway play *A Raisin in the Sun*, Amiri Baraka's play *Dutchman*, and Sonia Sanchez's poem *We BaddDDD People*. The articulation of the morals that fed the imagination of young activists is expressed in chants that echoed cries for freedom, including, "What do we want? Freedom! When do we want it? Now!" and their belief that what they imagined and hoped would actually become a reality through their collective efforts.

Imagination is a practice of freedom. Robin D. G. Kelley describes the Black radical imagination as "a collective imagination engaged in an actual movement for liberation."[9] Linking their imaginings to their actions, women during the Movement used a combination of strategic preparation and spontaneous execution to bring about social change. They exhibited a form of Theo-moral imagination in action with a womanist expectation that freedom would become a reality not simply for themselves, but for all persons. When Alice Walker created her four-part definition for "womanist," in addition to being "Committed to survival and wholeness of entire people, male *and* female" she describes one of the ways that this was made possible for the Black community through the moral imagination of Black women's visions of freedom as a possibility in lands they had not yet tread but believed they would because they were "Traditionally capable as in: 'Mama, I'm walking to Canada and I'm taking you and a bunch of other slaves with me.' Reply: 'It wouldn't be the first time.'"[10]

Imagination is also a tool of resistive resilience made possible in the acknowledgment that despite the reality, what currently is will not always be, because new ways forward are constantly revealed through God-guided imagination. As I spoke with women who were active during the Civil Rights Movement, understandings of God, as revealed most convincingly during the living out of faith in fear-inducing encounters, led the women to act in ways that centered justice as a moral mandate for them. Actively engaging in the struggle was something they believed they "had to do."

An understanding of God's role not only in their current situation, but also their future pushed Churchwomen in the Movement to act creatively and courageously, grounded in a lived religion of justice and freedom. This courage enabled women to walk *to* freedom in the mid-nineteenth century and walk *for* freedom in the mid-twentieth century. These women ultimately understood God as a just liberator, and they believed the injustice they experienced through personal interactions and structural policies would not always exist because they believed God would ultimately bring about change.

The arch of the moral universe was long, so they joined with others to actively push against societal systems in an effort to bend it toward justice.[11] This faith statement often quoted by Martin Luther King Jr. reflects a vision of ultimate victory for those who joined the fight. Religious women activists believed scripture—including Proverbs 29:18, where there is no vision, the people perish; Psalm 23, God is with you in the face of trying times; or Proverbs 3:6, in all your ways acknowledge God and your paths will be clear—supported God's vision for justice and freedom, and their faith became foundational in stretching their imagination. God was believed to be wise, powerful, and present in all places at the same time. They understood the God of the Bible to be the God who "made ways out of no ways" and delivered their foreparents from slavery. This was the same God they could look to as they hoped for a fully realized freedom for themselves and their children's children. They had to keep their eyes on the prize of freedom and not let the reality of the moment stop them from pressing forward.

Believing in a Better World

> We are building up a new world (3x)
> Builders must be strong.
>
> Courage sisters don't be weary,
> Courage brothers don't be weary,
> Courage people don't be weary,
> Though the road be long.[12]

With tears in her eyes, Beatrice Soublet describes what she imagined and hoped for at the age of nineteen when she was protesting, sitting-in, and being arrested as a student at the all-women's Bennett College in Greensboro, North Carolina. She believed she was taking action to create a better world for the children she would have some day. She hoped,

> [T]hat they wouldn't have to endure growing up being told that they couldn't go places because of their color and they couldn't be in this school and they couldn't sit there. And having their change thrown down on the counter instead of put in your hand. They wouldn't have to go through these little daily indignities . . . You couldn't try on clothes. You'd have to take them home [and hope they fit], and just treated like you're not worth anything. I didn't want my children to ever experience that.[13]

Her passionate belief in, and vision of, a society that respected the full humanity of her future children and others was what kept Beatrice focused and committed to the cause of justice and freedom when she was a sophomore in college. The vision to change society that young women such as Beatrice were pursuing in the mid-1950s and 1960s and the struggle to realize it was a fulfillment of the prayers of their parents and grandparents. Therefore, it became clear to some of them that their future children could also be the manifestation of their hopes and dreams.

Beatrice's family included a long line of Race men and Race women. Their confident and creative actions to create a better world were a part of her ethos so it seemed natural that she would do her part in the ongoing freedom struggle. Raised in the church in Louisiana, with both grandfathers as pastors, Beatrice was steeped in a vision for humanity that she lifted from her grandfathers' sermons and the lives of her parents whose understanding of God's word was reflected in their daily actions. Beatrice knew from her family that faith could undergird courage and she says the spirit of doing something to make things right for people is in her DNA. She knew the stories of her grandfather taking a group of teachers to a convention in Baton Rouge and then turning around and taking them back home when they were denied access to the motel rooms they reserved before arriving. She watched and listened attentively when her mother would speak up in department stores letting White women who believed it was their right to be served before anyone else know, "my daughter and I were here first." These influences helped shape her Theo-moral imagination in ways that resulted in her joining the ongoing struggle for justice and freedom when she saw an opportunity.

Margaret L. Evans grew up in the small Southeast Missouri town of Kennett. Her father, Cleo Green, was a self-educated man who did not have the opportunity for formal education after leaving school to work and support his family. He believed that women should bring as much as they could to the family, so he sent his wife to college. Unfortunately, Margaret's mother met someone else in college and did not return home. Her father, who she called her hero, raised her on his own until he later re-married. Green was determined that his family would never be poor or struggle and he ensured that his daughter had as many opportunities as possible. As she described it, as a child she "did the things that White kids did" and in her view, that allowed her to dream.

Margaret's father arranged for her to take private piano and voice lessons with White women who would only offer her lessons at night with the curtains closed so other White people would not see them. She was always the only Black student, but her father made sure that her dreams were not limited. He encouraged her to explore music as much as she could but cautioned that some White people would not be open to her and she might get her feelings hurt traveling to music events with White students from her newly integrated high school, where she was one of 17 Black students out of 500. Through a changing society where those in power fought to retain the inequities of the past, her father taught her not to cower down to anyone.

Margaret believed that a better world was possible, and her father created the opportunities for her to live in a liminal space. Although she wanted to go to the Juilliard School for music, she went to Lincoln University in Missouri and got married while she was in college. She had two children and began focusing on the public policy track of social work, believing that real change happened at higher legislative levels. Margaret felt that Black people needed to keep their eyes on the prize, and work to create a level playing field going forward. This vision was inspired by her father who gave her room to dream and imagine a world that was better than the one most experienced.[14]

More often than not, familial influences could go another way. In New Jersey, despite not receiving any support from her mother, aunt, or grandmother, who each believed the racial and gendered injustices Black women faced would always exist, Rose Davis Schofield imagined a better world linked to God's plan for her and others. She explains, "I just thought we would all be working together that we would have one goal, I thought that was what God wanted us to do. I might have been naive and I might still be naive but I just think that's what He wants."[15] The singular goal that Rose believed everyone should be working toward was equality, so she went to protests and mass meetings regularly to do her part in the fight toward the equality and justice that was consistent with the moral vision she was given by God as a teenager in Elizabeth, New Jersey.

Many of the women I interviewed expressed an understanding of God that was based in a belief that even if things were not currently good, God had the power to speak life into dead situations and societies that were operating counter to the will of God. Therefore, through their Theo-moral imagination, the women could "call those things that be not as though they were,"[16] manifesting a counterculture through God that centered on a radical love made known through justice. Despite what they saw and experienced in the current moment, they would not place limits on what an omnipotent God revealed to them, believing it could ultimately become a reality. Because their Theo-moral imagination was rooted in what God had revealed to them, they worked both within and against society to create the change they envisioned and imagined as possible, pushing and protesting whenever an opportunity presented itself.

Liminal Assessment

Anthropologist Victor Turner studied adolescents who participated in rites of initiation that resulted in liminal spaces for a short, designated window of time. In his 1964 essay, "Betwixt and Between: The Liminal Period in *Rites de Passage*," Turner writes of a period of margin or "liminality" as persons undergo initiations as rites of passage.[17] The liminal space is a time of almost but not yet during which initiates are living in or between multiple worlds at the same time. For Turner, during the liminal period, the subject is "structurally, if not physically, 'invisible.'" He characterizes these invisible beings in transition as having nothing—"no status, property, insignia, secular clothing, rank, kinship position, nothing to demarcate them structurally from their fellows."[18]

Attributes of structural and physical invisibility can be ascribed to many women who existed in liminal spaces because of both their race and gender during the civil rights era.[19] Liminality is a threshold space, a crossing from one reality into the next.[20] Such space suggests a singularity of identity that Black women will never be able to accomplish because they are always both Black and female among other identities. The women of my study were often in the liminal space of almost, but not yet, achieving full freedom and wholeness of dignity in the broader American society.

Liminality is also a stage of reflection and assessment; one leaves behind old habits, and considers the society, the cosmos, and powers that generate and sustain the persons who are in the liminal space.[21] Women during the Civil Rights Movement realized that they were in spaces that were at times foreign to them, yet they reflected on what could be and envisioned a society known for real justice and freedom, and many believed God would sustain them in the liminal space until they were able to live fully free.

By virtue of their position in society, Black women were often in a location of "almost but not yet" in their work environments, in the church, and the wider community. In general, they were not feared in the same ways as Black men who were prohibited from social interactions with White women, as a result of White ideological framings of the alleged sexual danger Black men posed. Black women were "trusted" to do menial and often invisible work in the homes and businesses of Whites, creating a closer proximity to witness Whiteness.[22] White women and men openly made plans around Black women that might negatively impact the Black community, assuming that Black women could not think critically or would not act strategically with the information. However, many Black women played along with White assumptions, but were savvy enough to carry important information back to the Black community.

Women's Political Council leader, Jo Ann Gibson Robinson, shared the experiences of Black women that were relayed to her during the Montgomery Bus Boycott. In one such instance, a Black maid expressed love for the White family that she worked for and she believed that they loved her too. Unbeknownst to each other, the husband and wife would both give the maid a few extra dollars for the boycott. This Black maid's liminal position became obvious when the family she worked for entertained their White neighbors. Robinson explains:

> [W]hen neighbors visited this home to deplore the boycott activities of the audacious blacks, the man and wife joined in the conversation as if they felt the same way. When she, the maid, was called in to bring food or drinks to the guests, each of the two hosts would wink at her to assure her that they were merely being polite hosts.[23]

This woman felt close with the family and expressed love for them but found herself in a liminal space. The White family she worked for financially supported the boycott, yet in the presence of other Whites, despite such winks of supposed assurance, both the guests and the employers who did not acknowledge and speak up for her and others rendered this Black woman and her desires for justice and freedom invisible.

Many of the women in my study were operating in a liminal period that at times lasted for decades; as they fought for justice they were able to imagine because a more just society had been revealed to them by God and supported by the constitutional documents of the United States. When Marjorie Wallace Smyth was a young child, she crossed boundaries and made assessments from a liminal position. She recalls:

> I was the feisty one . . . , when we went shopping to a store called Parisian and they had the White water and Colored water, I would rush to the White water to see how it would taste and my sister would get so angry. "You're not supposed to do that!" I would say oh well.[24]

Marjorie crossed the threshold and realized the water was equally wet and satisfying in the department store that integrated their dollars in the till but maintained segregated "accommodations" for their Black and White customers. Her mother died when she was young, so her older sister's admonishment was based in fear associated with her responsibility to protect Marjorie, but this threshold crossing became a regular practice for Marjorie who knew, even as a child, that one day the duplication of segregation would not exist because she tasted the water and could no longer see it as better or distinct. She could now imagine the not yet realized possibility of equal access without the need for duplicate and segregated provisions.

These imaginative actions offered Black women new access to social and political power, justice, and freedom. The well-quoted aphorism that what the mind could conceive, and the heart could believe, they would work collectively to achieve, was constantly tested. When society grappled with whether the seemingly impenetrable structures could be reconfigured more justly, it was often Black women who experienced life from the most marginalized positions and used their positionality to creatively imagine a different society, who insisted that change was not only possible, it was also necessary.

Theo-moral imagination plays an important role in social change. Women participating in the Movement faced choices that took place in the liminal space of what was and what could possibly become.[25] They sought to live their lives in ways that centered on actions taken by people, who though currently without formal power acknowledged by White society, nevertheless challenged White structures of power and acted in ways that brought freedom for all. Reflecting on the Movement, Bernice Johnson Reagon stated, "The movement gave all of us choices about how we would live, and it gave us a chance to act as people with power."[26]

Forming a Critical Faith through Experience

Marjorie Wallace Smyth was only ten years old in 1955 when an encounter shook her spiritual core and caused her to engage in serious theological inquiry. As a young girl growing up in an all-Black area of Birmingham,

Alabama, she experienced one loving reality in her immediate community, and an opposing reality in the all-White areas of her hometown. Out of her many experiences with racial separation and opposition, the ones that took place at a local church were the most jarring.

> [W]e would go to Church School and pass the White churches walking, and I could not figure out how the children would come out and call us Niggers, and Sambos and what was the other cartoon they used to call us, Little Rascals, Buckwheat, that's the one, and I just couldn't imagine how they prayed to the same, did they pray to the same God? I used to ask my father how could they pray to the same God? They must have a different God than our God, I just couldn't believe it, I just never could understand.[27]

When asked how she was able to conceptualize the "different God" that Whites worshipped, who she thought must be the cause of such hatred toward Blacks, she replied,

> No, it didn't make sense. That's what was so puzzling [to] me. Did they have two Gods? My father taught us there was just one God and from what I've learned in Church School and our pastor getting up to speak to us, there was only one God. So, there couldn't be a Black God and a White God, so something was wrong. Something was wrong. Then you would have every once in a while, one person [who] would know a white person that was so kind and was so different. But I didn't know any of them.[28]

At the tender age of ten years old, her conflicting experiences in racialized religious spaces made Marjorie realize something was wrong. Her lack of personal familiarity with kindhearted White persons shaped her understanding of whether or not the God that White persons worshipped would act in ways that were kind toward others. For her, persons who believed in and followed God should reflect the character of God. If their actions were unkind, maybe it was because their God did not require kindness but instead accepted or even encouraged hatred. Marjorie and her friends walked past a White church and were verbally attacked and sometimes even spat at by young people of similar age but of a different cultural and religious upbringing. These White children lived near her neighborhood and one might assume were from similar socioeconomic backgrounds, yet her Black presence triggered a response from them that challenged the messages Marjorie had been taught at home and in church about God and people—lessons of love, kindness, and the equality of humanity. For Marjorie, the internal battle was not simply in the words used, but the underlying understanding of God as revealed in those words and corresponding actions.

The assumed presence and influence of God at the White church made the location of Marjorie's encounter with hatred on her way to Church School significant. Racist name calling in non-church settings did not generate the same theological dissonance and subsequent inquiries as in the spaces where God was particularly believed to be present. Were the young people being taught lessons of hatred by older White people with whom Marjorie had no personal experiences of exhibiting kindness? She struggled to stretch her imagination to make sense of what she knew and what she experienced. As a young girl growing up in Birmingham, it appeared to Marjorie that one group of followers of God could love others in the face of hatred, and another group of followers spewed hatred in response to appeals for love and unity.

Marjorie's experiences ultimately led her to decide that based on their actions there was no way for the God of the White children and the God she knew as a Black child to be the same. She could not imagine how the same God could produce mean, hate-filled, exclusionary people at one church, and loving persons oriented toward inclusion in her church which was just blocks away. In an experience-based, lived theological assertion, the ten-year-old Marjorie concluded simply "they must have a different God than our God."[29]

In his "Letter from Birmingham Jail," published eight years after Marjorie's revelation, Martin Luther King Jr. also implied that based on their silence in the face of injustice White Christians must serve a different God than the one who was worshipped in the Black Church tradition. He noted that as he traveled throughout the south,

> . . . I have looked at the South's beautiful churches with their lofty spires pointing heavenward. I have beheld the impressive outlines of her religious-education buildings. Over and over I have found myself asking: "What kind of people worship here? Who is their God? Where were their voices when the lips of Governor Barnett dripped with words of interposition and nullification? Where were they when Governor Wallace gave a clarion call for defiance and hatred? Where were their voices of support when bruised and weary Negro men and women decided to rise from the dark dungeons of complacency to the bright hills of creative protest?"[30]

King also drafted a prayer to the God Blacks worshipped for an unknown occasion that reads,

> O God our eternal Father, we praise thee for the gifts of mind with which thou hast endowed us. We are able to rise out of the half-realities of the sense world to a world of ideal beauty and eternal truth. Teach us, we pray thee, how to use this great gift of reason and imagination so that it shall not

be a curse but a blessing. Grant us vision that shall lift us from worldliness and sin into the light of thine own holy presence. Through Jesus Christ we pray. Amen.[31]

King's supplication was a prayer of thanksgiving for mental capacities to see beyond the secular into the sacred. It was also a prayer of guidance that requested that God teach them how to use the gifts of reason and imagination in ways that would expand opportunities for greater freedoms without placing limitations on them or on future generations. King's acknowledgment of a gift of imagination highlights one of the most powerful theological capacities that enabled the sociopolitical change necessary during the Civil Rights Movement to be viewed as a possibility. The imagination was often considered a dangerous tool in oppressed communities because it provided desires for states of thriving that would shake and shatter the power systems that benefited from taking advantage of those with less formal power. As a young Black girl growing up under that soul-draining system of Jane Crow, imagining that you could do the things that you saw a young White girl doing and acting on those thoughts could lead to serious consequences.

A Theo-moral imagination challenges the potential of imagination as a curse because it makes room for the creative liminal space that only exists in the mind of the individual, through a vision initiated by God. King's prayer for vision that could lift the oppressed from where they were into God's own holy presence recognizes the need to see things not simply through the eyes and experiences of those who were facing troubles, but also through the eyes of God.

The Imaginative Second Sight

In *The Souls of Black Folks*, W. E. B. Du Bois explores the concept of "double-consciousness" which he describes as the two-ness of "an American Negro; two souls, two thoughts, two unreconciled strivings; two warring ideals in one dark body, whose dogged strength alone keeps it from being torn asunder."[32] This well-known concept is complemented by the lesser analyzed notion of second sight. Second sight, according to Du Bois, is seen as a gift. As I identify an imaginative second sight in the women during the Civil Rights Movement, it is a gift from God that allows individuals to see beyond what is physically before them. It is a future-oriented form of sight offered as a gift not only for the benefit of the individual, but often for the community.

During the Civil Rights Movement, Doris Brunson was a teacher at Wadleigh High School in New York City. She believed it was her responsibility to help students see a world where they could become anything they could imagine, and she was determined to use her classroom to prepare them to walk through any doors of opportunity that opened. Doris believed that a legacy rich in the power to survive and overcome ran through their veins just as it pulsed through hers. She believed that it was a combination of God's guidance and the examples of Black women who made choices to value their humanity in the face of inhumane treatment that pushed her to step up and help in whatever ways she could.

> [God] guides you. He leads you. He's there because He says things have been terrible for your people for so long. And if you don't go out and be a part of the protest against it; if you don't go and speak up or sing or walk with your fists up in the air, you're not helping. You've got to let the world know that they must treat you and your race, all the people around you, with respect and with deference because you deserve it. I think what went through my mind several times when I was out [protesting], I would think about the stories that I had heard about the slaves and how they were dragged here. And I remember hearing stories about women who used to throw themselves over the sides of the ships, even though they were chained to other people, because they were pregnant, and they didn't want their child to be born into the life they were leading. They didn't even get here to know how bad it was going to be, but they knew it was bad that they were snatched and chained and dragged off on these ships and everything. You think about that and you say well their blood is running in my veins. Now the dichotomy there is that the blood of the people who were chaining them ran in my veins too.[33]

Doris understood it to be God and her African ancestors calling her into the struggle for freedom and guiding her. Through the examples of the courageous women during the Transatlantic slave passage, she believed God provided a vision that allowed the imagination to see what was to come. This was all she needed to make a moral choice, even if it was viewed by others as extreme.

In 1963, after participating in a few smaller protests that she saw advertised in the newspaper or at times simply stumbling upon a protest on the streets of New York, Doris decided to take her little hat—signaling her respectability as a teacher—and travel by train to Washington, DC, for the March on Washington. She did not go with a group or know anyone there. She recalled walking and talking with a White man as they navigated the masses who gathered on that day from around the nation. She was proud of the leaders of the Movement who took the stage that day. She knew that she would not be highlighted as one of the leaders whose words or songs would go down in history, but she described feeling valuable at the march, believing that the presence of her small petite body among the thousands made a difference. In her words, "my body was one of the bodies they had to count." She was there for herself and there for the future of her students. When the story was told in the days and years to come, she imagined that her individual impact was important to the collective advancement.

Seeing beyond what is immediately before you was a gift of imaginative second sight that was not believed to have origins in the natural realm, but the spirit realm that did not have human limitations. Maintaining focus on what was revealed through the Theo-moral imagination was important, especially when the manifestation of what was revealed seemed slow to be realized.

Keep Your Eyes on the Prize, Hold On

In June 1956, during the height of the Montgomery Bus Boycott, Judge Walter Jones of the Montgomery Circuit Court issued an injunction, supported by Alabama Attorney General John Malcolm Patterson, that forbade the NAACP from raising funds, collecting dues, or recruiting new members.[34] Although the NAACP denied the accusations that they were the ones who organized the Bus Boycott or employed Autherine Lucy to integrate the University of Alabama, they complied with the injunction which basically banned NAACP activities in the state. Despite the ban, Doris Dozier Crenshaw and other young people would stop by Raymond and Rosa Parks's home on Mills Street every day after school where Rosa Parks continued to hold meetings for the NAACP Youth Chapter. Crenshaw recalls that as they sat around her table, she taught them about the injustices Black people were facing.[35] Parks's work with the NAACP was not limited to the formal organization. She was committed to helping young people not only imagine a better world but feel powerful enough to fight for it. Her eye remained on the prize of freedom which required the ability to visualize a time when the limitations being placed on Black people would not exist and opportunities would be available for the young people she trained and mentored. She ensured they would not only have academic preparation but also a historical cultural grounding that gave them insights into tools and methods they could utilize to excel.

The steps people took to continue the work of the NAACP when it was formally banned or under attack motivated both young and old throughout the South. In Atlanta, Pearlie Craft Dove recalls when John H. Calhoun, a Trustee and Sunday School Superintendent of Big Bethel A.M.E. Church and the Atlanta Branch NAACP President, jumped out of a high window from a building in Atlanta's Fourth Ward during the mid-1950s to protect the names of NAACP members when White men tried to forcefully obtain the membership list. The names and contact information of NAACP supporters would almost certainly put them in jeopardy for economic and physical retaliation by members of the White Citizens Council, Ku Klux Klan, and many White businessmen. Calhoun was later arrested for refusing to release the membership records. Dove described this action as indicative of the types of lessons she learned in resistance and the religious role models she had at Big Bethel. Subsequently, as a professor at Clark College (now Clark Atlanta University), she worked to protect student activists even if she did not directly engage in more public acts of resistance. She provided assignments while students were in jail and made sure that their academic work was able to continue so graduations for the activists would not be impacted. She wanted to make sure that students and faculty kept their eyes on the prize and were prepared to take advantage of whatever opportunities the freedoms they were fighting for would offer.

For some, the preparation was intellectual and gaining access through education became the main focus. For others, the preparation was also mental, and the right mindset became the way to not get stuck in the past and miss the opportunities that were on the horizon. While going to sit-ins and spending time in jail as a result, Bessie Smith Sellaway believed, much like Martin Luther King Jr.,[36] that the laws would change and then the people would change, so she began to make it a practice to "project in your mind that things were going to get better."[37] She did not allow what she saw and experienced in the physical to limit what she believed would be possible in the near future.

Acting on what God has helped you to see and imagine requires a relationship with God that trusts that what is revealed is actually possible for those willing to allow God to work in and through humanity to make it so. As Lillian Sue Bethel described it,

> [T]o know yourself is to know God. I know that may sound strange but to me that's the way it goes. You are an extension of Him in a sense. Without God there's no you; without you there's no God. I don't want to sound philosophical or anything but I think you can understand where I'm coming from.[38]

Knowing yourself and knowing the God within yourself creates conditions through which you can better connect to the Divine in order to hear and respond to the voice of God. Lillian described time periods when what you are able to imagine in the future leads you to act in ways that others may not understand, noting you have to "be true to yourself. You can't always do what somebody else wants you to. You have to follow yourself. You follow what you know is right, what God tells you is right in however He tells you. It doesn't matter what somebody else thinks or does."[39] As God speaks, the sparks to imagine what is possible with God become ignited in the lives of those with spiritual eyes and ears to see and hear. A Theo-moral imagination meant new ideas and ways of living that honored their full humanity as young Black women, because they knew God to be responsive to the needs of people who were in a real relationship with God.

For many of the women, what they imagined during the Civil Rights Movement has not fully come to fruition in the twenty-first century, but they believe that it can still be realized through the current generation if they know the power of their history and allow their lives to be guided by and connected to God. A Theo-moral imagination can be fueled by knowing that if God has done it before, God can do it again. Peggy Lucas describes it in this way.

> [A]s a people, we've been through quite a bit and God has just been with us and . . . sometimes it seems like we're going forward sometimes we're moving backwards but we have to rely on our faith and on God to continue to be with us, and we have to be, you know, guided by [the knowledge] that He loves us and He wants the best for us. God is just an awesome God and its during your trials and the hard times that you know that no one else but God could do the things that were done in the Civil Rights Movement, you know, with the people being killed and hanged and shot and bombed in addition to being mistreated, you know, all kinds of mistreatment. We are overcomers. We are. We're a very strong people. How could we survive all the things that we've been through even slavery? We are strong people, and the young people need to know that and cherish our heritage and we need to teach them.[40]

Teaching younger people their heritage and helping them tap into some of the faith practices that guided those who came before them includes opening themselves up and allowing a God-given Theo-moral imagination to shape their actions and push them beyond human limitations.

Asking God What to Do

Many of the women who made the choice to become active during the Civil Rights Movement, believed they were doing what they had to do. While the majority of the women that I interviewed were young high school and college students during the Movement, others like Rosa Brown, Pearlie Craft

Dove, and Jayme Coleman Williams were already out of college and working in their careers. Jayme, a woman of deep faith, always believed the Lord would provide a way to overcome whatever was being faced. In 1956, after fourteen years teaching at Wilberforce University, she joined the faculty at Morris Brown College in Atlanta. Although she grew up as she describes "a daughter of the parsonage" while her father pastored A.M.E. churches in Kentucky, Atlanta was a place with more blatant racist and segregationist practices than she had encountered before. Now solidly below the Mason-Dixon line, she did not like having to explain to her daughter why she could no longer eat in the tearoom at the department store in Atlanta as she had become accustomed to doing in Dayton. Jayme quickly became involved in the NAACP, serving as the advisor for the NAACP Youth Council as the burgeoning Civil Rights Movement was beginning to gain traction. After two years in Atlanta, she and her husband McDonald Williams moved to Nashville to teach at Tennessee State University. To her dismay, faculty members at Tennessee State were not very active in the Movement, however once again, Jayme became the advisor for the NAACP Youth Council and served on the executive board of the Nashville Branch of the NAACP from 1960 until she left the city in 2003.

Nashville in 1960 was the hotbed of student activism, led primarily by collegians from Fisk University, American Baptist College, Meharry Medical College, and Tennessee State University. As a professor and Youth Council advisor, Jayme found herself right in the middle of the action and worked to encourage young people to find their place in the struggle. As she describes it, "We got there just in time to get involved. We went to all of the mass meetings. They had a mass meeting every Monday night. And we transported students from the campus to the site." She believed that Dr. Walter S. Davis, then President of Tennessee State, was sympathetic to the students, but like other state-funded institutions, he had to walk a thin line in order to not risk having state appropriations taken away. She nor her husband, who would go on to establish and lead the Honors College at Tennessee State, feared becoming as active as they could be in their support of the students, but they were also aware that their methods of support did not always need to be on the front line. As Jayme explains, "When the kids went on the Freedom Rides, Kelly Miller Smith, who was helping to organize it, said to me that he thought I should go with them, because they needed an adult along. And I say okay, you know, fine. I'm going to get ready to get on this Freedom bus, and go to Birmingham. And I told Mac and he said, 'are you out of your mind?' He said, 'all you're going to do is get a migraine on the bus.' [her husband interrupts the interview to say that was the bus Klansmen set on fire in Anniston]. I was supposed to be on it. I would have been there if it had been left to me." Thankfully, she was not on the bus that day, but she continued to work closely with college and high school students as they were shaped into leading activists during the Civil Rights Movement, including John Lewis, Bernard Lee, and James Bevel, and she is clear to note that Diane Nash was the real leader of the group.

When I conducted my initial interview with her at the age of 92, she said she thanks God for life, and when she prays she still asks God to "open up vistas of service for me," as she asks the spirit to show her what to do.[41] She draws from her favorite scripture in Philippians 4:11 which reminds her that in whatever state or condition she is in, she can be content. While content in a sense, she actively worked to challenge systems of injustice, especially patriarchal systems that limit the advancement of well-qualified women in the African Methodist Episcopal Church, the academy, and beyond.

Bold Actions Amplified by God

Lydia Walker believes her actions, when she speaks up against things that are not aligned with the moral compass of God, are a part of the work that she is called to do as a Christian. "I think I'm doing the Lord's will" because "Jesus was a radical."[42] She gets upset when people do not rise up against injustice, believing that speaking up and challenging the status quo is the Christian thing to do. As she engaged in individual acts of resistance, she described feeling not only sanctioned by the Lord but also amplified by God. The work of a Christian required a radical orientation toward a society that is built on maintaining systems and structures of power for a few at the expense of many. Stepping out beyond your comfort zone in the face of potential danger was not easy, but the desire to fight back was not something civil rights women sought on their own; they felt their actions were directed and strengthened by God. Lydia's beliefs in many ways echo those of Bessie Sellaway, who draws on Philippians 4, including the declaration in the thirteenth verse that "I can do all things through Christ who strengthens me."

For many of the women, they inherited a faith and vision of humanity that was passed down from their grandmothers and mothers. It was a belief system which understood they were working in partnership with God to make the world better, especially for Black people who were being oppressed. When there was a need for inspiration and motivation to stand up for their own humanity and that of others, stories such as Alicia Roberts's memory of her mother throwing bricks at a White man for trying to take advantage of her grandmother come to the surface. Her mother talked about change so her family could live without worrying about being exploited, and Alicia wanted to be a part of the work that would allow her to see the change her mother envisioned. She took on her mother's imagined future and joined the Civil Rights Movement to help make it a reality.

Similarly, Barbara Ann Adams associates her great-grandmother with her first memories of activism. When speaking about women of that generation she shared, "those women were just born with wisdom. [They] had so much even though they had so little."[43] As Patricia Hill Collins argues, there are two modes of knowing—knowledge and wisdom, with experience being the differentiating factor between the two. The limitations of educational systems that women like Barbara Ann's grandmother encountered may have limited formal knowledge, but it did not prevent the acquisition of wisdom, which was more important for the survival of the family and community. Sarah Frierson recalls her grandmother challenging a White man who did not want to call her Mrs., but instead called her aunt. So, her grandmother told him to "tell her sister hello." This experience was a clear example for Sarah of how to push back when you are not given the respect you deserve and to not allow others to name or categorize you in ways that are not of your choosing.

The bold actions of these women to fight back in words and deeds created a template for what their daughters and granddaughters would do in the mid-twentieth century as they found their voice in the Civil Rights Movement. The ability to see things as they were, and then have the realms of possibility stretched through a Theo-moral imagination, often meant the realization of the vision would lead them to become even bolder as they put what God showed them to the test.

Eberta Lee Spinks

Imagining Beyond
the Visible Reality

Long before the steel cotton curtain of racialized violence was pulled back by Mamie Till Bradley's refusal to allow her son Emmett Till's murder in Money, Mississippi, to be covered up, or Nina Simone belted out the piercing critique in the lyrics of "Mississippi Goddam," the state's violent reputation was well established, especially among Black people throughout the United States. Mississippi was a place with a deep history of racialized divisions that set Whites on one path and Blacks on another, and perpetual segregation was clearly conveyed as the desired end for Whites. When Eberta Lee Spinks was born in 1914, she was the fifteenth of her parents' eighteen children.[1] A missionary from the age of four, she helped others in the community under the direction of her mother. This included taking freshly picked flowers and home-cooked meals to neighbors who were sick to brighten their day, giving milk and hand-churned butter to anyone who wanted it, and chickens to those in need, so families in the community could be fed. Her family did not sell anything that they were able to grow or raise on their farm in Sumrall, Mississippi; they gave it away.

Growing up in such a large family, it was not as if the Lees did not have needs, but what Spinks remembers most from her childhood was the sense of community and taking care of others which was ingrained in her at an early age. Around age five, Spinks and her friend, Winsie Mae Shelton, became very sick with typhoid malarial fever and the community rallied together to support the two families by scheduling times to stay with them overnight and "keep watch" so the parents were able to rest. Unfortunately, young Winsie Mae died from the fever, but Spinks said, "the Lord had something for me to do" and she believed it was the Lord that kept her and brought

Left to right, George Gaddy, Velma Jordan, Rev. Ceceil Newell, and Eberta Lee Spinks honored by the NAACP in Laurel, Mississippi. Source: *Laurel Leader-Call.*

her through that health scare. Stepping up to help others within her small Black community was what she saw modeled by her family and neighbors, who drew close to support each other during times of illness. This ultimately taught her that where there was unity, there was strength, a lesson that stayed with her throughout her life.

The Lees were a deeply Christian family and both of her parents made sure that she and her siblings were raised in the knowledge of the Christian faith. As she described,

> My dad, he carried the bigger children to prayer meeting on Wednesday night, and we little sleepyheads, who would go to sleep, Mama taught us at home. She taught us . . . we sat around that rocking chair with that big, wide, pretty apron on, and she would tell us about Jesus. And what he wanted, expected of us. And so, after that, my mother, she was the president of the Missionary Society. And she did a very fine job. I had an aunt; she was a state missionary. My daddy's sister. And my grandfather, he was a preacher. One of my brothers, Hardy Lee, he was a preacher. And a lot of my first cousins, they were preachers. And so, we were taught God's

word, and we had to live up to it. And so, she would tell us what the Lord wanted us to do, and how we were supposed to treat them as parents.

My daddy, he would carry the older children to prayer meeting on Wednesday night. And he was the chairman of the deacon board, and he was superintendent of the Sunday School.[2]

Hickory Grove Baptist Church in Sumrall and around her mother's feet were the places of Theo-moral formation for Spinks and her siblings. Surrounded by a family who believed, and did their best to live, according to Christian teachings shaped her own commitment to doing what she understood to be right.

Her family moved to Hattiesburg, where her father worked at the Newman Mill. The faith that was taught at home and church was reinforced in school, especially during fifth grade. At that time Mrs. H. B. Mott was her teacher, and prayer was a daily part of the morning ritual in school. Mott also taught her students the Sunday School lesson for the week on Friday, and before they left school for the weekend, she told them she expected to see them in church on Sunday.[3] There was no separation between what they learned in seemingly secular and sacred spaces. Spinks referred to her fifth-grade teacher as a preacher, and Mott at one point signed her name as a State Evangelist.[4] The role of evangelist was often relegated to women who spoke boldly of the faith and brought others to Christianity through their preaching, even if their proclamation was not categorized as such within the patriarchal religious organizations who only saw men as preachers. The religious influence on Spinks and others was consistent and it was not relegated to within ecclesial walls. As time moved on, a lived religion was evident not only in the churches, homes, and schools, but also in street protests and civil rights assertions.

The student-led efforts of the Civil Rights Movement were not restricted to the popular sit-ins that garnered much media attention and support in the early 1960s. By 1964, Bob Moses and the Council of Federated Organizations (COFO), which included SNCC and other civil rights organizations, planned a much bigger effort with the aim to disrupt the severe racial disparities in the Mississippi education system and voting population. Although her grandmother had always warned that she should never go to Mississippi, as a college student Gwendolyn Zoharah Simmons began asking questions and finding out information about a three-month Freedom School effort being organized by COFO to make educational and political interventions in the magnolia state. Despite her fears about Mississippi and her grandmother's threat to not allow her to return home to Memphis if she joined the SNCC work there, Zoharah summoned the courage to apply for the Freedom Summer project and she was accepted.[5] Even after finding out during her training at Western College for Women (now a part of Miami University) in Oxford, Ohio, that two White men and one Black man, who Zoharah had seen days before at the training session, were murdered in Mississippi for doing the work she was preparing to do, she did not allow fear to stop her.[6]

Cynthia Griggs Fleming describes the relative egalitarian atmosphere of SNCC, including access to leadership. Gender for women was not seen as a limiting and oppressive factor in the way that race and class were. She notes that many SNCC workers were accustomed to having women in their families work outside of the home and exercising authority inside the home, so seeing women, especially those who were willing to equally risk their lives for freedom became an accepted practice among the younger activists in SNCC.[7] However, of the forty-four project locations throughout Mississippi during Freedom Summer, Zoharah became one of only a few Black women project leaders. Her courage was molded by the woman who welcomed her into her home and into her life as the leader of the Laurel, Mississippi, Project. Zoharah describes the first meeting in this way,

> Laurel didn't have an infrastructure when we got there and little by little we started meeting people. We had to sleep in Hattiesburg, the next town over, thirty miles to the south, and go up in the day looking for people. Finally, I had a name of an NAACP member named Eberta Spinks, and I went and knocked on her door. When she opened it, I was stumbling trying to figure out how you ask somebody: "Can I live with you? And put you in danger of being killed and your house being burned and everything?" How do you ask somebody that who's never laid eyes on you before, right? So I was sort of stumbling around trying to figure out how to say it and she looked at me, because I had on blue jeans (we had sort of a uniform, and I had on a blue jean jacket and my blue jeans), and she said, "Are you one of those Freedom Riders?" And I didn't know if that was good or bad, and I said, "Yes, ma'am." And she said, "Come in, I've been waiting on you all my life." And she was in her late fifties.[8]

At the time the Freedom Summer workers arrived, Eberta Spinks was actually fifty years old, married and helping to raise children (her own two—Hazel and Charlie, and foster children), some of whom were grown and out of the house at that point. Her husband worked at the Masonite plant and she worked at the Tant's Packing Company in Laurel for twenty-three years until she left in 1964 to begin working with the Movement. There had been some effort to rally Black men and women to register to vote throughout Jones and Forrest County for years, but the progress was slow. When young people began making their way into the state and working one-on-one with Black Mississippians to prepare them to fully exercise their right to vote, White violent resistance ominously increased. The COFO office that was in Queensborough was burned by the Klan. And as a result of fear, many doors of churches and Black businesses had been closed to the young SNCC workers in Laurel until they encountered Spinks who saw them as the manifestation of who she imagined years earlier God would use to bring about change.

Eberta Lee Spinks was a woman of deep faith, courage, and vision rooted in the knowledge of and love for her community. She often told Zoharah, "God is on our side. I'm not giving up. I'm not letting people drive me away from the movement. I'm in the movement 'til death if need be."[9] As Spinks described it, local leader Clarence Collins asked if students could stay with her, and she was sick at the time, so that was her concern since she felt she would not be able to cook for them. When she was asked how much she was going to charge, she responded, "Charge? I ain't going to charge nothing." But she did want to talk to her husband first. When she and her husband spoke about the potential of housing the students and he said "Bert, anything you want to do, you do it, because I know it'll be right, whatever you do." They prayed over it and she also felt her sickness leave reflecting, "When my mind was sure enough made up, the Lord touched my body, and healed my body."[10] The healing seemed to be a sign from God saying that she should open up her home to the students.

After the COFO office was burned down, the concern of their three-bedroom home also being targeted and burned was something Mrs. Spinks brought up to her husband before deciding to house multiple student volunteers. She confided to her husband, "We might get our house burned," and he replied, "That's why we're paying insurance."[11] Her husband's support and confidence was all she needed to open her door to Zoharah and the many other students who piled into her home, filling the two bedrooms and overflowing in sleeping bags throughout the house, leaving one bedroom for Mrs. Spinks, her husband, and son Charlie.

The Masonite plant where Mr. Spinks worked was unionized, which enabled the Spinks family to stand up in ways that appeared bolder than others whose employment was more precarious. Zoharah recalls that many of the women Mrs. Spinks recruited from her church to safely house the twenty-six Black and White volunteers who descended on Laurel, were also married to men who worked at the Masonite plant.[12] The union protected these families from economic repercussions on their jobs that would be the normal response for having White women living in Black homes, however physically violent repercussions linked to White men's fears of miscegenation were still a possibility. The presence of a Klan headquarters in Jones County made the threat of home attacks all the more real for Zoharah, but she quickly learned to trust in Mrs. Spinks, Mrs. Clara Clayton, and the other women who housed students and put their trust in God because they saw a better future on the other side of the Movement and would not be stopped by momentary fear.

There is a long tradition of self-defense in the Black community that often enabled the nonviolent strategies of the SCLC, SNCC, CORE, and other organizations to be actualized. Mrs. Spinks was also one of a number of women throughout the South who sat up at night with a shotgun on her lap to protect the nonviolent students, including many White women who were staying with her, from the potential violence their presence might attract. In addition to women like Spinks, Historian Akinyele Umoja brings to the forefront groups of primarily Black men, including the Deacons for Defense and Justice, who were armed, well organized, and kept Black activists safe during the day and Black communities who housed and fed Black and White summer volunteers safe at night.[13] This was particularly true in Mississippi where former military men often worked as armed bodyguards for local Movement leaders and carried guns to Mass Meetings to protect those nonviolent activists in attendance.[14]

Spinks and other women provided free food, clothing, and protection to the many young students who flooded Mississippi during the summer of 1964. Most students made their way south with a small suitcase and no real provisions that could independently sustain them for three or more months. The extra bodies in what were often already full homes meant that more food had to be purchased, additional utilities were used, clothing had to be washed, and other forms of care and labor provided. The families gave willingly, and the students did their best to create the conditions for change while they were in Mississippi, which they hoped would remain through the efforts of local leaders after they left. Young Movement leaders including Gwendolyn Zoharah Simmons and Marsha Moore had a great influence on Spinks's activism. Spinks not only housed the students, but she put her own body on the line doing what she could to make lasting change possible. A SNCC Incident Report from October 28, 1964, indicates that as a result of the work she and seventeen other voter registration workers and prospective applicants were doing in McComb, MS, Mrs. Spinks was roughed up and had her arm badly twisted by a state investigator while the FBI was present.[15]

When the student volunteers purchased a station wagon to expand the reach of their work, they could not get it, so they put the vehicle in Spinks's name as the Mississippi Freedom Democratic Party (MFDP) president for Laurel. Spinks often ended up driving the station wagon around to pick up people from throughout the county so they could vote, even before she had a driver's license.[16] She picketed, protested, and sat-in to integrate Kress's store and the dining area at the Pinehurst Hotel. It was at the Pinehurst Hotel where Mrs. Spinks was the spokesperson for the action, so when they were told to leave or the police would be called, she responded with an economic argument, "We're going to stay right here . . . It looks like to me the more you serve, the more money you'd make here and you'd be glad to serve anybody." When the police arrived, and they asked her if she and the others in the integrated group she led were told to leave she replied, "Yes, but we ain't going . . . We didn't come to leave. We came to be served."[17] The FBI was there along with a White woman who worked with the Movement as an observer. Spinks was taken to jail for the Pinehurst action and when she spoke to her daughter Hazel on the phone from jail to request the medication she would need while there, she said, "Don't be afraid. Because, ain't nothing going to happen to us." She asserted, "If anything happens to us, blood's going to run down the street like water."[18] The men in the jail were nice to her after she made that intrepid statement while they were within earshot. Spinks became the County Chairperson for the MFDP, and she led voter registration efforts in Laurel and throughout the rural areas of Jones County.[19] While the majority of the students in Freedom Summer stayed only for a few months in 1964, others including Gwendolyn Zoharah Simmons, the Laurel project leader, stayed until December 1966.

Eberta Spinks was also not afraid to confront White men who tried to threaten her. In January 1966, businessman, farmer, and committed voter registration activist Vernon Dahmer was murdered by the Mississippi White Knights, who firebombed Dahmer's home and business after he publicly offered to collect and pay the poll taxes for Blacks who could not afford them. Following this, Spinks's boldness seemed to grow exponentially. When a White man who worked in furniture came to her house to warn her about the voter registration activities she was engaged in, he asked her, "You know what you're doing? That's what Vernon Dahmer got killed about." Without fear or intimidation, she once again replied, "Yes. But you know what? If anybody bothers me, it's going to be blood running down the street like water. Now, you can put that in your pipe and smoke it." She said the man got up, left, and never came back again.[20] When asked if she was afraid when approached by the man who offered a threat of warning she responded,

"Nooooo, no, no, no. You see, I prayed, and I asked God. I asked him for our protection. And He protected us."[21] God gave Eberta Lee Spinks a vision that gave her the freedom to do whatever she and others were capable of without limitations. This vision extended beyond their current reality, but because it was placed in her mind by God she embraced it fully. She did not have to physically see it to know that it could actually exist one day as their new lived reality. Spinks believed, "When you trust God, your work is done. All you've got to do is get at it."[22]

Eberta Lee Spinks died in 1996.

"Which Side Are You On?"

A Theology of Movements
for Liberation

For many people who have been actively committed to the struggle for justice, the commitment has not simply been based on their own desires, but on what they feel is a calling, a personal compulsion to take the risk and do the work even if others disagree. It is an intentional choosing of sides. This ethic of compulsion during struggles for Black freedom is often rooted in what I identify as a theology of movements for liberation.

Born out of a love of life and a respect for creation, and filled with resilience, hope, determination, and trust in the Divine, Black faith has operated in many forms throughout the continent of Africa since the beginning of humanity. Black faith traveled with African explorers who made their way west to the soils of South, Central, and North America before European colonizers laid claim to occupied lands and sought to exploit resources and eradicate long-standing peoples and cultures. Black faith was fully alive before Black women, men, and children were kidnapped and forcefully brought to the Americas and assumed to be without religion or faith traditions by White European Christians. Black faith provided the strength to endure unimaginable horrors during more than two hundred and fifty years of chattel slavery in South and Central America, the Caribbean, and the United States. Black faith on American soil drew from a different relationship with and understanding of God than the White forms of Christianity practiced by enslavers and their supporters. This dissimilarity of beliefs and practices anchored in lived experiences speaks to a core difference of theologies in general and Christian theologies in particular.

For some, it may seem repetitive to distinguish or work to differentiate a theology of movements for liberation from what might be considered "traditional" Christian theology. However, the projects of liberation theologies, particularly in the Americas, have made it clear that not all systematic theologies have the same understanding of God and God's relationship to humanity and other forms of creation. Liberation theologies are often built on the principle that God has entered into a covenant with the poor and oppressed, a belief which inspires a quest for and commitment to freedom in all areas of life. These theologies use a particular lens to engage the sacred and secular, where God is actively involved with humanity in the fight against oppressive elements throughout society. As a result, liberation theologians work to critically challenge oppression enacted by individuals, organizations, and institutions through their words and actions. As I explore a theology of movements for liberation through the lived experiences of Black women religious leaders during the first few years of the Movement for Black Lives era, there are traditional sources that I draw from based on frameworks outlined by Black liberation and womanist theologians. These include songs, sacred texts including novels and short stories, and experiences of Black women, as well as the incorporation of theological virtues of Freedom Faith, Courageous Resistance, and Moral Imagination noted in previous chapters.

Traditional Western theology draws from sources of scripture, tradition, reason, and experience that are primarily oriented toward White male dominance. There are examples of this throughout the history of the United States including the colonizers—many of whom initially fled Europe in search of religious freedom but shut down the religious liberty of persons they encountered as the original occupants of the land as well as those they enslaved and forced to produce the wealth of the new nation. Other examples include the theologies of Klansmen that were anything but liberative toward many persons including Blacks, Jews, and Roman Catholics; the theologies of the Quakers who were among the first White religious groups to oppose slavery (although they initially benefited from the institution); and other Whites who were supportive of equal opportunities for any of the aforementioned groups. Liberation theologies make justice and transformation central elements of desired ends. Liberation theologies name differently their revelations[1] from God because their contextualization requires distinctive sources to generate their understandings. These liberation theologies are part of a liberative school of thought, where each theology is influenced by the context in which they were generated.[2]

Songs

Songs are a source of a theology of liberation movements. It is through sociopolitical protest songs, with lyrics often created in moments of contestation from the lived experiences of the people, that we are able to understand the theo-ethical beliefs and motivations of many who participate in liberation movements. In the global Movement for Black Lives (M4BL),[3] there are many songs that form regional and global canons for Movement Music. Some of these songs, such as "We Shall Overcome," draw from previous struggles for justice and liberation including songs of the Civil Rights Movement, and often they were initially anchored in spirituals and later in rhythm and blues. Other contemporary songs such as "Alright," are created from the pains of stymied progress in the twenty-first century using hip-hop and other popular music forms to communicate messages.[4]

Women, including Karen Anderson, Traci Blackmon, Leslie Callahan, and Pamela Lightsey, shared their experiences with me as religious leaders in the Movement for Black Lives era, and noted a few songs they identified with and connected to the struggles of resistance on streets throughout the United States.[5] Karen Anderson and Traci Blackmon, pastors who were both active in Ferguson, Missouri, during the uprising, mentioned "Ella's Song" by Sweet Honey in the Rock, as one they often sang with younger protesters. The popular chorus, "We who believe in freedom cannot rest. We who believe in freedom cannot rest until it comes," like many of the song's other lyrics, is taken from a speech that Ella Baker delivered in 1964 after the murders of James Chaney, Andrew Goodman, and Michael Schwerner in Mississippi, and speaks to the realities of anti-Black violence and racial injustice that will continue to limit humanity's progress if these issues are not faced and dealt with. At the core of the belief system that undergirds this statement is a desire to work for freedom that is actualized in the lives of everyone without classification. "Ella's Song" bridges the generations of freedom fighters by lifting the words of Miss Baker, a senior sage in the twentieth century, who many consider to be the godmother of the Civil Rights Movement. Baker became active in justice work that challenged social and economic incongruities faced by northern Blacks in the 1930s, first working with the National Association for the Advancement of Colored People (NAACP), ultimately becoming the national director of branches, and later helping form and shape the structure of the Southern Christian Leadership Conference (SCLC), and the Student Nonviolent Coordinating Committee (SNCC). Throughout her life, Baker was a champion of young people and grassroots leaders. These characteristics, as well as her participatory democracy framework, were attractive to young M4BL leaders, who have been astute students of previous freedom struggles and found themselves drawn to the non-hierarchical structures of communal leadership models that Baker promoted, along with her understanding that the work of freedom is a long game, and until it was obtained for everyone the work of freedom fighters will not end. This song, with lyrics that include the words of a senior strategist and freedom fighter of the 1960s, has given people light across many generations to find their way forward in the twenty-first century.[6]

Janelle Monáe's repurposed "Hell You Talmbout" was the song that professor Pamela Lightsey noted for its ability to tap into a history of resistance and use that legacy as a way of propelling people to action during twenty-first-century movements. Monáe changed what was a "pop" bonus track on her 2013 album *The Electric Lady*, into a protest song in the fall of 2015 through performances with members of the Wondaland artist collective. She offered the song to the broader community as something they could adjust to fit their needs by including the names of victims of police and state-sanctioned violence from their own communities into the say her/their name chant, replacing the lyrics of the original song. The drums, which are the only instruments used in the protest version of the song, create a percussive bassline that Lightsey describes as harkening back to slave uprisings. The call-and-response structure of the song—"Sandra Bland, say her name; Sandra Bland, say her name"—makes it easily portable and shareable in diverse settings. These rhythms, which can be recreated with the human body through hands and feet, also call for communities to stand up, speak out, and creatively resist the structures which keep Black lives bound. Unlike Monáe's often other-worldly lyrics and aesthetics, "Hell You Talmbout" tethers us firmly to the realities of the present time and space with this-worldly cries of inquisition.

Pastor Leslie Callahan focused on "Fight for You," a song by gospel, R&B, and hip-hop genre-bending artist Mali Music, that she sees "as a loving manifesto" for the Church. Callahan explains "the sentiment of the song is I'll fight for you because of who you are. I won't let them take you on. I won't let them hurt you." Inspired by this song, she wrote a sermon that she preached at her church, St. Paul's Baptist in Philadelphia, on August 23, 2015.[7] In the sermon, she draws links to the Black Lives Matter Movement and the opportunity the Movement represents for the Church to be who and what it is called upon to be. The song reminds her that we should all be preaching, teaching, leading, and living through means that do not diminish the capacity to hold and be the light of God in a dark world. Callahan prophetically connects the song to the biblical text Ephesians 6:10–20 where the writer describes putting on the whole armor of God to fight the structures that oppress and limit.

In 2018, the Black Youth Project 100 (BYP 100) released an album, "The Black Joy Experience: Freedom Songs and Liberation Chants from the Movement," that included songs, chants, and spoken word directly from and inspired by the M4BL. In June of 2020, the BYP 100 held a virtual-live

Black Joy Experience Juneteenth Celebration dubbed "Freedom Is Coming," amidst the pain of multiple pandemics of the global COVID-19 health crisis and the ongoing pandemic that Black lives were reminded of in the killings of Ahmaud Arbery, George Floyd, Breonna Taylor, and Tony McDade which ran across the large and small screens of televisions, computers, and smartphones. Using lyrics as a vehicle for speaking out and rhythms as a way to carry people forward, songs continue to be one of the key sources within theologies of movements for justice.

Scripture

As noted in the forming Freedom Faith chapter, there are distinctions between the scriptural text that liberation theologians draw from based on their experiences. The exodus and eschatological scriptures for liberation by a God who could lead them *out* of oppression were put forward as central by early Black male theological leaders. This is compared to the scriptures used by grassroots Black women civil rights activists where the Psalms, the Prophet Isaiah, and the Gospels dominated their Biblical references of a God who was with them *in* the struggle. In a similar way, the biblical texts which anchor the activism of Movement for Black Lives–era religious leaders differ from the previous, but consistent themes can be recognized within each. The religious leaders I interviewed in the second decade of the twenty-first century had access to formal seminary training unlike the majority of women during the mid-twentieth century.[8] Now equipped with theological tools and training, these women have what some call "the learning and the burning," blending critical intellect with spirit-led inspiration. They turn their focus to a text from the prophet Micah as well as the gospels of Matthew and Luke as foundational words for their approach to Movement work. I argue these scriptures form a critical component of a contemporary theology of liberation movements.

Among the women leaders highlighted in this chapter as well as through my experiences as a participant observer of messages featured on protests signs at marches and preached through physical and virtual pulpits and platforms, one of the most-often sourced Movement texts is taken from Micah 6:8, "He has told you, O mortal, what is good; and what does the Lord require of you but to do justice, and to love kindness, and to walk humbly with your God?" At times, this verse serves as a type of shorthand fill-in for deeper conversations around the challenge to move beyond theology as God-talk and to actively get involved and engage within the ethical justice work at hand as God-walk.

For Pamela, Micah 6:8 is the text that chronicles what she tries to do as she moves throughout the world unfettered by what society often categorizes as "othered" through her identities and communities. For her, this text not only outlines a moral mandate for living and addressing injustice wherever it exists, but it is also a caution to Movement leaders who become arrogant and neglect to do the work of justice in humility as they work alongside God. Her counsel for humbleness in leadership seems to be necessary whether or not the individuals acknowledge a Divine partnership in the work of justice. The wisdom of Pamela's mother, who taught her that "a bird can only fly so high, and then it must land," echoes as a reminder to maintain a sense of groundedness as you do the work and not allow others to lift you beyond the community in ways that lead you to feel you are above and separate or perhaps even free from them.

Karen also mentioned Micah 6:8 as a text she and others often drew upon in their grassroots efforts during the Ferguson uprising in 2014, and in other places throughout the nation since that time. "That to me is a prophetic call, and action word. It's not to talk about justice, it's to *do* justice, to get engaged with it."[9] Moving beyond discourse and theory to praxis and direct engagement continues to be a theme throughout the lives of the Black women I interviewed who are drawn to activist work as a part of their Christian identity. Turning to Matthew 35:31–46, Karen continued to articulate the way she feels the Bible speaks to the context in which she offers grassroots religious activist leadership. When the disciples asked, "When did we see you hungry?" and Jesus said, "What you do for the least of these, you do for me," represents a Biblical exchange that shapes Karen's outlook for undertaking the work that she feels she cannot stop doing; she is not doing it for a singular individual, but for Jesus.[10] Karen feels an inward pull to do whatever she can for those who are impacted daily by oppressive systems, structures, and practices which seek to silence and prevent them from living lives full of the dignity, respect, and opportunities that everyone deserves. It is an ethics of compulsion that women who were active during the Civil Rights Movement also described.

Luke 4:18–19 is the passage of scripture that Leslie sees as connected to the work of those who answer God's call to remain dedicated to justice. In this text, Jesus is back in his hometown of Nazareth after receiving popular acclaim for teaching in synagogues throughout other parts of Galilee. He stands in the synagogue on the Sabbath to read a passage from the scroll of the prophet Isaiah. Leslie and others, like Fannie Lou Hamer during the Civil Rights Movement, read this ancient text in conversation with their present-day encounters with God and the work God is calling them to do. "The Spirit of the Lord is on me, because he has anointed me to proclaim good news to the poor. He has sent me to proclaim freedom to the prisoners and recovery of sight for the blind, to set the oppressed free, to proclaim the year of the Lord's favor." This scripture grounds the activist work Leslie feels called to do as something the Spirit of God equips and, in many ways, requires her to do in collaboration with others. The proclamations of good news, freedom, and the year of the Lord's favor are empty rhetoric without working to make those things a reality for those who are poor, imprisoned, unable to see, and bound by oppression. The labor to create justice is not a singular act; it is a call to challenge and change systems that work against liberation for all of creation. Drawing from the prophet Isaiah, the embrace of the Lukan text in the twenty-first century marks a lineage of justice seekers who allow the Spirit of God to rest on them and empower their fight for those who do not have the awareness, access, or ability to fight for themselves.

Traci articulates a theology of movement work in Luke 13:10–17, as illustrative of what she and others are called to do throughout the world. In the passage, we see a woman who has been bent over for years. Traci explains, "I am cognizant in that scripture that Jesus describes the cause of being bent over as the spirit, but never locates that spirit in the woman." Traci describes her revelation from God showing "the healing was in the coming [for the bent over woman] . . . The healing in the text is in the movement to the center . . . the text says *as* she was coming, Jesus declared her healed. He declares her healed *before* he touches her." For Traci, her "theology of movement work is that those who are most hurting, those who are in the most pain, those who have been crippled most, those who are so bent over that they can't see up, must be brought to the center for healing to occur." As she reads the scripture, "Jesus interrupts what we think is necessary to do what is essential," so it is imperative from her perspective for the Church broadly to break the business-as-usual routines that prevent them from helping persons who find themselves struggling on the margins of society.[11]

Unlike the texts that systematic and organic theologians have drawn from in twentieth-century movements, each of these passages the twenty-first-century women religious leaders point to as ones that shape the grassroots work they have participated in during the Movement for Black Lives reflect a call narrative for the women, which does not permit passive awareness of issues in lieu of active resistance of them.

In the words of Charlene Carruthers, many movement activists in the twenty-first century see "Movement building [as] spiritual work."[12] Leaders, including Brittany Packnett Cunningham, Bree Newsome Bass, and Opal Tometi, have publicly articulated Christian faith traditions that they draw on for strength and direction when facing challenges. Other activist leaders including Patrisse Cullors and Erica N. Williams embrace an expansive African spirituality that we see reflected in Yoruba, Christian, Muslim, and other practices.

Sayings

Public proclamations are often made through non-formal avenues during protest gatherings and planning sessions, and they serve as unifying tools in movement work. In previous twentieth-century movements, some of these sayings included, "Freedom Now," "One man, one vote," and "Black power." Some civil rights activists described times of intragroup conflict when someone would break out in a song that culminated in a chant, and brought the hearts and minds of the young activists back together as they worked to fight against the systems that put limitations on the flourishing and progress of Black citizens. As a participant observer in many grassroots organizing actions in both the twentieth and twenty-first centuries, I have heard numerous sayings and chants proclaimed as rallying cries and ways of bringing people together. A few of the sayings which originated from a particular moment and context continue to be used at various gatherings while others have been designed to speak to more specific issues such as immigration status or a living wage.

One chant of unity, "The people united will never be divided," was identified by Karen as the saying that most reminded her of the activist work she participated in during the Ferguson Movement. These words provided a vocal reminder to remain united as smaller factions arrived, often from outside of the community, with a goal of undermining the efforts to keep the focus on the police and political systems that supported the corrupt manipulation of the laws in ways that continue to fleece and disadvantage the majority Black community of Ferguson and the surrounding areas. Karen and other grassroots activists watched as the national media spun and sensationalized stories about what was happening in the aftermath of the murder of Michael Brown, which differed greatly from what they were experiencing on the ground. By coming together, the hope was that their united efforts and consistent messaging would allow more pressure to be placed on local people in power, so that substantive change could happen.

"The people united will never be divided," was also a recognition that spreading seeds of disunity was often used as a tool to splinter power before it was able to coalesce and form in ways that could become operationalized against forces who sought to maintain political and social authority. The results of the activists' unified struggle became evident in 2020 with the election of Ella Jones as Mayor of Ferguson after serving as the first Black person elected to the Ferguson City Council in 2015 in the aftermath of the uprising. Additionally, without major support from outside donors, 2020 also bore witness to the election of Cori Bush, who describes herself as a "nurse, pastor, single mom, and Ferguson-made activist," as the US Representative from the MO-01 District.

The Ferguson Movement and others also used the chant "No justice, no peace," with great regularity as a statement that forewarned of ongoing direct-action challenges to systems and persons whose actions were inconsistent with what the activists believed justice required as a response to the offense. As Traci reflected on the chant, she also noted that "No justice, no peace" could also be understood as the homophone "Know justice, know peace." She believes that justice and righteousness are the same, and notes that we can understand the saying as both "a statement of resistance and as a statement of salvation."[13] The knowledge of what justice is and what it requires, and the commitment to do the work necessary to achieve it, can ultimately lead to peace for the communities involved. The chants can operate at both levels of understanding for those participating in the struggles.

In the midst of the theological declaration that Black Lives Matter, there became an additional call to ensure that there was inclusivity even within the Black community by stating that "All Black Lives Matter," which is a proclamation Leslie mentioned. This notes the intentional inclusion of Black lives that some people and institutions, particularly in the Black Church, may reject and deem as invisible. All Black lives include Black trans lives, Black incarcerated lives, Black disabled lives, Black poor lives, Black young lives, Black old lives, and all others. As a theological statement, we may also add two implied words to this saying to state, All Black Lives Matter to God.[14] This can help counter views of humanity which may say and act otherwise.

Another chant, mentioned by Leslie and known by all of the participants, that has been incorporated in many planning sessions and public actions, as a rallying cry and ethical mandate was an excerpt from Assata Shakur's statement, "To My People" which was broadcast nationally on July 4, 1973.[15] As the Movement for Black Lives began to draw from the strategies and sayings of inspiring leaders from previous movements, Black women in particular took the following section of Shakur's statement as a call to action: "It is our duty to fight for our freedom. It is our duty to win. We must love each other and support each other. We have nothing to lose but our chains." It is at once a collective cry of deontological expectations and theological requirements of love and liberation. I, like many other movement participants, have repeatedly chanted this as either a call-and-response or in unison with each repetitive round growing in sonority and conviction, often with so much passion and fervor that the chant itself becomes a transformative spiritual experience that inspired deeper commitments to the ongoing work in the struggle for justice.

There are times when the clarity about the end results of the direct-action efforts do not lead to comfort because the odds are so highly stacked against achieving the goal. Speaking the proverbial "truth to power" often comes at a cost, sometimes personal and other times communal, and while necessary, speaking out in this way is not always easy. Pamela draws from a saying that pushes for internal fortitude in the face of external fear. Versions of the words "Speak your mind, even if your voice trembles" often attributed to Gray Panther founder Maggie Khun with similar statements from Audre Lorde, have shown up on various items from t-shirts to bumper stickers. For Pamela this saying is a push to speak up whether in a faint whisper or loud voice, with courage or trepidation. The act of speaking important thoughts is a way of actively engaging the powers and not cowering to them. This statement, unlike the others which are utilized as an external proclamation of being within the community, engenders more of an internal reflection for self-motivation to speak publicly about specific issues. In many instances, statements remembered in isolation are often not enough. It is the communal recalling and public proclamations that nourishes the ground of activism.

Sermons, Speeches, and Statements

Although women such as Prathia Hall and Fannie Lou Hamer could deliver sermons and speeches that would rival if not surpass the power and eloquence of any of the male religious leaders who dominated the Civil Rights Movement, women did not have the opportunity to lay claim to the pulpit as pastors and consistently set the spiritual and sociopolitical tone for a congregation during the traditional Movement period.[16] Activists today can draw from the sermons and speeches of Black women pastors and well-recognized religious leaders who they can access in person or through recorded forms especially in social media. Through formal and informal pulpits as sacred spaces, Black women religious leaders have both the opportunity and responsibility to hear from and speak on behalf of God through their embodied voices and experiences, which has led to more expansive understandings of what God can do in Movement leadership and through whom. These women use their power and position to often speak both prophetically by calling *out* unjust systems and structures, and pastorally by calling *in* those who are trapped on the margins and made invisible or even disposable by society. While this is certainly not the case for all Black women in ministerial leadership, without feeling the need to explain their commitments to anyone within the denominational structures in which they operate, Black women Movement pastors and religious leaders, including Karen, Traci, Leslie, and Pamela create space to regularly honor the sacredness of all Black lives.

On one Sunday morning, in July of 2016, I visited St. Paul's Baptist Church in Philadelphia where Leslie is the Senior pastor. On that day, the congregation joined in the holy sacrament of communion and, as pastor, Leslie was dressed ceremonially in a long, white, ministerial robe. After a beautiful service anchored by singing and the preaching of a sermon from Luke 10:20–37, Leslie left the pulpit and greeted members and visitors in the congregation. I was talking to a friend who attends the church when I noticed that the pastor had partially opened her robe on that warm day to reveal a black t-shirt with white letters stating Black Lives Matter that she was wearing underneath her vestment. I asked if I could take a picture, and she happily obliged, saying that was a normal type of thing for her to wear to church on a Sunday morning. A few years later, in September of 2019, I visited St. Paul's again during Leslie's tenth pastoral anniversary celebration. Traci Blackmon preached the Sunday morning sermon as the guest preacher, and she wore a black t-shirt with rhinestone lettering saying "Made to Worship," draped with a long clergy stole made of a burlap-type fabric with purple large-font lettering of the words "Do Justice, Love Mercy, Walk Humbly, Micah 6:8" on one side and the words of Womanist Ethicist Katie Geneva Cannon, "Do the work your soul must have, KGC" on the other side. Again, I asked if I could take a picture and she, too, obliged. The full embodiment of their commitments to Black lives are evident not only in what they say through the sermons, but also in their aesthetic presentations and proclamations from their positions of power behind the sacred desk within the pulpit.

The women's sermons themselves are written and delivered in ways that show a distinct view of the challenges that people face within society and the role that the Church/religious organizations and Black women play in painting clear pictures of what is at stake for Black women, men, and children.

Pastor Leslie D. Callahan preaches consistently at St. Paul's Baptist Church in Philadelphia, and she is also an in-demand preacher in progressive pulpits around the nation. Her sermons are known for their spirit-filled power and social justice critiques. She ensures that the faith she preaches and teaches about is a living faith that is concerned with the real experiences of people whose lives are impacted by systems and structures that are designed to limit their full flourishing. One year after the murder of Michael Brown in

Rev. Leslie D. Callahan, PhD, St. Paul's Baptist Church, July 10, 2016. Source: AnneMarie Mingo

Ferguson, Missouri, Leslie joined "The Black Scholars National Gathering: Lessons from Black Lives," convened by Pamela Lightsey, which I also partici- pated in from August 7–8, 2015. In 2014, drawn to what she was witnessing in the media as forces occupied Ferguson, Pamela flew from Boston where she was the Associate Dean of Community Life and Lifelong Learning at the Boston University School of Theology and was present to bear witness, live-stream video that could expose what was happening on the ground in the midst of the Ferguson uprising, and be an accessible veteran activist for those who needed support. When she convened the gathering in 2015, she brought young activists from St. Louis/Ferguson who she met during her time there together with scholars from around the nation to collaboratively share, learn, and create the public statement "Learning from Black Lives Conversation: A Statement of Solidarity and Theological Testament."[17]

During this gathering, Brittney Cooper, a professor at Rutgers University and member of St. Paul's Baptist Church, delivered the opening plenary address in which she plainly stated the Church has not earned a spot in the movement in Ferguson and elsewhere as Black Lives Matter was forming into a national movement. She explained that the Church earns its way back into a place of relevance by actually telling the story of Jesus Christ because it is the most compelling revolutionary narrative around. She implored the professors, pastors, and activists present that "if we teach our own [Christian] story right, people will break down the walls to come [to the Church]," and reminded everyone that God is here for the questions we have to ask about the systems in which we live. Standing in the legacy of a radical Christ and pressing God for deeper understanding of the present are ways of accessing what this era of Black Freedom Struggles calls for.

During a second plenary address at The Gathering, J. Kameron Carter, a professor at Duke University at the time, called-in those present and said, "the Black Church needs to be re-churched by Black Lives Matter." In the final plenary on the second day, Traci Blackmon, who had been invited to the protest space by young activists at the start of the Ferguson uprising as a pastor who was accessible to a community in need, described the killing of Michael Brown as a truth-telling moment for the Black Church. Reflecting what Cooper described the previous day regarding the church's relevance for young people where the Church in most communities walked away from struggles those young people now faced, Traci's experience with the activists leading in Ferguson clearly revealed that "the Church would no longer be grandfathered into leadership." Traci pushed further and challenged the religious scholars and pastors present, saying, "the church IS Ferguson. Stop trying to make them [young activists] be church, and join the church that they are. They need black scholars and spiritualists."[18] Through her experiences, she explained that grassroots activists want a church that is not stuck inside the building but is present in places of need. The messages from local activists who at that time had spent nearly one full year showing up in protest on the streets of Ferguson every day was that the work they were doing was work of liberation centered in love for humanity, which was the work of God, and it was therefore nonnegotiable.

On the fourth Sunday of August 2015, in a sermon preached less than two weeks after her return from the Ferguson gathering of scholars, drawing from Mali Music's song "Fight for You," (referenced in the songs section), Leslie pushes the Church universal through the church she pastors locally to hold the light of God and get involved in the struggle and fight for justice. In the sermon, the lyrics of the song are put in conversation with the Biblical text of Ephesians 6:10–20, and the lived experiences of people in her congregation and community. Many of the ideas Leslie shared reinforced themes discussed during the Ferguson gathering, and were consistent with the beliefs she had been preaching to her congregation over the years. She told the members and visitors on that Sunday, "our job is to stand side-by-side and back-to-back to fight what is outside of us, and not to fight each other on the inside."

Drawing from Ephesians 6:12, she reminds those who will listen that we wrestle against powers and principalities of evil. We wrestle against systemic evil and ways of being in the world that are trying to snuff out our life. It requires vigilance and a commitment to fight. In listening to the recorded sermon it is clear she wanted to distinguish between the systems of evil at work in people and not the people themselves. She explained to her congregation, "the systems are organized, and they pay attention to us. If we are going to fight we have to know what it is that we are fighting. We are fighting systems. We are fighting sophisticated and well put together systems. Sometimes we think we have defeated the opponent that we think we are fighting, but they are actually simply agents in a system that pops up in another place." In imagery reminiscent of Agents in *The Matrix* series of films, we are able to clearly see that without changing the system at its core, the impact the system has by oppressing others in order to sustain themselves will continue. As a pastor who preaches in the way theologian Karl Barth suggested with the Bible in one hand and the news in another, Leslie made a direct connection to the systems and agents of the system through her congregation's familiarity with the political rhetoric of the day, noting it's not White people who they are fighting, it's systems. "You know how I know it's systems, 'cause Ben Carson ain't White. Marco Rubio ain't White. Bobby Jindal ain't White. And it's not just the Republicans." Preached more than a year prior to the 2016 presidential election, these men were showing themselves to be non-White agents of the Republican system who worked against communities of color in a way that could clearly be understood as Leslie preached.

As I watched and listened to a video recording of the sermon through St. Paul's website, I could hear Leslie relaying the messages from the streets of Ferguson and other places as she encouraged the universal Church through the people in the local church to do the work of fighting for each other to be able to live fully. She chided them for closing the doors of the church on people who they deemed as not like them and shutting themselves inside ecclesial walls.

> [T]he church is often more outside of the doors—[outside] the building than it is inside. And the church of the street is trying to evangelize the church in the building because we shut the doors, after we've already been infected [with the virus of social evil]. We shut the doors. We shut the doors on the life giving and creative intentions and energy of young folks. Oh, we shut the doors on all of them. And not just young folks, on the opposite [age] spectrum we shut the door again and forget that those who built and who established the very congregation whose doors we've shut are no longer able to be in the building, and we forget entirely about the service that they give and we lock out their wisdom, and their knowledge, and their energy. We shut the doors . . . We've proven by the fact that we've shut the doors that we've already been infected by the virus. And we're dying in the church . . . Because we don't know who to fight for.[19]

The church, which has ignored the critically engaged energies of young people and grounded wisdom of older people who are no longer able to be actively involved in its physical life, is dying inside of an edifice where its myopic gazing practices of what a church looks like and what it does has left it disconnected from the people for which God has called them to fight.

Leslie's sermon continued and she asked those listening what they are covered in as their armor when the church joins the Movement for Black Lives, and suggested that they cover themselves in the armor of God:

> The content of the pieces of armor are virtues. They are Christian virtues like truth. The kind of truth that makes it possible to worship God. The kind of truth also that makes it possible to see through the circus of things and into deeper matters that keep you from being asleep when you are supposed to be awake. You have righteousness; not self-righteousness but the virtue of right relationship that I have to believe is connected in the mind of this Jewish writer to the idea of justice which always goes with righteousness in the Old Testament. You got truth and you've got righteousness which is right relationship with God and with other people. Also, known as justice. You've got salvation. You've got the concept of full and complete deliverance. And you've got a way out of the places where you've got to get out of. And a way into the places where you need to go. Salvation is connected to the concept of peace and well-being, and on your feet you've got whatever it is that makes you ready to share, and not share with your mouth. Do you notice that the sharing of the gospel happens with your feet? Lots of times the church shares the gospel with our mouth. And our feet are not in it. We have no actual skin in the game.[20]

The Theology of Movement requires that we move outside of the comfortable and simultaneously suffocating walls of the Church and into the communities where injustice exists, to fight for and with those who are, as Leslie observes, "experiencing some of the worst of what the powers can do."

Contrary to early criticisms by persons familiar with Black freedom movements of the twentieth century such as the US Civil Rights Movement and the Black Power Movement who expected to see a designated charismatic, and most-often, male leader to represent the movement, the Movement for Black Lives is not a leaderless, but a leader-full movement where many people are able to speak from the communities that they represent. Leaders during the Black Lives Matter era have studied the previous movements and they have created more inclusive structures in an Ella Baker style of participatory democracy within leadership, where multiple leaders understand and are committed to both local and broader struggles, which also prevents one leader from being isolated and picked off socially, politically, and physically.

One of the women in the M4BL whose voice has been rising up from the community and gaining access to, and influence with, persons in power is Brittney Packnett Cunningham. Thrust into the national spotlight during the Ferguson uprising, Cunningham's voice and impact have been felt from her native Missouri as a member of the Ferguson Commission, to the White House as a member of President Obama's Task Force on 21st Century Policing, to co-founding Campaign Zero, to becoming a regular contributor on cable news networks. As a speaker, she weaves her lived experiences as an educator, with her social justice commitments, and her radical faith tradition that seeks freedom. She was raised within the Black liberation tradition of the National Baptist denomination where her activism was equally yoked to her faith. In an interview with the *Christian Recorder* she explains, "I don't think I had a choice. My father was a pastor and both he and my mother very clearly ascribed to activism and social justice work as a duty of our faith. I was in a stroller at my very first protest. The films that raised me were not Disney movies as much as they were documentaries like *Eyes on the Prize* by Henry Hampton, films like *Roots,* and books like the *Autobiography of Frederick Douglass*. To paraphrase Jay Z, 'I didn't choose this life. This life chose me.' But I'm deeply thankful to have been raised in that tradition and understanding that faith without works was dead."[21]

Cunningham's father, Ronald B. Packnett, a Yale Divinity School graduate, served as pastor of Central Baptist Church in St. Louis, Missouri, from 1985 until his early death in 1996 when Cunningham was twelve years old. Her mother, Gwendolyn Packnett, who is also an ordained minister, was a social worker and higher education administrator before she retired from the

University of Missouri-St. Louis in 2015 as the assistant vice chancellor for academic affairs. Shaped by her father's freedom-seeking faith and her mother's justice-focused education, Brittany Packnett Cunningham identifies as "a proud Black woman of faith who believes that freedom is within our grasp."[22] When asked what the Church needs to change moving forward, she replied,

> We can begin by recognizing that there is only one Savior—and none of us are Him. Our superiority and savior complexes do nothing to end injustice—only our solidarity does. Solidarity requires two critical shifts:
>
> First, that we are led by those who are most affected by an injustice. We do not get to dictate the mode or the medium of freedom for others—we can only follow the lead of the vision they set for themselves, asking permission to be useful in the movement and spending our privilege to achieve the win.
>
> Second is that we love beyond charity. Charity is food and has its place—people need to be fed, housed, and fueled in the here and now. But charity is only concerned with feeding 500 people on a single day; solidarity is concerned with replacing the systems that leave 500 people hungry in the first place. Solidarity is concerned with recognizing the power inherent in those who are marginalized and supporting them in exercising it to achieve justice and liberation.
>
> Anything less than solidarity is a paternalistic exercise to save people who don't need saving—they simply deserve our support.[23]

As the Movement for Black Lives continues to form and shape around commitments to justice in various ways, we have seen the use of public statements from groups that are accustomed to speaking to institutions and organizations. Two such statements were primarily written under the leadership of Black women who are theologians and activists. They are: the "Statement from Black Presidents and Deans, Schools and Departments of Theology and Religion" coauthored by Pamela Lightsey in June 2020 declaring that "the survival and thriving of Black people in this nation and globally in our unapologetic commitment," with fifteen signatures from presidents and deans, and capturing over forty additional signatures of scholars of religion and African American studies, including mine;[24] and the "On Black Lives Matter: A Theological Statement from the Black Churches" released for Juneteenth in 2020, and primarily written by Theological Ethicist Eboni Marshall Turman, with eleven additional pastors and ministry leaders in New York City as signatories, before receiving additional support by nearly 700 additional Black pastors and theologians, including me, who signed-on in support virtually of the call to "emphatically repudiate the evil beast of white racism, white supremacy, white superiority and its concomitant and abiding anti-Black violence."[25]

From pastors, to professors, to grassroots activist practitioners, in the twenty-first century, Black religious women's audible and written voices are impacting society in ways that have wider and deeper reach than was possible in previous movements.

A Liberative Social Ethic of Compulsion

While there are some experiences that were particular to the eight Civil Rights Movement–era women I primarily share about in this book, there are other experiences that have a universal quality for many of the women I have been able to learn from over years of research. Throughout my oral history interviews with over forty women who were active during the Civil Rights Movement, and interviews with women who are active in the Movement for Black Lives, without the ability to hear what one another were saying, many of them used almost identical language to describe their commitment to activism. Without fail, at some point during the interview they stated that taking the risk for themselves, their current community, and the potential of the more just society they imagined for the future was something they simply "had to do." This sense of the work of liberation as something that they had to do does not limit their own agency, even if the commitment to step up to act was not as much desire as a sense of call from God.

The women consistently noted their inability to do anything other than the activism and work for change to which they had committed their lives. Whether as a one-time act, something they sought out to participate in as often as possible, or work in which they engaged in a leadership or organizing capacity, they spoke about feeling compelled to act in ways that would result in long-term communal justice and freedom. What they saw in the daily inequities of Black women, men, and children, and what they heard in the vitriolic rhetoric often hurled at them created an insatiable desire to see the world change for the better, and that was something to which they could not turn a blind eye or deaf ear.

This inner compulsion was both a source and framework, driving the women to first analyze a situation, then imagine what ought to be as God revealed it to them, and finally work pragmatically to find ways to realize those visions. This is an ethics that takes its shape within the contours of the morals of the community. A distinctive element of a virtue ethics is the sense that there are no other options outside of the one being acted upon. Black Churchwomen who chose to actively engage in Movement work did not need to deliberate or decide their actions by group consensus because they were already morally formed by their heritage, their faith, and their experience to act as often as possible in service of justice and freedom. The Black community provided the necessary moral tools including lessons from sermons and church school, values and virtues modeled by parents and grandparents, and reinforcement from the community that the opportunities they received were not solely for themselves (as Nana Rosa reminds us, it was bigger than that), but they had a responsibility to make things better for those who would come behind them. As the women reflected on their actions, they consistently analyzed the situations they encountered with a clear sense of moral judgment and resolve to change the situation.

These Black Churchwomen were historically, and are contemporarily, doing the work of justice as they work for the common good. It is, in the words of Katie Cannon, the work their souls must have. They understand faith as an anchor and guide for radical resistance of any system or structure that limits human flourishing. Through their lived experiences and understanding of history, they know that not all who profess to be Christians are living out a religion that is good in the broadest ethical way. When White Christians enslaved Africans and forcibly brought them to the Americas, the Black women knew that particular religion was not good. When White Christians, including women, did all that they could to reinforce the construction of White superiority that saw Black life as disposable during the periods of enslavement, Reconstruction, and Jim Crow, Black women knew the religion these White Christians embraced was not good. When White Christians sat comfortably silent in church on Sundays in the face of Black death at the hands of police officers who may have worshipped next to them in pews, Black women knew that practice of religion was not good.

"Have You Got Good Religion?" is the refrain and more common name for the spiritual "Certainly Lord," which was often invoked in mass meetings during the Civil Rights Movement. The inquisition requires an examination of the character of the religion that a person professes and lives by. Challenging the ethical concept of the common good in the religious ethos that spurred many Black churches to action and lulled many White churches into silence, Black Churchwomen knew that religion could take on *bad* characteristics, such as when practitioners burned crosses on front lawns of Black homes and bombed churches with parishioners inside. As a result, these Churchwomen distinguished between those types of religious expressions rooted in evil and *good* religion. The titular question also implies an ethical mandate that seeks human flourishing and the resultant highest good that requires virtues reflective of a deep faith.

A theology of movement picks a side. It fights to center and make *good* religion normative. For those who understand God as one who is a collaborator with people who are actively bending the arch of the moral universe toward justice, they have inherited the ability to discern between good religion and bad religion. For them, there is no possibility for a lukewarm, partially committed religion. There is a need to be certain that they have got good religion where their faith, courage, and imagination are shaped by a relationship with God that pushes them to do justly, love kindness, and walk humbly with God.

Bree Newsome Bass
Choosing a Religion of Freedom and Justice

In the pain-filled aftermath of the murders of nine men and women inside Charleston's Mother Emanuel A.M.E. Church on June 17, 2015, when the images of the twenty-one-year-old killer brandishing guns and the confederate flag were publicized, many saw that deadly White supremacist act as the last straw and decided something had to change. Less than two weeks later, when Bree Newsome ascended a thirty-foot flagpole on the Statehouse grounds in Columbia, South Carolina, on June 27, 2015, she did so after a condensed period of physical preparation that taught her how to safely climb up and repel down a metal pole, and an intense period of spiritual preparation of prayer and fasting. It was with this spiritual and physical strength that she snatched the symbol of secession, treason, and hatred as represented by the confederate flag from the privileged perch from which it had flown since 2000. The flagpole on the statehouse grounds was considered a compromise when the confederate flag was removed from South Carolina's capitol dome where it had flown since 1961 when it was officially raised in honor of the Civil War's centennial. However, the flag was more commonly understood as a response to civil rights activism led by young Black people throughout the south.[1]

Brittany Ann "Bree" Newsome Bass was born in 1985, and grew up primarily in Columbia, Maryland. Her father, Rev. Dr. Clarence Newsome, is a Baptist minister, scholar, former president of Shaw University, former Dean of Howard University Divinity School, and former president of the National Underground Railroad Freedom Center. Her mother, Lynne Newsome, is an advocate for education who works toward solving the achievement gap.

Brittany "Bree" Newsome Bass Taking Down Confederate Flag, June 27, 2015. Source: AP Images

Clarence Newsome recalls that his daughter had a longtime passion for, and commitment to, helping people. She grew up hearing her grandmother tell stories of a neighbor who was brutally beaten by the Ku Klux Klan for adhering to the Hippocratic oath as a Black doctor but defying hypocritical Jim Crow racist practices in the south, by medically treating a White woman. Newsome Bass also learned the stories of family members who died by lynching and the history of her ancestors who can be traced back to the slave market in Charleston.[2]

An artist—filmmaker, musician, composer, writer—Newsome Bass began blending her creativity and sociopolitical critique early. In high school, her animated short film *The Three Princes Idea*, earned her a $40,000 scholarship from the National Academy of Television Arts & Sciences. Her work caught the attention of the Academy director who described it as a "combination of intellectual horsepower and creative range." Newsome Bass attended New York University's Tisch School of the Arts where her public service announcement promoting increased voter turnout, "Your Ballot, Your Voice," won the grand prize in a competition sponsored by NYU and MTV. She graduated with a degree in Film and Television.

Although raised in a household where social change through faith and education were central, it was voting rights suppression in North Carolina that moved Newsome Bass from support on the sidelines to direct action. She was arrested in 2013 in association with political activism when she and five others sat-in and occupied the office of South Carolina Speaker of the House Thom Tillis, who later became a US Senator in 2015. The murder of Trayvon Martin also sparked a flame in her as she described Martin as her generation's Emmett Till, and she joined protesters in the streets of Ohio and Florida to raise awareness around police and state-sanctioned violence against Black bodies. It was after the murder of the nine churchgoers, practitioners of the faith she had been born and raised within, that she had a "crisis of faith" that pushed her to take an action that might cost her life. As a part of her preparation, in addition to reading scriptures, praying, and fasting, the final decision to go forward with the planned action was made after Newsome Bass asked her "prayer warrior" sister to pray for her. She did not tell her parents about her plans. They found out as the world did. The fear and need for covering and protection through prayer was heightened because of the deeply entrenched feelings about the confederate flag in the south and the place of physical vulnerability Newsome Bass would be in while attached to the flagpole. She was more concerned about potential retaliation that might involve her being shot or someone electrifying the metal pole while she was harnessed to it.[3]

One day after President Barack Obama eulogized the slain pastor of Mother Emanuel A.M.E. Church and South Carolina Senator Rev. Clementa Pinckney, a small group of activists who decided enough was enough, made an early morning trip to the South Carolina Statehouse to remove the symbol of hate which had flown proudly despite the tragedy wrought to families and the nation under its banner. Police officers arrived as Newsome Bass was about halfway up and began commanding her to come down. "You're doing the wrong thing," they told her. In response, she quoted from the book of Isaiah, "What kind of fast have I chose? Is it not to break the yoke of oppression?" She further let the officer know that she was prepared to be arrested but would not come down until she removed the flag. Video recorded during the action captures Newsome Bass making a declaration in an echo to the story of David and Goliath that she read before taking on the task. "You come against me with hatred, oppression, violence. I come against you in the name of God. This flag comes down today!"[4]

This day was not a moment when you had to ask or wonder in the words of the Movement song "which side are you on." It was evident which side Bree Newsome Bass had chosen in the fight for justice and freedom and she was clear in expressing that more than one side existed as she responded to the officers in the moment and to potential critics who would see her bold and decisive actions as disruptive and destructive.

In the video we hear her quoting Psalm 27 as she bravely braced herself while descending, "The Lord is my light and my salvation—whom shall I fear? The Lord is the stronghold of my life—of whom shall I be afraid?" You can also hear other members of the nearby group begin to collectively applaud and proclaim through call-and-response what has become known in activist circles as Assata's Chant, "It is our duty to fight for our freedom, it is our duty to win. We must love and protect each other. We have nothing to lose but our chains." As Newsome Bass was led away in handcuffs, she repeated Psalm 23 and made a public statement about which side she was on in the fight for freedom and which side she believed God to also be on. Newsome Bass saw her action on that day as a part of her duty as a woman of faith. "I see no greater moral cause than liberation, equality, and justice for all God's people. What better reason to risk your own freedom than to fight for the freedom of others?"[5]

The removal of the confederate flag was not Newsome Bass's idea. It was a direct action that had already been researched and planned by an interracial group of activists from Charlotte, North Carolina. The group discussed the symbolism of having a Black woman remove the flag instead of reifying motifs of White saviors. The team of about fifteen people, including climbing trainers, photographic surveillance, and a liaison who would greet the police and let them know it was a nonviolent action, were selective in who would serve as the person to assist Newsome Bass on that day. One factor that pushed her comrade, James Tyson, to participate in the action was the fact that unlike the United States and South Carolina state flags, the confederate flag was not lowered to half-staff following the murder of Emanuel A.M.E. pastor and State Senator Pinckney because state laws prohibited it. The flag which had been embraced by the man accused of murdering nine Black Christian worshippers continued to fly as Pinckney's body lay in state at the capitol with black fabric covering the windows so those grieving and paying their respect would not have to see it outside. As Newsome Bass described, their nonviolent direct action was always about more than the flag, "It's not just about a piece of fabric that flaps next to [a] metal pole . . . It's about the ideology and that's why we thought it was important—the symbol of a black woman taking it down and handing it to a white man."[6]

It took Newsome Bass about ten minutes to climb up the thirty-foot flagpole and unhook the flag. James Ian Tyson, who allowed her to stand on his back to climb over the four-foot gate and the base and spotted her in the climb, wanted to make sure that she was up high enough before the officers arrived so that she could not be easily pulled down. Black and White officers arrested the Black and White pair of activists who were charged with defacing monuments on state capitol grounds, a misdemeanor carrying fines of up to $5,000 and three years in prison. As the Black officer led Newsome Bass away she was praying and he asked her why she felt the Holy Spirit led her to do it. She was as open with him as she could be at that moment. For her, it was "a calling as a human being, it's a calling as a child of God, to fight on behalf of the oppressed."[7]

In a press release issued during the direct action and emailed to the media by organizers, they shared, "We took this task in our own hands because our President, Governor, mayors, legislators, and councilmen had a moral duty to remove the flag but failed to act . . . We could not sit by and watch the victims of the Charleston Massacre be laid to rest while the inspiration for their deaths continue to fly above their caskets . . . We removed the flag today because we can't wait any longer. It's time for a new chapter where we are sincere about dismantling white supremacy and building toward true racial justice and equality."[8] Social media quickly celebrated Newsome Bass's brave actions describing her as a superhero, flooding timelines with her image near the top of the flagpole with the confederate flag in her hand, prompting the hashtags #KeepItDown and #FreeBree to trend as funds were raised for the legal fees she would incur.[9]

Shortly after her release on bond, Newsome Bass continued to speak and draw attention to the activist work that she and others were committed to. Newsome Bass was a mainstage speaker at the Wild Goose Festival (a gathering of Progressive Christians) in North Carolina on July 11, 2015, along with Tyson. The festival also drew other religious activists whose work throughout the United States was gaining broader awareness, including Rev. Traci Blackmon, then a part of the Ferguson Commission, Rev. William Barber, whose Moral Mondays were expanding, and immigrant advocate Alexia Salvatierra. After her speech, Newsome Bass was introduced to Blackmon and the two religious activists embraced and encouraged each other. As Blackmon thanked Newsome Bass, with tears in her eyes she let the warrior for justice know, "you lit my fire." Newsome Bass responded, "y'all lit my fire in Ferguson."[10] These fire-starting women were on the same side fighting along with the God of liberation who wants everyone to be free.

Not only were activists in Ferguson and other cities motivated by the bold actions of this real-life superhero, but her own parents were inspired. Rev. Dr. Clarence Newsome described it this way: "She took a moral stand for justice and harmony and progress . . . She has helped me understand how all of us need to be more courageous in promoting social change in our society."[11] Two years after this most well-known action, Newsome Bass reflected on other Black women, including Takiya Thompson, who were inspired to take action and bring down confederate statues and markers in their areas: "I just see this shifting in the consciousness, and people just kind of reaching a point where we just can't be quiet anymore, because I think there has been, in some ways, this belief that we keep ourselves quiet in order to survive. But staying quiet is also like its own form of death. I think people are just tired of living that form of death."[12]

Bree Newsome Bass understood her action on that Saturday morning as an extension of her faith and her connection to struggles throughout the African Diaspora, and a continuation of the work that she was doing in North Carolina. "I removed the flag not only in defiance of those who enslaved my ancestors in the southern United States, but also in defiance of the oppression that continues against black people globally in 2015, including the ongoing ethnic cleansing in the Dominican Republic . . . I did it in solidarity with the South African students who toppled a statue of the white supremacist, colonialist Cecil Rhodes. I did it for all the fierce black women on the front lines of the movement and for all the little black girls who are watching us. I did it because I am free."[13] In response to breaking the law through the removal of the flag, in the tradition of Aristotle and Martin Luther King Jr., Newsome Bass explained that there are times when unjust laws must be broken. She later clarified, in an interview, "Yes, I broke the law, but laws can also be unjust. And I feel that the law that protects that symbol of hate is an unjust law."[14]

"Have You Got *Good* Religion?"

All of us have the capacity to live lives of faith, courage, and imaginative change. Throughout my years interviewing and spending time with Black Churchwomen and religious activists from both the twentieth and twenty-first centuries, I have found their "everydayness" to be the most inspiring. These women are not out of reach; they are not so extraordinary that I cannot see myself in them and be motivated to take on similar risks for the sake of the good that I imagine for the world in which we live. Most of the more senior of these women are nearly octogenarians yet still active in various aspects of freedom movements as they live out the often-quoted words of Ella Baker from 1964, "Until the killing of black men, black mother's sons, becomes as important to the rest of the country as the killing of a white mother's son, we who believe in freedom cannot rest until this happens."

There are similarities across the generations, but one of the differences between the eras of the civil rights and Black lives movements is the greater centering of intentional care and rest among activists in the twenty-first century. As a part of what I see as a womanist ethics of care, Black women activists today frequently study and are mentored by activists from previous movements who share out of their lived experiences the necessity of stepping away from direct engagement for mental and physical health. The elder mentors also promote having enough people actively involved in the movement, so the work does not completely stop as one leader steps back to care for herself. This is one of the benefits to creating organizations with the focus on developing multiple leaders and not placing all the responsibility and expectations on one charismatic person that the media can elevate or deflate, or the opposition can figuratively or literally kill.

Women I interviewed who were leaders during the Civil Rights Movement, including Gwendolyn Zoharah Simmons and A. Lenora Taitt-Magubane, and those I read narratives about such as Fannie Lou Hamer, describe how the trauma of the physical and psychological violence they faced, particularly in the southern freedom movement, resulted in moments when they were encouraged and at times forced to leave the intense context of battle and step away from the front lines. Zoharah and Lenora each described examples of movement activists who "stayed in" too long without time to disengage and recharge, and as a result experienced a type of mental break that they were not able to return from. In the current movements in the second and third decades of the twenty-first century, Black women including Tricia Hersey, known as the Nap Bishop of the Nap Ministry, and groups such as Rest for Resistance QTPoC Mental Health, argue for rest *as* resistance and a radical tool for community healing. Today, social movement organizations regularly incorporate and model care for the mental health of leaders and communities as central to their work. As Audre Lorde notes, "caring for myself is not self-indulgence, it is self-preservation, and that is an act of political warfare."[1]

The news provides daily reminders of the wars Black lives continue to fight not only in the United States, but throughout the world as made evident in the many means through which anti-Blackness shows up in almost every area of society. As a result, the virtuous work of freedom faith, courageous resistance, and Theo-moral imagination remains necessary. The virtues that the twentieth-century women drew on from within their segregated Black communities continue to offer methods of using a liberating faith to keep twenty-first-century women anchored in ancestral wisdom and spiritual strength as they embark on deep and transformative forms of engagement with the systems and structures that seek to limit human flourishing today.

When Alicia Garza, Patrisse Cullors, and Opal Tometi created the #BlackLivesMatter hashtag and expanded it into a global Movement for Black Lives (M4BL), they understood their mission within a legacy of resistance as they joined the ongoing liberative work of justice in collaboration with other predominantly Black and Brown organizations. When the M4BL launched their Vision for Black Lives in August 2016, the vision was "endorsed by over 50 Black-led organizations in the M4BL ecosystem and hundreds of allied organizations and individuals."[2] Much like the Student Nonviolent Coordinating Committee (SNCC) which as its name indicates served as a coordinating committee with two representatives from each of the affiliated organizations of local and regional bodies during the Civil Rights Movement, the Movement for Black Lives identifies as a part of an "ecosystem of over 170 Black-led organizations."[3] During the twentieth century, SNCC and the National Council of Negro Women (NCNW) were two of very few organizations with Black women in positions of significant public leadership. Black women often bring holistic perspectives, strategies, and commitments in a womanist approach to activism that is "committed to the survival and wholeness of entire people, male and female."[4] No longer pushed to the background as in the past, many of the organizations in the twenty-first century including #BlackLivesMatter, BYP100 (Black Youth Project 100), Southerners on New Ground, Millennial Activists United, Black Feminist Futures Project, and others have been created by and/or are led by Black women and femmes. They work to intentionally counter the patriarchal, misogynist, heteronormative, and ableist structures of the past civil rights organizations.

In historic and contemporary movements, Black faith and activism often meet in spaces of Black resistance. However, in the contemporary movements, faith is not always expressed in the form of one of the major world religions. While there were diversities of belief during historic movements, the openness to non-Christocentric expressions is more accepted in grassroots activist spaces today as formal and informal leadership expands beyond the ordained clergymen of the past. This openness and expansion of faith forced the historical Black Church into an awakening that revealed their presumed position as the vanguard of justice movements to no longer be their reality. Despite revisionist memories of "their day," historical records verify that most Black churches were not actively involved in the Civil Rights Movement for various reasons, yet the work of the movement was often associated with a liberative Christian belief system. However, many churches, pastors, and members ceded their position as the moral community leaders when they became comfortable with the initial wins of the Civil Rights Movement through changed laws and stopped fighting for the full rights of all. The prosperity gospel era ushered in a sense of individualism that reeked of White capitalist notions of self-advancement that are antithetical to a more communal African ethos. Many Black churches strayed away from agitating and holding political and communal leaders accountable in local struggles, especially those impacting young people. Once fewer legal discrimination practices created openings for new employment and housing opportunities, some Black pastors and members with financial resources leveraged their social mobility and moved from Black city centers to the suburbs. At times, communities were forced to disperse as "urban renewal" plans disrupted social connections, creating a form of neighborhood transience that Omar McRoberts and others describe.[5] Often church members and leaders who no longer lived within the neighborhood traveled to the

Black church community only on the weekend for specific experiences (e.g., hair appointments, church, and occasional social gatherings) in the physical spaces that remained tightly or at times loosely anchored to the locale and therefore were not present or actively involved, thus creating a lacuna of leadership. The young people who were left behind with under-resourced school systems, inadequate safe housing, limited health options, absent elder leaders, and more found themselves on the receiving end of an anti-Black system that thrives in times of apathy in lieu of consistent activism.

I believe "Black Lives Matter" is a theological statement through an assertion of the dignity of life as ordained by the Creator.[6] It is a necessary statement of humanist worth in the midst of the often absent and silent Black Church. The organizational leaders in the twenty-first century often openly draw from a broader sense of Black spirituality and faith than their predecessors. As I have traveled and participated in various actions around the nation and observed others through grassroots journalists in social media, I have noticed spiritual practices that may not be recognizable to the casual observer because the rituals have not been overtly named as such. One such example is an experience I had in Ferguson, Missouri, during the one-year commemoration of the murder of Michael Brown. Following an afternoon with participants in the "The Black Scholars National Gathering: Lessons from Black Lives," I met up with a friend from college who lives in the area, and she drove me to see the place where Michael Brown was killed near the Canfield Green Apartments. At that time, a memorial of stuffed animals, flowers, notes, and candles marked sacred space in the middle of the street, anchored at the place where Brown's head and feet lay for 4.5 hours on that fateful August afternoon.[7] The previously blood-drenched section of asphalt was repaved—making the new section even more noticeable to even the casual viewer who made a pilgrimage to that place.[8] However, the city could not erase or pave over the pain of the community. Cars entering and leaving the parking lots of the apartment complex or driving down Canfield Drive had to be mindful of the area the community deemed as sacred after the life of "Mike Mike," one of their communal sons, was taken. I also noticed a half-moon-shaped concrete inlay in the sidewalk with a black image of a dove ascending in correlation to the spot where Brown died. At the time of the one-year commemoration of the death of Michael Brown, votive candles outlined the marker.[9] These were semi-permanent and permanent markers drawing from sacred practices for the honoring of Black lives.

The marking of sacred space was also evident when I visited the area across the street from the City of Ferguson Police Department and Municipal Court where in August 2015 people had gathered every day for nearly a year after the killing of Michael Brown to protest, pray, and maintain a consistent presence long after the media cameras left. I was drawn to the sound of drumming by KB, a Black trans Jewish man I met briefly in one of the sessions of the Black Scholars National Gathering, so I walked toward the spot where he and a small group were gathered. As I approached, I noticed some things that indicated the presence and enactment of spiritual practices. While there were portable chairs and even an empty wheelchair that formed an outer border, I saw colorful handwoven blankets that had been placed in a large pattern on the asphalt and various candles were lit marking the inner borders of the blankets. Sage and other forms of incense were burning in the area where people stood, and there were pillows available if anyone desired to sit within the blanketed space. In the moment of my walking up and seconds before stepping on the blanket to approach the small group the sacredness of the space resonated with me, and I paused to address them from the margins. I mentioned my observation, and those gathered within the area confirmed that a designation of a sacred space from which to consistently protest the injustices of the Ferguson police department and other agencies was indeed their goal. Within an African worldview, there is no separation between the sacred and secular and in these instances of socio-political-religious activism through sacred remembrance of lives taken by state-sanctioned violence this blending is evident through acts of communal protest.

In the early stages of the Movement for Black Lives a critique was offered and intergenerational tensions began to be stoked with some persons who lived during the civil rights era and may have participated in some ways but were not necessarily grassroots leaders. They were looking for a lone charismatic heterosexual male Christian leader to step from behind the pulpit and grab the microphone to speak as "the voice" of the people. This idea of a singular leader was exactly what the organizers in the twenty-first century knew to avoid, as they pushed back on the notion that they were leaderless and embraced the reality that they were leader-full. In the spirit of Ella Baker, they looked to local leaders within communities to rise up and address the concerns that they were closest to and most impacted by. If assistance was necessary, other leaders from outside of the community would walk and work alongside those within the community.[10]

Many of the grassroots organizers I have studied and observed in the second decade of the twenty-first century continue to agitate at local levels to push for systemic changes that shape the lived experiences of Black people throughout the United States and beyond. We see the virtues of freedom faith, courageous resistance, and moral imagination in the work of numerous contemporary justice-centered organizations of which I will briefly note a few.

The Samuel DeWitt Proctor Conference (SDPC), cofounded by Dr. Iva E. Carruthers, Dr. Frederick D. Haynes III, and Dr. Jeremiah A. Wright Jr., and incorporated in 2003, continues to expand its reach and impact on society under the leadership of Executive Secretary Dr. Iva E. Carruthers. SDPC holds as its mission "to nurture, sustain, and mobilize the African American faith community in collaboration with civic, corporate, and philanthropic leaders to address critical needs of human rights and social justice within local, national, and global communities. SDPC seeks to strengthen the individual and collective capacity of thought leaders and activists in the church, academy, and community through education, advocacy, and activism."[11] Each year, the SDPC hosts a conference for clergy, laypersons, seminarians, and thought leaders from the Church, Academy, and broader community who are committed to learning, strategizing, and increasing the influence of their grassroots justice work in their local communities. Living out their biblical mandate to do justice, the SDPC also advocates at the US Capitol, hosts legislative sessions, publishes resources, and leads numerous initiatives that enable them to work with and on behalf of the most vulnerable and marginalized persons throughout the world.

Fair Fight Action, founded by Stacey Abrams, the daughter of two United Methodist pastors and a fierce fighter for justice, aims to "promote fair elections around the country, encourage voter participation in elections, and educate voters about elections and their voting rights. Fair Fight Action brings awareness to the public on election reform, advocates for election reform at all levels, and engages in other voter education programs and communications."[12] While often credited for the "Blue Wave" in the historic elections for the state of Georgia in 2020, the work of Fair Fight has deep roots and an expansive reach throughout the United States. Abrams who was also shaped in the rich HBCU tradition as a graduate of Spelman College describes the connection to her faith and activism in this way: "My faith is central to the work that I do, in that I not only hold Christian values, but my faith tradition as a Methodist tells me that the most profound demonstration of our faith is service."[13]

Formed by Rev. Dr. Pamela Lightsey in mid-August 2020 at the invitation of Rev. Michael McBride to support the goals of the Black Church Political Action Committee, the Blaque Political Collective (BPC) is described as "Black LGBTQIA+ activists; working on intergenerational public policy issues from multigenerational perspectives; squaring the circle by bending the rules."[14] Through bi-weekly Facebook live events that were also broadcast to YouTube, the BPC reached over five thousand people with their first event and thousands more with each subsequent one. Their team members represented expertise in the critical political geographies of Texas, Georgia, Florida, Pennsylvania, and Illinois. Within less than three months, the BPC hosted multiple conversations through their Facebook live events and text-a-thons to increase political education and engagement. Lightsey's efforts to bring the Black Church and Black LGBTQIA+ communities together to focus on common challenges are also centered in her womanist commitments as she stresses "genuine engagements that lead to healing need to happen for the protection and wellbeing of the entire Black community."[15]

A critical faith can be a tool for freedom, and a liberating religion can offer strategies of ongoing resistance and resilience, especially to forces of oppression rooted in a culture of racism and White supremacy. In the lived experiences of women from the civil rights era we see ways they actively claimed freedom through resistance by drawing on a faith fashioned in ways that sustained and delivered their fore parents and they believed could do the same if not more for them. The critical faith and liberating religion, once bedrock for many Black denominations and churches, has become unstable sand with little space for the movements of the twenty-first century to use as a foundational support on which to build their activism. Today, the Black Church does not hold the central position it once garnered within the communities where Black people live, survive, and thrive. Its silence and absence in ongoing struggles post the historic Civil and Voting Rights Act of the 1960s has left many activists curating other spiritual and moral communities of support.

The stories of civil rights era women including Lillian Sue Bethel, Doris Virginia Brunson, Peggy Lucas, Rose Davis Schofield, Bessie Smith Sellaway, Marjorie Wallace Smyth, Beatrice Perry Soublet, and A. Lenora Taitt-Magubane, offer broader understandings of the faith commitments that undergirded past victories. These women, who remained active in justice movements throughout their lives, provide examples for people who want to join the constant struggle to work for the consistent goal of freedom for all of creation. Women who took on the fight in the twentieth century can point to their faith and belief that the work they were doing in the words of Nana Rosa was bigger than themselves as a part of what has sustained them in their efforts decades later. The work of justice and social change was and is God's work and they see it as such.

Today we see the ongoing challenge of discerning what Good Religion is as observed in the actions of the people professing their faith as leaders and followers. In *White Evangelical Racism: The Politics of Morality in America*, Anthea Butler offers a clear critique of conservative evangelical activism from the US Civil War through the racial unrest of 2020, identifying evangelicalism as a political movement that is synonymous with cultural whiteness and holds racism as a central feature in the political choices this brand of evangelicalism supports.[16] As White conservative evangelicals, Southern Baptists, and others support laws and practices that limit human flourishing and reinforce fissures as a result of racism, sexism, classism, ableism, heterosexism, and more, some Black evangelicals such as Rev. William Barber fight to reclaim the category for acts of the common good. Historic Black churches including the African Methodist Episcopal Church and Progressive National Baptist Convention are bringing the voices of younger leaders to the forefront as they begin to once again do the radical work of justice. The absence of the Black Church in areas of struggle including LGBTQIA+ rights, health care, environmental justice, living wages, and more has been long and they must find ways to work alongside those who have been filling in the gaps. In the refrain of the song "Certainly Lord," often sung during the Civil Rights Movement, the question "Have you got good religion?" forces us to critique not only what is verbalized as belief, but what is realized in action. As it has for millennia, Micah 6:8 still proffers a liberative ethics and challenge of reflection—"He has told you, O mortal, what is *good*; and what does the Lord require of you but to do justice, and to love kindness, and to walk humbly with your God?"

Appendix

Brief biographical sketches for some of the women interviewed associated with this research.

Barbara Ann Adams—Ms. Adams participated in this research while at Ebenezer Baptist Church. She was born and raised in Atlanta, Georgia. She was baptized at Ebenezer at the age of six by Reverend King, Sr. During the Civil Rights Movement, she marched to integrate hotels, and one day was seen on television participating in a march when she had called out sick from work. She integrated the YMCA on Edgewood by herself when others did not show up.

Karen Anderson—Rev. Anderson, D.Min. was born in Detroit, but has called St. Louis, Missouri, home since her family moved there when she was in elementary school. As a registered nurse, prior to entering full-time ministry as a pastor, she worked in healthcare administration for over thirty years. During the Ferguson uprising, she served as pastor of Ward Chapel A.M.E. Church in Florissant, Missouri, board president for Gamaliel's Metropolitan Congregations United, board member of Magdalene St. Louis, and on the cabinet of the Interfaith Partnership and Flourish St. Louis.

Lillian Sue Bethel—Ms. Bethel was interviewed as a member of First A.M.E. Bethel Church. She was born in Albany, Georgia, and raised between there and Florida before moving to New York City after graduating from High School. After the sudden death of her mother in New York, Bethel returned to Albany where she attended Albany State College (now University). She joined efforts to protest the treatment of Freedom Riders and was arrested in 1961 along with almost forty other students who were all summarily expelled from the College.

Traci deVon Blackmon—Rev. Blackmon was born and raised in Birmingham, Alabama, which shaped how she sees both the world and herself. She worked as a registered nurse and healthcare administrator for over twenty-five years. At the time of our interview, she described herself as a pastor, denominational leader, and co-laborer in the struggle for justice. During the Ferguson uprising, a young person in the community reached out to her as the pastor of Christ the King United Church of Christ in Florissant, Missouri. She also serves as the Associate General Minister of Justice and Local Church Ministries for the United Church of Christ.

Rosa H. Brown—Mrs. Brown was born and raised in Atlanta, Georgia and interviewed as a member of Big Bethel A.M.E. Church. She was shaped as a student at Washington High School and Spelman College. Born in 1920, she was older than many of the other research participants when she became active in the Civil Rights Movement in the early 1950s. She and other office workers from Atlanta Life Insurance Company protested the low levels of hiring of Black workers at the U.S. Post Office and supported other efforts. During the Movement, she was a member of Big Bethel A.M.E., which was pastored by Reverend Harold Bearden at the time.

Doris Virginia Brunson—Ms. Brunson was interviewed as a member of Abyssinian Baptist Church. She was raised in New York City, but born in Manning, South Carolina, after her parents traveled back to where they were from as the time neared to make sure their child was born in the South. During the Civil Rights Movement, she attended Abyssinian when Reverend Samuel DeWitt Proctor was the pastor. She taught at Wadleigh High School for many years, and became involved in the Movement in the 1960s because of her desire for equality and to motivate younger persons.

Leslie Dawn Callahan—Rev. Callahan, PhD was raised in the coal mining region of southern West Virginia, and it was there that she grew up in the Pentecostal tradition. After serving as a religious studies professor at the University of Pennsylvania and New York Theological Seminary, she became the first woman to serve as senior pastor of St. Paul's Baptist Church in Philadelphia, Pennsylvania, in 2009. Her justice commitments led her to Ferguson to support the pastors and community during the uprising.

Margie Davis—Ms. Davis was born and raised in Fairfield, Alabama, just outside of Birmingham. She was interviewed as a part of Big Bethel A.M.E. Church. She became active in the Civil Rights Movement in 1963 while a student at Fairfield Industrial High School. During this time, she attended Galilee Baptist Church in Fairfield where Reverend E. J. Walker served as pastor.

Pearlie Craft Dove—Dr. Dove was born and raised in Atlanta, Georgia, and participated in the research as a lifelong member of Big Bethel A.M.E. Church. During the Civil Rights Movement, she was a professor at Clark College (now Clark Atlanta University), and she supported students who missed class because of their activism.

Margaret L. Evans—Ms. Evans grew up in Kennett, Missouri, and participated in the research as a member of Big Bethel A.M.E. Church. Raised primarily by her father, Evans was taught that she could do anything that others could do. Connected to the arts and education, she found her place in activism through the public policy side of Social Work as she fought for change.

Maxine Smith Frere—Ms. Frere's parents left central Florida and moved to New York in the 1940s after returning from the war. She participated in the research as a member of First A.M.E. Bethel Church. Her father taught her that no one was better than her, and reminded her that both her mother and grandmother were considered rebellious. She was one of the first six Black students to integrate Theodore Roosevelt High School. At age seventeen she joined the organization Black Liberty for Black Unity where she and others practiced karate, learned Swahili, and learned to make explosives as a part of self-defense and self-determination. She became a nurse through Harlem Hospital School of Nursing because she wanted to help people.

Sarah P. Frierson—Ms. Frierson was born and raised in Bishopville, South Carolina, and was active in the Civil Rights Movement starting in 1963 in New York City. She participated in this research as a member of First A.M.E. Bethel. She was a part of an activist family where her grandparents, mother, aunt, and uncle were active, and her children were involved in various actions with her from 1965 to 1969. She attended First A.M.E. Bethel under the pastoral leadership of Reverend Richard Allen Hildebrand in the Civil Rights Movement era, but she shares that she was not very active at the church during that time.

Cassandra Gould—Rev. Gould, D.Min. was born in Demopolis, Alabama, and as the daughter of an activist, she has been committed to the fight for justice for all of her life. During the Ferguson uprising, she pastored Quinn Chapel A.M.E. Church in Jefferson City, Missouri, but was often present in the streets of Ferguson with young activists or challenging the governor and other state leaders. She served as Executive Director of Missouri Faith Voices and more recently began serving as the senior faith strategist for Faith in Action.

Ernestine Lee Henning—Supervisor Henning was born in Memphis, Tennessee, into a family of fourteen children, and she and is the oldest of her six sisters (Sandra Faye, Brenda, Elaine, Joan, Peggy Jane, and Susan Carlotta). She was first arrested in March 1960 along with forty students from LeMoyne and Owen Colleges for refusing to leave two Whites-only public libraries. The Lee Sisters were written about in the July 15, 1965, issue of *Jet* magazine, where Simeon Booker wrote, "Oft Arrested: When 17-year-old Elaine Lee of Memphis, Tenn. showed up for youth council meetings, she was a hero. Members of her family have been arrested 17 times for civil rights activities and claim the title of the 'Most Arrested Family' in the country." She later served as a Missionary Supervisor in the A.M.E. Church.

Linda Jolly—Ms. Jolly was born and raised in Atlanta, Georgia, and participated in the research as a member of Big Bethel A.M.E. Church. She started attending Big Bethel as a child with her grandfather. She later attended West Hunter Street Baptist Church, where Reverend Ralph David Abernathy was pastor, from about age eleven through her teen years. She and other teens traveled to Savannah with Reverend Abernathy and did a wade-in demonstration at the all-White Tybee Island Beach.

Pamela R. Lightsey—Rev. Lightsey, PhD, grew up in West Palm Beach, Florida, and was shaped in a community of that allowed her to see the move of the Spirit outside of the church. She is the first, out, Black lesbian elder in the United Methodist Church. In the early days of the Ferguson uprising, she flew from Boston, where she was a professor and administrator at the time at Boston University School of Theology, to be present with the activists. As a minister, scholar, veteran, and justice advocate, she was uniquely positioned to document the experience through livestreams that countered the skewed narratives of corporate media. She is the author of *Our Lives Matter: A Womanist Queer Theology*.

Peggy Lucas—Ms. Lucas was interviewed as a member of Ebenezer Baptist Church. She was born and raised in Birmingham, Alabama, in the Dolomite community. Her father, Louis Lucas Jr. was an activist and he supported the activism of Peggy and her oldest sister Shirley. Lucas was a student at Miles College in Fairfield, Alabama, and a member of the Alabama Christian Movement for Human Rights Choir (the primary Movement Choir in the state). During the Movement she was a member of St. John Baptist Church in Dolomite with Reverend Clark. She was drawn to the Civil Rights

Movement because of Dr. King's philosophy of nonviolence and the need to challenge unjust laws. She also understood that there was a need for young people to effect change in Birmingham because adults could lose their jobs for participating in direct action. She was arrested during the Birmingham sit-ins and held in solitary confinement for a period.

Esther McCall—Ms. McCall participated as a member of Abyssinian Baptist Church. She was born in Bladen County, North Carolina, and attended business school in Raleigh, North Carolina. Her older sister lived in New York City, and would send newspapers and magazines to the family who would read them around the table at night. Ms. McCall moved to New York City around 1950 to have more opportunities. She was a member of the political club at Abyssinian and went to the March on Washington with that group after a White friend of Adam Clayton Powell Jr. paid for members to go. She was in charge of the total membership for the church and was well trusted by Reverend Powell.

Geneveive Mitchell—Ms. Mitchell was born in Walterboro, South Carolina, and lived in Rock Hill, South Carolina, and Fort Pierce, Florida, before moving to New York City. She participated in the research as a member of First A.M.E. Bethel Church. The 139th Psalm allowed her to release the pain of the past, and Isaiah 54:17 offered strength when thinking about the Civil Rights Movement.

Alicia M. Roberts—Ms. Roberts was born in Bessemer, Alabama, and participated in the research as a member of Ebenezer Baptist Church. She was active in the Civil Rights Movement beginning in 1963 while a student at Miles College, and as a musician she would often step in and play the piano during mass meetings if she saw there was a need. During the Movement she attended St. Paul C.M.E. Church where Reverend I. F. Lynch served as pastor.

Rose Davis Schofield—Mrs. Schofield participated in the research as a member of Big Bethel A.M.E. Church. She was born and raised in Elizabeth, New Jersey, and became active through the efforts of the NAACP and Reverend Watts who served as the pastor of Mt. Teaman A.M.E. where Schofield attended as a teenager. She was arrested along with other teenagers for blocking access to a construction site in Elizabeth that Black companies were not permitted to bid on.

Paulette Scott—Ms. Scott was born and raised in Atlanta. After a Vacation Bible Study lesson from Daddy King (Reverend Martin Luther King, Sr.), she joined Ebenezer Baptist at the age of eight, and participated in this research while still a member. She described being shaped by three groups:

parents (morals and values), church (ethics and love of God), and Girl Scouts (service). She attended Koinonia Camp in Americus, Georgia with Martin Luther King Jr., and while there the Klan shot into the buildings. She never imagined Dr. King belonging to the world; she saw him as her pastor.

Bessie Smith Sellaway—Mrs. Sellaway was born in Round Oak, Georgia, and raised in Atlanta during her formative years. During the Civil Rights Movement she was a member of Lindsey Street Baptist Church, where Reverend Alexander pastored, and she was interviewed as a member of Ebenezer Baptist Church for this research. She became active in the Movement while a student at Spelman College because of her past experiences of seeing how people looked down upon one another and treated one another with disrespect and hatred, and because she believed in what Dr. King and others were doing. She valued their sacrifices and wanted to help do something to make life better for all of us. Sellaway was arrested twice for protesting in Atlanta.

Ann P. Sheriff—Mrs. Sheriff was born in rural Mississippi, about thirteen miles outside of Canton. She participated in the research as a part of Abyssinian Baptist Church. When she was thirteen, civil rights workers came to the area where she lived and stayed for a couple years through Freedom Summer. She and her cousin, Angie, were selected to attend a conference in Meridian, Mississippi, and Fannie Lou Hamer was identified as their representative. Other members of her family were also active, including a cousin who loaned his truck to the Movement to pick up children, and her mother, who confronted people when not treated fairly.

Gwendolyn Zoharah Robinson Simmons—Dr. Simmons was born in Memphis, Tennessee, and became active in the Civil Rights Movement while a student at Spelman College in Atlanta. Simmons became one of the few Black women project leaders during the 1964 Freedom Summer efforts of SNCC in Mississippi. She worked full-time in the Movement in Georgia, Alabama, and Mississippi for seven years. Simmons was raised in the Baptist denomination and has been devoted to the practice of Sufi Islam for over fifty years. She worked as staff at the American Friends Service Committee for twenty-three years. She earned her PhD from Temple University and is an emeritus professor of religion and Africana studies at the University of Florida. Dr. Simmons continues to mentor younger activists and work as an active member of the SNCC Legacy Project, Circle of Elders, and other groups.

Marjorie Wallace Smyth—Mrs. Smyth was interviewed as a member of First A.M.E. Bethel Church. She was born and raised in Birmingham, Alabama, and was active in the Movement while a student at Carver High School in

Birmingham, where her niece Linda also became involved with her, as well as at Tuskegee Institute in Tuskegee, Alabama as a student, and when she moved to New York City. During the Movement she attended St. Luke A.M.E. Church in Birmingham, pastored at the time by Reverend A. Thomas. She was initially drawn to the fight for equal rights for all and better treatment for Black people in her neighborhood.

Beatrice Perry Soublet—Mrs. Soublet is a member of Our Lady of Lourdes Catholic Church in Atlanta and was interviewed as a part of Big Bethel A.M.E. Church where her daughter was a member at the time. She was born and raised in New Orleans, Louisiana, and became active in the Civil Rights Movement while a student at Bennett College in Greensboro, North Carolina. She was drawn to the Movement because she felt it was her responsibility to work for change and did not want her children to live through the abuse of segregation. Her brother was also active in the Movement. She was arrested during a sit-in in Greensboro along with other students from Bennett College.

Deborah Aramenta Stuckey—Ms. Stuckey was born in Bishopville, South Carolina, and remembers always pushing back on things that she did not believe were right. Along with her sister and cousins, Stuckey was active in the Civil Rights Movement in Bishopville in the late 1960s, starting at the age thirteen while a student at Dennis High School. She participated in the research as a member of First A.M.E. Bethel Church, and during the Movement she attended New Bethel A.M.E. in Bishopville, where Reverend Williams served as the pastor at that time.

A. Lenora Taitt-Magubane—Dr. Taitt-Magubane was interviewed as a member of Abyssinian Baptist Church. A native of New York City, Taitt-Magubane was raised between there and Trinidad. She was active in the Civil Rights Movement throughout the 1960s and 1970s. She became involved in the Movement because she experienced segregation laws firsthand when she attended Spelman and became active to change those laws. She served as the president of the Canterbury Association, which was a part of the Episcopal Church in the Atlanta University Center, while a student. She was arrested in connection with her work with the Committee on the Appeal for Human Rights (the Atlanta Movement) and was also a leader with SNCC. She continued her activism in New York.

Johnsie Williams Thomas—Mrs. Thomas grew up in Leaksville, North Carolina (now known as Eden, NC). She participated in the research as a long-standing member of Abyssinian Baptist Church. Her grandfather owned many houses in North Carolina that he left to the family. Those resources gave the family stability. Her father, who was president of the PTA and a union organizer, was considered the mayor in Leaksville, and he and his brothers, who served in WWII, were not afraid to stand up to anyone. She is a graduate of Bennett College where she was a biology major and chemistry minor. While a student, she actively supported the Civil Rights Movement by participating in sit-ins at Woolworth, marching, and babysitting for mothers so they could go vote. During the Civil Rights Movement she was a member of Mt. Sinai Baptist Church in Eden, pastored at the time by Reverend F. C. Smith.

Lydia Walker—Ms. Walker participated in the research while a member at Ebenezer Baptist Church. She is a graduate of Spelman College and Atlanta University. Inspired by her father who was a former president of the local NAACP, she often took individual stands during the Civil Rights Movement, including riding in the seat directly behind the bus driver, cutting up her Rich's department store card in protest, and refusing to make her son attend the all-Black school and instead driving him to an elementary school where he became the first to integrate. She believes Jesus was a radical, so rising up against injustice is the Christian thing to do.

Jayme Coleman Williams—Dr. Williams was born in 1918 in Louisville, Kentucky, as a daughter of an A.M.E. pastor. She participated in this research as a member of Big Bethel A.M.E. Church. She and her husband Dr. Mc-Donald Williams were active during the 1960s while teaching at Tennessee State (A&I during the 1960s) University in Nashville, Tennessee. She led NAACP Youth efforts in Nashville and was an important leader and adviser for the Nashville Student Movement. Her brother, Dr. Frederick D. Coleman Jr., was also active in the Clarksville, Tennessee, area during the 1960s. She attended St. John A.M.E. Church in Nashville where Reverends J. M. Granberry and Peter G. Crawford served as pastors during the Movement.

Joyce Carpenter Young—Rev. Young was raised in Anniston, Alabama, where she became active as a teenager under the leadership of her pastor Reverend Nimrod Quintus "N.Q." Reynolds. She participated in every mass meeting at Seventeenth Street Baptist Church, but her mother would not let her march. She agreed to integrate the previously all-White YMCA, when her pastor spoke of the need in 1967. She continued her justice work when she moved to Atlanta. She participated in this research as a part of Big Bethel A.M.E. Church.

Notes

Introduction. "Ain't Gonna Let Nobody Turn Me Around"

1. One account of Bess's suspicious death can be found in Tananarive Due and Patricia Stephens Due's *Freedom in the Family: A Mother-Daughter Memoir of the Fight for Civil Rights*, 299–300. George Calvin Bess's funeral program was also accessed from his sister Cherrye Bess-Branch's Flickr page. https://www.flickr.com/photos/cherryebess/6364538313

2. Discussion with Cynthia Mingo, June 20, 2019.

3. Tallahassee Civil Rights Oral History Collection, 1957, 1978, FSU Special Collections and Archives. Series 1, Transcripts 1978, Box 1, Folder 5, King Solomon DuPont. DuPont was also the first Black person to run for political office in Tallahassee since Reconstruction.

4. See Gary Moore, *Rosewood: The Full Story* (Manantial Press, 2015); AnneMarie Mingo, "Restoring Rosewood: Movements from Pain to Power to Peace," *Practical Matters Journal*, no. 5 (Spring 2012): 1–23; and Tameka Bradley Hobbs, *Democracy Abroad, Lynching at Home: Racial Violence in Florida* (Gainesville, FL: University Press of Florida, 2015).

5. I will often use the first names for the women after the first full use of the name. I understand and respect the importance of utilizing full names and titles, especially for Black women of this generation. However, I made this naming choice to limit confusion between the last names from the time period when many of them were active in the Civil Rights Movement and their names in the twenty-first century when I conducted interviews with them.

6. Carrie Patterson and Wilhelmina Jakes were the two students who refused to give up their seats when a White woman was seated near them. After being refused a refund of the ten cents they each paid to ride the bus, the cause for which they remained seated sparked a movement that cost the Bus Company and the city much more than

twenty cents. The Tallahassee bus boycott, which lasted from May 26, 1956, through January 1957, has received much less attention than the well-known Montgomery bus boycott that took place during the same time. However, newspaper accounts show that at that time both boycotts were held up as successful examples of the ways Black communities could come together to cripple the economic foundation of the bus companies in a way that ultimately caused them to support integrated seating on the buses. See Tananarive Due and Patricia Stephens Due, *Freedom in the Family: A Mother-Daughter Memoir of the Fight for Civil Rights* (New York: One World Book, 2003); and Glenda Alice Rabby, *The Pain and the Promise: The Struggle for Civil Rights in Tallahassee, Florida* (Athens, GA: University of Georgia Press, 1999).

7. See Tallahassee, Florida, McCrory's sit-ins in Rabby, *The Pain and the Promise: The Struggle for Civil Rights in Tallahassee, Florida*, 91–94.

8. Rosa Brown, Interview with AnneMarie Mingo, Personal Interview, Atlanta, GA, May 12, 2007.

9. Eduardo Medina, "In the Twilight of Life, Civil Rights Activists Feel 'Urgency to Tell Our History," *New York Times*, February 19, 2022, https://www.nytimes.com/2022/02/19/us/civil-rights-movement-oral-history.html. This article features Vivian Washington Filer, who is a member of my home church whom I have referred to as "Aunt Viv" for all of my life and is one of the women whose stories of activism shaped my early awareness.

10. Martin Luther King's colleague, C. T. Vivian noted that King wrote the phrase, "Redeem the soul of America" on the window at the Southern Christian Leadership Conference headquarters. Hilda Raye Tompkins, "To Redeem the Soul of America: The Leadership Challenges Martin Luther King, Jr. Faced and Managed as Leader of a Social Movement" (PhD dissertation, University of Georgia, 2009). Coretta Scott King noted, "women, if the soul of the nation is to be saved, I believe you must become its soul," Page Smith, *Daughters of the Promised Land, Women in American History* (New York: Little, Brown and Company, 1970), 273.

11. While the women in this study are all Black and associated with a Black Church, I intentionally use the term "Black Churchwomen" in response to the language used throughout the 1960s and 1970s by the National Committee of Negro Churchmen, later known as the National Committee of Black Churchmen. This committee wrote the Statement on Black Power that was published in the *New York Times* on July 31, 1966. This statement, which is a significant guidepost in the creation of Black Theology, was signed by forty-eight persons, which included Dr. Anna Arnold Hedgeman, the only woman and only layperson to sign. James H. Cone and Gayraud S. Wilmore, eds., *Black Theology: A Documentary History, 1966–1979* (Maryknoll, NY: Orbis Books, 1979), 22–30.

12. Tracey E. Hucks, "Perspectives in Lived History: Religion, Ethnography, and the Study of African Diasporic Religions," *Practical Matters*, no. 3 (Spring 2010): 13. Hucks describes participant engagement as a series of multiple blurrings between human devotees and their sacred spirits through experiences that result from their shared beliefs.

13. Author telephone conversation with Angela M. Dixon, April 3, 2018.

14. I will often refer to the Civil Rights Movement as simply "the Movement," with the capitalization noting the reference to the more generally understood social actions and events during both the traditional and "long" Civil Rights Movement periods. Other social movements will be referred to by the full name with which they are most commonly associated. I use a capitalized Black to reference the sociological group of peoples of African descent, and I also use a capitalized White to reference the group of peoples of European descent. If reference is made to a particular color such as a white crayon, I will use the word in the lowercase form. While I recognize that the group of people that I refer to as Black have had an interesting history of being named and naming themselves in America, including African, Nigger, Negro, Colored, Black, Afro-American, and African American, I use Black as an all-encompassing descriptor to include those from continental Africa and throughout the African Diaspora. Unless a part of a direct quotation, this will be the language used throughout.

15. Some of the significant texts that widen the scope of the Movement by foregrounding the contributions of women include Bettye Collier-Thomas and V.P. Franklin, eds., *Sisters in the Struggle: African American Women in the Civil Rights—Black Power Movement* (New York: New York University Press, 2001); Vicki L. Crawford, Jacqueline Anne Rouse, and Barbara Woods, *Women in the Civil Rights Movement: Trailblazers & Torchbearers 1941–1965* (Bloomington: Indiana University Press, 1990); Belinda Robnett, *How Long?, How Long? African-American Women in the Struggle for Civil Rights* (New York: Oxford University Press, 1997); Rosetta Ross, *Witnessing and Testifying: Black Women, Religion, and Civil Rights* (Minneapolis, MN: Augsburg Fortress, 2003); Deborah Gray White, *Too Heavy a Load: Black Women in Defense of Themselves 1894–1994* (New York: W. W. Norton and Company, 1999); and Betty Livingston Adams, *Black Women's Christian Activism: Seeking Social Justice in a Northern Suburb* (New York: New York University Press, 2016), which focuses on women's roles prior to World War II. This list excludes important recent biographical accounts of women leaders, including Barbara Ransby's *Ella Baker and the Black Freedom Movement: A Radical Democratic Vision* (Chapel Hill: University of North Carolina Press, 2003); Chana Kai Lee's *For Freedom's Sake: The Life of Fannie Lou Hamer* (Urbana: University of Illinois Press, 1999); Katherine Mellen Charron, *Freedom's Teacher: The Life of Septima Clark* (Chapel Hill: University of North Carolina Press, 2009); Danielle McGuire, *At the Dark End of the Street: Black Women, Rape, and Resistance—A New History of the Civil Rights Movement from Rosa Parks to the Rise of Black Power* (New York: Alfred A. Knopf, 2010); and Jennifer Scanlon, *Until There Is Justice: The Life of Anna Arnold Hedgeman* (New York: Oxford University Press, 2016), as well as many autobiographical accounts written by Movement women.

16. General Civil Rights Movement survey books include the trilogy by Taylor Branch, *Parting the Waters: America in the King Years 1954–1963* (New York: Simon & Schuster Paperbacks, 1988); *Pillar of Fire: America in the King Years 1963–1965* (New York: Simon & Schuster Paperbacks, 1988); and *At Canaan's Edge: America in the King Years 1965–1968* (New York: Simon & Schuster, 2006); Clayborne Carson, David J.

Garrow, Gerald Gill, Vincent Harding, and Darlene Clark Hine, eds., *The Eyes on the Prize Civil Rights Reader: Documents, Speeches, and Firsthand Accounts from the Black Freedom Struggle 1954–1990* (New York: Penguin Group, 1991); Bruce J. Dierenfield, *The Civil Rights Movement,* Revised Edition (United Kingdom: Pearson Education Limited, 2004, 2008); and Aldon D. Morris, *Origins of the Civil Rights Movement: Black Communities Organizing for Change* (New York: The Free Press, 1984). Women community organizer texts include accounts of SNCC women in Faith S. Hosaert, Martha Prescod Norman Noonan, Judy Richardson, Betty Garman Robinson, Jean Smith Young, and Dorothy M. Zellner, eds., *Hands on the Freedom Plow: Personal Accounts by Women in SNCC* (Urbana: University of Illinois Press, 2010).

17. Belinda Robnett, *How Long? How Long? African American Women in the Struggle for Human Rights,* see chapters 3 and 5. Sociologist Belinda Robnett offers the categories of bridge leaders and formal leaders to distinguish between the leadership of women who served as grassroots connectors or bridges within the community and the leadership of those in the institutional hierarchy of the Black Church—primarily men. Changes in societal structures are noted as she explores a more inclusive type of leadership, which was the result of the equally intense work and physical risks taken by women as they struggled for rights.

18. Samuel K. Roberts, *African American Christian Ethics* (Cleveland, OH: Pilgrim Press, 2001), 3–7. The knowing of God stretches far before and beyond the encounters through White Christians, however Roberts references a particular period within primarily North American experiences.

19. James H. Cone, *God of the Oppressed* (Maryknoll, NY: Orbis Books, 1975, 1997).

20. Traci C. West, *Disruptive Christian Ethics: When Racism and Women's Lives Matter* (Louisville, KY: Westminster John Knox Press, 2006), 68.

21. Melanie L. Harris, *Gifts of Virtue, Alice Walker, and Womanist Ethics* (New York: Palgrave Macmillan, 2010), 55–58.

22. Charles Black, Emory University Human Rights Week 2008 Panel—"The Legacy of the Civil Rights Movement on Human Rights Today," March 24, 2008.

23. Some works include Harvard Sitkoff, *Toward Freedom Land: The Long Struggle for Racial Equality in America* (Lexington: University Press of Kentucky, 2010); Angela D. Dillard in *Freedom North: Black Freedom Struggles Outside the South, 1940–1980* (New York: Palgrave Macmillan, 2003); Jacquelyn Dowd Hall, "The Long Civil Rights Movement and the Political Uses of the Past," *Journal of American History* 91, no. 4 (March 2005): 1233–1263; Sundiata Keita Cha-Jua and Clarence Lang, "The 'Long Movement' as Vampire: Temporal and Spatial Fallacies in recent Black Freedom Studies" *Journal of African American History* 92, no. 2 (Spring 2007): 265–288; Steven F. Lawson, "Long Origins of the Short Civil Rights Movement, 1954–1968" in *Freedom Rights: New Perspectives on the Civil Rights Movement,* eds. Danielle L. McGuire and John Dittmer (Lexington: University Press of Kentucky, 2011), 9–37.

24. *Open Wide the Freedom Gate* is the title of Dorothy Height's memoir about her life as one of the most influential Black women of Civil and Human Rights struggles

of the twentieth century. Dorothy Height, *Open Wide the Freedom Gate: A Memoir* (New York: PublicAffairs, 2003).

25. Cindy Rugeley and Montgomery Van Wart, "Everyday Moral Exemplars: The Case of Judge Sam Medina," *Public Integrity* 8, no. 4 (2006): 381–394.

26. Belinda Robnett, *How Long? How Long? African American Women in the Struggle for Civil Rights* (New York: Oxford University Press, 1997), 19–22.

27. This includes: Katie G. Cannon, *Black Womanist Ethics* (Eugene, OR: Wipf and Stock Publishers, 1988); Emilie M. Townes, *Womanist Justice, Womanist Hope* (Atlanta, GA: Scholar's Press, 1993); Marcia Y. Riggs, *Awake, Arise & Act: A Womanist Call for Black Liberation* (Cleveland, OH: Pilgrim Press, 1994); Rosetta E. Ross, *Witnessing and Testifying: Black Women, Religion, and Civil Rights* (Minneapolis, MN: Augsburg Press, 2003); Marla F. Frederick, *Between Sundays: Black Women and Everyday Struggles of Faith* (Berkeley: University of California Press, 2003); James Cone, *Black Theology and Black Power* (Maryknoll, NY: Orbis Books, 1969, 1997); Major J. Jones, *Christian Ethics for Black Theology: The Politics of Liberation* (Nashville, TN: Abingdon Press, 1974); James H. Cone and Gayraud S. Wilmore, eds., *Black Theology: A Documentary History, 1966–1979* (Maryknoll, NY: Orbis Books, 1979); and James H. Cone and Gayraud S. Wilmore, eds., *Black Theology: A Documentary History, Volume two: 1980–1992* (Maryknoll, NY: Orbis Books, 1993).

Chapter 1. "We Shall Overcome"

1. Scholars include Emilye Crosby, ed., *Civil Rights History from the Ground Up: Local Struggles a National Movement* (Athens, GA: University of Georgia Press, 2011); John Dittmer, *Local People: The Struggle for Civil Rights in Mississippi* (Urbana, IL: University of Illinois Press, 1994); Aldon Morris, *The Origins of the Civil Rights Movement: Black Communities Organizing for Change* (New York: Free Press, 1984); and Charles M. Payne, *I've Got the Light of Freedom: The Organizing Tradition and the Mississippi Freedom Struggle* (Berkeley: University of California Press, 1995).

2. The U.S. Civil Rights Movement is considered a precursor and model for the anti-war, women's, and LGBT movements that formed primarily in the last quarter of the twentieth century.

3. The lack of a push for credit or recognition is one of the reasons the recovery work of the narratives and experiences of Black women who were active in the Civil Rights Movement is so important since so many of them allowed men to take center stage in recognition for the work they initiated and sustained. There are times when the women's names are found in passing in the narratives of men or they are mentioned in conversation, but in general it has only been within the past two decades that women have revealed the more substantive influence and role they had in the Movement.

4. Enslaved Africans were a part of the Spanish expeditions into Florida and South Carolina in the 1500s

5. The National Committee of Negro Churchmen began meeting and releasing statements in 1966 and was formally organized in November 1967. With 300 members

from twelve denominations, they were a collection of male pastors, Bishops, and one woman—Dr. Anna Arnold Hedgeman with the National Council of Churches in New York. Their position statement on Black Power published in the *New York Times* on Sunday, July 31, 1966, is one of the foundational Black liberation theology texts.

6. Consent was given by the women to be referred to by their real names. Emory University IRB #00005138. I will often use the first names of the women not out of cultural disrespect, but to maintain clarity as many of the women have married since their days in the Civil Rights Movement. In some instances, I will use pseudonyms for the protection of persons revealed during the oral histories.

7. Lillian Sue Bethel, Interview with AnneMarie Mingo, Personal Interview, New York, NY, August 25, 2009.

8. Carlton Fletcher, "In the Shadow of Jim Crow," *Albany Herald*, July 23, 2010, https://www.albanyherald.com/news/in-the-shadow-of-jim-crow/article_861d5b5a -2828-5f52-acec-115ff4f8fb56.html, Accessed February 19, 2020.

9. Doris Brunson, Interview with AnneMarie Mingo, Personal Interview, New York, NY, July 8, 2010.

10. Peggy Lucas, Interview with AnneMarie Mingo, Personal Interview, Atlanta, GA, November 6, 2010.

11. Peggy Lucas's maternal aunt lived near her family and helped to raise her. Her aunt was not active in the Movement and did not believe her mother would have been supportive, but that did not stop Peggy from participating with her father.

12. Peggy Lucas.

13. From 1964 to 1965 the State of Alabama changed the voter registration requirements four times in an effort to prevent Blacks from successfully registering to vote. In addition to a long form with information that provided details about housing and employment (that made retaliation easy), voter registration requirements included reading from sections of the Constitution and writing portions of the Constitution. See sample registration form in Alabama Department of Archives and History, http://www.alabamamoments.state.al.us/sec59ps.html.

14. Reverend Fred Shuttlesworth started the Alabama Christian Movement for Human Rights in 1956 after the NAACP was prohibited from operating in the state of Alabama. It was the most powerful civil rights organization in the state.

15. A program honoring the 40th year anniversary reunion of the Foot Soldiers of the 1963 Birmingham Civil Rights Movement lists both Peggy Lucas and her sister Shirley Fomby among those jailed. A copy of the program is in the author's possession.

16. Rose Schofield, Interview with AnneMarie Mingo, Personal Interview, Atlanta, GA, May 10, 2010.

17. Rose Schofield.

18. To be clear, the Black community was not monolithic. Everyone was not supportive of the goals of the Movement, or the widely shared values of uplift and advancement. Inter-communal strife existed, even as others fought external oppressors.

19. Beatrice Soublet, Interview with AnneMarie Mingo, Personal Interview, Atlanta, GA, April 14, 2010.

20. Belinda Robnett, *How Long? How Long? African-American Women in the Struggle for Civil Rights* (New York: Oxford University Press, 1997), 98–114.

21. See Act XII, *Laws of Virginia*, December 1662 (Hening, *Statutes at Large*, 2:170), accessed through the Library of Congress. Amaryah Jones-Armstrong also examines the structural role of White supremacy through the notion of White inheritance.

22. Stetson Kennedy's 1959 *Jim Crow Guide: The Way It Was*, is now accessible online and provides one historical view of the origins and methods of navigating Jim Crow laws and practices in the United States. https://www.stetsonkennedy.com/jim_crow_guide/. Accessed December 16, 2021.

23. Thomas Dixon, *The Clansman: An Historical Romance of the Ku Klux Klan* (New York: Grosset & Dunlap, 1905); D. W. Griffith, *The Birth of a Nation*, Motion Picture (New York, 1915); David M. Chalmers, *Hooded Americanism: The First Century of the Ku Klux Klan, 1865–1965* (Garden City, NY: Doubleday and Company, 1965); Wyn Craig Wade, *The Fiery Cross: The Ku Klux Klan in America* (New York: Simon and Schuster, 1987). By the mid-twentieth century, the Klan also targeted Jews, Catholics, organized labor advocates, and Whites who actively supported civil rights. Also see Glenda Elizabeth Gilmore, *Gender and Jim Crow: Women and the Politics of White Supremacy in North Carolina 1896–1920* (Chapel Hill: University of North Carolina Press, 1996).

24. See Ibram X. Kendi, *Stamped from the Beginning: The Definitive History of Racist Ideas in America* (New York: Nation Books, 2016); and Carol Anderson, *White Rage: The Unspoken Truth of Our Racial Divide* (New York: Bloomsburg, 2016), 7–38.

25. The use of "Klan" and "Klansmen" here is both a specific and broad term used to categorize White supremacist organizations who used physical and emotional violence as tools of terror against Blacks and other marginalized groups. The Klan's activities were not limited to areas of the traditional South. High Klan activity also took place in states including Pennsylvania, Ohio, Indiana, Oklahoma, Colorado, and Washington. Examples of Klan retaliation that had ramifications for the families of women in this study are included in some of the overviews of the women earlier in this chapter. Also see, Ida B. Wells, speech delivered at the National Negro Conference, *Proceedings: National Negro Conference*, 1909, 174–179.

26. Angela D. Sims, *Lynched: The Power of Memory in a Culture of Terror* (Waco, TX: Baylor University Press, 2016).

27. Darlene Clark Hine, *Hine Sight: Black Women and Re-Construction of American History* (Brooklyn, NY: Carlson Publishing, 1994), 87–108; Bobby M. Wilson, "Historical Spaces of African Americans," in *Contemporary Ethnic Geographies in America*, eds. Ines M. Miyares and Christopher A. Airriess (Lanham, MD: Rowman and Littlefield, 2007), 79–80.

28. Waltraut Stein, "White Citizens' Councils" *The Negro History Bulletin* 20, no. 1 (October 1, 1956): 21. Referencing "The Bite," *Time*, December 20, 1954, 20.

29. Joyce Shaw Peterson, "Black Automobile Workers in Detroit, 1910–1930," *Journal of Negro History* 64, no. 3. (Summer 1979): 177–190.

30. Some women left the South and Middle West as they sought to escape rape and the threat of rape by White men. Darlene Clark Hine, "Rape and the Inner Lives of Black Women in the Middle West," *Signs* 14, no. 4 (Summer 1989): 912–920.

31. Dennis C. Dickerson, "The Black Church in Industrializing Western Pennsylvania 1870–1950" in *Western Pennsylvania Historical Magazine*, no. 64 (October 1981): 329–344.

32. See Daniel M. Johnson and Rex R. Campbell, *Black Migration in America: A Social Demographic History* (Durham, NC: Duke University Press, 1981), 74–78; Isabel Wilkerson, *The Warmth of Other Suns: The Epic Story of America's Great Migration* (New York: Random House, 2010); and Nell Irvin Painter, *Exodusters: Black Migrants to Kansas after Reconstruction* (Lawrence: University Press of Kansas, 1986). Also see Davarian L. Baldwin, *Chicago's New Negroes: Modernity, The Great Migration, and Black Urban Life* (Durham: University of North Carolina Press, 2007); Ira Berlin, *The Making of African America: The Four Great Migrations* (New York: Penguin Group, 2010); Timuel D. Black, *Bridges of Memory: Chicago's first wave of Black Migration,* Volume 1 (Evanston, IL: Northwestern University Press, 2003); Steven Hahn, *A Nation under Our Feet: Black Political Struggles in the Rural South from Slavery to the Great Migration* (Cambridge, MA: Harvard University Press, 2003); Nicholas Lemann, *The Promised Land: The Great Migration and How it Changed America* (New York: Alfred A. Knopf, 1991); Carole Marks, *Farewell—We're Good and Gone: The Great Black Migration* (Bloomington: Indiana University Press, 1989); Milton C. Sernett, *Bound for the Promised Land: African American Religion and the Great Migration* (Durham, NC: Duke University Press, 1997); Joe William Trotter Jr., ed., *The Great Migration in Historical Perspective: New Dimensions of Race, Class, and Gender* (Bloomington: Indiana University Press, 1991).

33. Keeanga-Yamahtta Taylor, *Race for Profit: How Banks and the Real Estate Industry Undermined Black Homeownership* (Chapel Hill: University of North Carolina Press, 2019); Richard Rothstein, *The Color of Law: A Forgotten History of How our Government Segregated America* (New York: W. W. Norton and Company, 2017).

34. This prohibition was also necessary to save the lives of young men who were at even greater risk of being murdered for the slightest offense to Whites whether real or imagined. Marjorie Wallace Smyth recalls her father giving additional lectures to her brothers regarding where they could or could not go. "The girls never went anywhere by themselves anyway, but he would tell them places that they could not go, where they were never to go. To never go alone, and how to protect themselves." Marjorie Wallace Smyth, Transcript of interview, 6.

35. Bobby M. Wilson, "Race in Commodity Exchange and Consumption: Separate but Equal," *Annals of the Association of American Geographers* 95, no. 3 (2005): 587–606.

36. See Richard Kluger, *Simple Justice: The History of Brown v. Board of Education and Black America's Struggle for Equality* (New York: Vintage Books, 1975); James T. Patterson, *Brown v. Board of Education: A Civil Rights Milestone and its Troubled Legacy* (New York: Oxford University Press, 2001); Clarice T. Campbell, *Civil Rights*

Chronicle: Letters from the South (Jackson: University Press of Mississippi, 1997), 9; Nancy T. Ammerman, "The Civil Rights Movement and the Clergy in a Southern Community," *Sociological Analysis* 41, no. 4 (Winter 1980): 339–350.

37. Pearlie Clark Dove, Interview with AnneMarie Mingo, Personal Interview, Atlanta, GA, May 4, 2010.

38. Johnsie Williams Thomas, Interview with AnneMarie Mingo, Personal Interview, New York, NY, August 6, 2010. Bennett College is a United Methodist Church related institution. Other Black colleges and universities such as Florida A&M University, that were not related to religious institutions also held daily or weekly chapel and vesper services during the mid-twentieth century.

39. A. Lenora Taitt-Magubane, Interview with AnneMarie Mingo, Personal Interview, New York, NY, July 29, 2010.

40. Lefever, 39.

41. Pearlie Clark Dove.

42. Lillian Sue Bethel.

43. Taitt-Magubane archives, "Jail Schedule 1961" Box 1, Folder 14.

44. See chapter 3 for illustrations of the academic risks taken by Lillian Sue Bethel and A. Lenora Taitt-Magubane.

45. "Harlem Union Launches New Economic Campaign: New Program," *Amsterdam News* 40, no. 42 (October 21, 1961): 1, 30.

46. Gene Roberts and Hank Klibanoff, *The Race Beat: The Press, the Civil Rights Struggle, and the Awakening of a Nation* (New York: Vintage Books, 2006).

47. News surrounding Till's murder was covered in at least ten issues of *Jet* from September 1955 to July 1964.

48. Pat Smalls and Rose Fofana interviews with AnneMarie Mingo, Harlem, NY, August 5, 2010, and August 5, 2009, respectively.

49. Taitt-Magubane papers, WERD broadcast notes for Sunday, Jan. 8, 1961, "This You Should Know," with Lenora Taitt as a guest, Box 1, Folder 14.

50. See Albert J. Raboteau, *Slave Religion: The "Invisible Institution" in the Antebellum South* (New York: Oxford University Press, 2004); C. Eric Lincoln and Lawrence Mamiya, *The Black Church in the African American Experience* (Durham, NC: Duke University Press, 1990); and E. Franklin Frazier, *The Negro Church in America* and C. Eric Lincoln, *The Black Church Since Frazier* (New York: Schocken Books, 1963, 1974).

51. Survival was an acceptable goal, but not all Blacks or Black churches were supportive of resistance during slavery.

52. C. Eric Lincoln, *The Black Church Since Frazier* (New York: Schocken Books, 1974), 107–108.

53. Patricia Pates Eaton, Interview with AnneMarie Mingo, Personal Interview, Harlem, New York, August 4, 2010. Patricia's uncle Fulton Ford also bailed out the Black Pharmacist in Clarksdale, Mississippi, who kept getting arrested, and as a result, the IRS came down on him and his cleaners business. See also, Davis W. Houck and Matthew A. Grindy, *Emmett Till and the Mississippi Press*, (Jackson: University Press of Mississippi, 2008), 69.

54. Black Masonic lodges were also occasionally used for gatherings.

55. Joanne Grant, "Godmother of the Student Movement" in *The Crisis* magazine, July/August 2001, 40.

56. Bayard Rustin, "Southern Negro Leaders Conference on Transportation and Nonviolent Integration, January 10–11, 1957," Yale University, Lillian Goldman Law Library.

57. Lawson did mission work in India in the 1950s for the Methodist Church, and he received his STB from Boston University in 1960. He organized and began teaching non-violence strategies in Nashville, TN, while doing work at Vanderbilt University after King persuaded him to go to the South to help. http://mlk-kpp01 .stanford.edu/index.php/encyclopedia/encyclopedia/enc_lawson_james_1928/, accessed December 18, 2011.

58. David F. Burg, *Encyclopedia of Student and Youth Movements* (New York: Facts on File, 1998), Student Nonviolent Coordinating Committee (SNCC), 184. Emphasis added.

59. Amelia Boynton Robinson, *Bridge Across Jordan*; Wyatt T. Walker, in Adam Fairclough, "The Southern Christian Leadership Conference and the Second Reconstruction, 1957–1973" in *South Atlantic Quarterly 80* (1981). This did not necessarily mean allowing their churches to be used.

60. The gendered use of clergymen is intentional considering the limited patriarchal practices surrounding ordination and formal church leadership during that era. Anecdotally, I have been told that a little less than 25 percent of the Black community actively participated in the Civil Rights Movement.

61. C. Eric Lincoln and Lawrence H. Mamiya, *The Black Church in the African American Experience* (Durham, NC: Duke University Press, 1990), 189.

62. Adam Fairclough, "The Southern Christian Leadership Conference and the Second Reconstruction, 1957–1973" in *South Atlantic Quarterly 80* (1981), 183.

63. See Wilson Fallin, *The African American Church in Birmingham, Alabama 1815–1963: A Shelter in the Storm* (New York: Garland Publishing, 1997). Allen Temple AME was bombed during a worship service on April 28, 1957.

64. Marjorie Wallace Smyth, Interview with AnneMarie Mingo, Personal Interview, New York, NY, July 7, 2012.

65. Amelia Platts Boynton Robinson, *Bridge Across Jordan*, 218, 78–81, 226–227, 232, 234.

66. Marjorie L. White, *A Walk to Freedom: The Reverend Fred Shuttlesworth and the Alabama Christian Movement for Human Rights, 1956–1964* (Birmingham, AL: Birmingham Historical Society, 1998). Interviews with Peggy Lucas, Alicia Roberts, and Marjorie Wallace Smyth.

Moral Exemplar. Ella Baker

1. Rosetta E. Ross, *Witnessing & Testifying: Black Women, Religion, and Civil Rights* (Minneapolis, MN: Fortress Press, 2003), 36. Ross also draws from John Britton's "Interview with Ella Baker: June 19, 1968," Ralph Bunche Oral History Collection,

Manuscript Division, Moorland-Spingarn Research Center, Moorland-Spingarn Collection, Howard University, Washington, DC, 2, as quoted in Catherine M. Orr's UNC Chapel Hill master's thesis, "'The Struggle Is Eternal': A Rhetorical Biography of Ella Baker."

2. Joanne Grant, *Ella Baker: Freedom Bound* (New York: John Wiley and Sons, 1998), 8.

3. Grant, 18.

4. Barbara Ransby, *Ella Baker and the Black Freedom Movement: A Radical Democratic Vision* (Chapel Hill: University of North Carolina Press, 2003), 14–15.

5. Ransby, 17.

6. Ransby, 17.

7. Ransby, 46. Ella Baker Papers, Schomburg Center for Research in Black Culture, New York, NY.

8. Ella Baker and Marvel Cooke, "The Bronx Slave Market." *The Crisis*, November 1935, pp. 330–331, 340.

9. Ross, 40.

10. Carol Mueller, "Ella Baker and the Origins of Participatory Democracy," in *Women in the Civil Rights Movement: Trailblazers & Torchbearers 1941–1965,* eds. Vicki L. Crawford, Jacqueline Anne Rouse, and Barbara Woods (Bloomington: Indiana University Press, 1993), 57. Ransby, 117.

11. Ransby, 117.

12. Ransby, 130.

13. Joanne Grant, *Ella Baker: Freedom Bound* (New York: Wiley and Sons, 1998), 114–115.

14. James Lytle, "Rev. Thomas Kilgore, Jr., Civil Rights Leader, Advisor to Three USC Presidents, Dies." https://news.usc.edu/10736/Rev-Thomas-Kilgore-Jr-Civil-Rights-Leader-Adviser-to-Three-USC-Presidents-Dies/. Accessed May 14, 2022.

15. In Friendship, https://kinginstitute.stanford.edu/encyclopedia/friendship. Accessed May 6, 2022.

16. Ella Josephine Baker, https://kinginstitute.stanford.edu/encyclopedia/baker-ella-josephine. Accessed May 6, 2022.

17. Grant 108; Ransby, 183–185.

18. Belinda Robnett, *How Long? How Long? African-American Women in the Struggle for Civil Rights* (New York: Oxford University Press, 1997), 96.

Chapter 2. "Woke Up This Morning with My Mind Stayed on Freedom"

1. Prathia Hall, Prathia Hall Pre-Interview: Tape 1 side A, Interview by Meredith Woods, October 4, 1999, Henry Hampton Collection, Washington University Libraries, 1.

2. Prathia Hall, "This Far by Faith" Episode 4, *Freedom Faith*, Transcript pages, 9–10. Emphasis added.

3. Gender and class inequities and other forms of oppression were challenged, but

not as much as race during the Civil Rights Movement. See Belinda Robnett, *How Long, How Long? African American Women in the Struggle for Civil Rights.*

4. During Ruby Hurley's tenure in her positions, the youth units grew from 86 to 280, and the Southeastern region of the NAACP became the largest region with more than 500 branches. Library of Congress, http://www.loc.gov/exhibits/naacp/the-civil-rights-era.html#obj14. Accessed November 2, 2019.

5. *Jet* magazine, October 6, 1955, Hurley was featured on the cover of the magazine dressed in a suit and staged taking a telephone call. The cover identified her as "RUBY HURLEY: She has had the toughest job in fighting for Negro rights in the South" and "Most Militant Negro Woman in the South," and her styling simultaneously supported the politics of respectability at work during the era.

6. Transcript of an interview with Mrs. Ruby Hurley; Director, Southeastern Regional Office of the National Association for the Advancement of Colored People; John H. Britton, Interviewer, Atlanta, GA, January 26, 1968, Ralph Bunch Oral History Collection, Manuscript Division, Moorland-Spingarn Research Center, Howard University, Washington, DC, 15.

7. C. Eric Lincoln and Lawrence H. Mamiya, *The Black Church in the African American Experience* (Durham, NC: Duke University Press, 1990), 12.

8. Rosetta E. Ross and Shirley T. Geiger, "Leading in Challenging Times: Martin Luther King, Jr., Ruby Hurley, and the Meaning of Black Leadership" in *The Domestication of Martin Luther King Jr.: Clarence B. Jones, Right-Wing Conservatism, and the Manipulation of the King Legacy*, eds. Lewis V. Baldwin and Rufus Burrow (Eugene, OR: Cascade Books, 2013), 68.

9. Taitt-Magubane.

10. Barbara Ransby, *Ella Baker and the Black Freedom Movement: A Radical Democratic Vision* (Chapel Hill: University of North Carolina Press, 2003); Charles Payne, "Ella Baker and Models of Social Change," in *Signs: Journal of Women in Culture and Society* 14, no. 4 (1989): 886.

11. Rosetta E. Ross, *Witnessing and Testifying: Black Women, Religion, and Civil Rights* (Minneapolis, MN: Augsburg Fortress, 2003), 34.

12. Oral History Interview with Ella Baker, April 19, 1977. Interview G-0008. Southern Oral History Program Collection (#4007) in the Southern Oral History Program Collection, Southern Historical Collection, Wilson Library, University of North Carolina at Chapel Hill.

13. Ella J. Baker, "Bigger than a Hamburger," http://www.amistadresource.org/documents/document_08_04_010_baker_hamburger.pdf. Accessed March 5, 2019

14. Voices of Democracy, "Ella Baker, 'Address at the Hattiesburg Freedom Day Rally' (21 January 1964)," http://voicesofdemocracy.umd.edu/ella-baker-freedom-day-rally-speech-text/. Accessed March 4, 2019

15. See Eddie S. Glaude Jr., *Exodus!: Religion, Race, and Nation in Early Nineteenth Century Black America* (Chicago: University of Chicago Press, 2000), 3–18; Gary S. Selby, *Martin Luther King and the Rhetoric of Freedom: The Exodus Narrative in America's Struggle for Civil Rights* (Waco, TX: Baylor University Press, 2008), 27–50; James Cone, *God of the Oppressed* (Maryknoll, NY: Orbis Books, 1975; United

Kingon: Seabury Press, 1997), 178; David Robertson, *Denmark Vesey: The Buried History of America's Largest Slave Rebellion and the Man Who Led It* (New York: Alfred A. Knopf, 1999), 53.

16. Emilie M. Townes, *Womanist Ethics and the Cultural Production of Evil* (New York: Palgrave McMillan, 2006).

17. Beatrice Soublet.

18. Located west of downtown Atlanta, the Atlanta University Center is the largest contiguous consortium of Historically Black Colleges and Universities in the United States. During A. Lenora Taitt-Magubane's time as a student there it comprised Morehouse College, Spelman College, Clark College, Atlanta University, Morris Brown College, and the Interdenominational Theological Center.

19. Taitt-Magubane.

20. A. Lenora Taitt-Magubane's activism is also featured in a text on Spelman College students in the Movement. See Harry G. Lefever, *Undaunted by the Fight: Spelman College and the Civil Rights Movement 1957–1967* (Macon, GA: Mercer University Press, 2005). It is certainly possible that Taitt-Magubane recalled her northern experiences in a more positive way than other scholars have described the racism, segregated spaces, and inequality in New York City during that time. See Wil Haygood, *King of the Cats: The Life and Times of Adam Clayton Powell, Jr.* (New York: HarperCollins, 2006), and Martha Biondi, *To Stand and Fight: The Struggle for Civil Rights in Postwar New York City* (Cambridge, MA: Harvard University Press, 2003).

21. Matthew 15:21–28 (NRSV). Some scholars who suggest that Jesus was corrected include Frances Taylor Gench, *Back to the Well: Women's Encounters with Jesus in the Gospels* (Louisville, KY: Westminster John Knox Press, 2004), 1–11; J. Martin C. Scott "Matthew 15.21–28: A Test Case for Jesus' Manners," *Journal for the Study of the New Testament* 63 (1996): 21–44; Jennifer Thweatt-Bates "Perfect Righteousness," *Leaven* 16, no. 1 (2008): 44.

22. Rosetta E. Ross, *Witnessing and Testifying: Black Women, Religion, and Civil Rights* (Minneapolis, MN: Augsburg Fortress, 2003), 110–113.

23. See Charles Marsh, *God's Long Summer: Stories of Faith and Civil Rights* (Princeton, NJ: Princeton University Press, 1997), 10–48.

24. Karen D. Crozier, *Fannie Lou Hamer's Revolutionary Practical Theology: Racial and Environmental Justice Concerns* (Boston: Brill, 2021).

25. Fannie Lou Hamer, "Sick and Tired of Being Sick and Tired," *Katallagete*, no. 8 (Fall 1968): 26. Karen D. Crozier, 166–170.

26. See more on Pierre Caliste Landry, Euell A. Nielsen, "Pierre Castile Landry, 1841–1921," July 13, 2016, https://www.blackpast.org/african-american-history/landry-pierre-caliste-1841–1921/. Accessed April 4, 2019; and Amistad Research Center, Tulane University, "Dunn-Landry Family," http://amistadresearchcenter.tulane.edu/archon/?p=creators/creator&id=133. Accessed April 5, 2019.

27. A school was named after Lord Beaconsfield Landry in the late 1930s and when it became a high school in 1942 it was the first named for a Black man in New Orleans.

28. Soublet.

29. Soublet.

30. Beatrice Perry Soublet, *Watch Words: Thoughts on Race, Water and War* (Bloomington, IN: AuthorHouse, 2008)

31. Janie Rambeau, *This Far by Faith,* "Freedom Faith," PBS, Produced, Directed, and Written by Alice Markowitz.

32. Prathia Hall, "Freedom-Faith" in *Hands on the Freedom Plow*, 178.

33. Psalm 145:18

34. Coretta Scott King in *Standing in the Need of Prayer: A Celebration of Black Prayer* (New York: Free Press, 2003), x.

35. Marjorie Wallace Smyth, Interview with AnneMarie Mingo, Personal Interview, New York, NY, August 2009.

36. Exodus 12:12–14. Also see JoAnne Terrell, *Power in the Blood: The Cross in the African American Experience* (Maryknoll, NY: Orbis Books, 1998), 17.

37. Jo Ann Gibson Robinson, 62.

38. Katie Geneva Cannon, "The Emergence of Black Feminist Consciousness" in *Feminist Interpretation of the Bible,* ed. Letty M. Russell (Pittsburgh, PA: Westminister Press, 1985), 35.

39. David L. Chappell, *A Stone of Hope: Prophetic Religion and the Death of Jim Crow* (Chapel Hill: University of North Carolina Press, 2004), 71–72; Hebrews 11:1.

40. Hall, *Hands on the Freedom Plow*, 176.

41. Prathia Hall Pre-Interview for "This Far by Faith": Tape 1 side A, Interview by Meredith Woods, October 4, 1999, Henry Hampton Collection, Washington University Libraries, Prathia Hall.

42. Bernice Johnson Reagon, "Since I Laid My Burden Down," in *Hands on the Freedom Plow*, 150.

43. Jacqulyne Johnson Clarke, "Goals and Techniques in Three Civil Rights Organizations in America" (PhD dissertation, Ohio State University, 1960). See also, Jacqulyne Johnson Clarke, *These Rights They Seek: A Comparison of the Goals and Techniques of Local Civil Rights Organizations* (Washington, DC: Public Affairs Press, 1962).

44. Smyth, 2009.

45. Ross, 140.

46. Prathia Hall was raised in Philadelphia, PA, and Kathleen Conwell was raised in Jersey City, NJ. They both did not limit themselves to the gendered religious politics of the south but used their voices in ways that sparked faith in others.

47. See Drew D. Hansen, *The Dream: Martin Luther King Jr., and the Speech that Inspired a Nation* (New York: Harper Collins, 2003). Bernice Johnson Reagon, shared as an audience member in a session at the Association for the Study of African American Life and History that I attended on September 28, 2012. It is known that King did not originate the phrase, but in the Black preaching tradition, King borrowed it from the prayers that he heard prayed in Georgia. Therefore, King's use of the phrase could have come from one or both of the women. Their prayers were known to have moved people physically as they prayed with power and conviction. King's use of the phrase in sermons began in November 1962.

48. Claude Sitton, Special to the *New York Times*, "VOTING DRIVE MET BY HOPE AND FEAR; Student Workers in Georgia Tell of Rights Campaign Hope for Negroes Seek Meaning in Lives U.S. Inquiry Under Way," September 11, 1962, p. 20.

49. Mama Dolly Raines, https://snccdigital.org/people/mama-dolly-raines/. Accessed June 19, 2019.

50. Coretta Scott King, x.

51. Bethel.

52. Charles Payne, *I've Got the Light of Freedom*, 273.

Moral Exemplar. Rev. Dr. Prathia L. Hall

1. Prathia LauraAnn Hall, Dissertation "The Religious and Social Consciousness of African American Baptist Women," Princeton Theological Seminary, 1997, i; Prathia Hall, Prathia Hall Pre-Interview: Tape 1 side A, Interview by Meredith Woods, October 4, 1999, Henry Hampton Collection, Washington University Libraries, 1.

2. Prathia Hall, "Freedom Faith," in *Hands on the Freedom Plow: Personal Accounts by Women in SNCC,* eds. Faith S. Hosaert, Martha Prescod Norman Noonan, Judy Richardson, Betty Garman Robinson, Jean Smith Young, and Dorothy M. Zellner (Urbana: University of Illinois Press, 2010), 172.

3. "Special Report—WOMEN IN MINISTRY," *The American Baptist,* July/August 1987, 22. It is interesting to note that Hall includes Paul Robeson and Nannie Helen Burroughs in a list of the best preachers. Proclamation of a liberatory message seemed more descriptive of preaching than a formal title.

4. Hall, "The Religious and Social Consciousness of African American Baptist Women," i–ii.

5. C-SPAN, "Civil Rights Movement in 1963," April 29, 1998, https://www.c-span.org/video/?104990-1/civil-rights-movement-1963. Accessed April 6, 2019.

6. Hall competed in the twenty-eighth annual oratorical contest at the annual convention of the Improved Benevolent Protective Order of Elks of the World, which met at Metropolitan Baptist Church in Washington, DC, in September 1958. "Little Rock Pupils Share in Elk Grants: Get $1000 each at 60th Confab." *The Chicago Defender (National Edition) (1921–1967),* September 6, 1958, 23.

7. Marjorie Hope, *Youth Against the World: Contemporary Portraits of The New Revolutionaries* (Boston: Little, Brown, and Company, 1965, 1967, 1970), 43.

8. Hope, 143

9. Johnson's speech in 1950 was attended by Martin Luther King Jr., who was a seminary student at Crozier near Chester, Pennsylvania. It was through this speech that King became captivated by Johnson's description of Mohandas Gandhi's satyagraha method for social change and prompted King to begin a deep study of Gandhi. See Martin Luther King Jr., *Stride Toward Freedom* (Boston: Beacon Press, 1958, 1986), 84.

10. Mitchell's mother, Lillie Carol Jackson, was the head of the local NAACP branch for thirty-five years, and Mitchell serves a legal counsel before becoming a leader at the state level. "Juanita Jackson Mitchell" in the *Baltimore Sun*, February 25,

2007. https://www.baltimoresun.com/features/bal-blackhistory-juanita-story.html Accessed July 11, 2019.

11. Hall's arrests include: Selma, Alabama, in October 1963, charged with contributing to the delinquency of a minor (her fifth arrest). See Ernestine Cofield "Expect Violence to Explode in Selma Vote Registration Drive (2)." *The Chicago Defender (National Edition) (1921–1967),* October 12, 1963. https://search-proquest-com .proxy.library.ucsb.edu:9443/docview/493131313?accountid=14522. Accessed June 28, 2019; Atlanta, Georgia, January 11, 1964, arrested with other Movement leaders attempting to integrate the Heart-of-Atlanta Motel. "Ga. NAACP Presses Governor on Banning Bias in Hotels." *New Pittsburgh Courier (1959–1965),* Jan 18, 1964, National edition. https://search-proquest-com.proxy.library.ucsb.edu:9443/docview/ 371637249?accountid=14522. Accessed June 28, 2019.

12. C-SPAN, "Civil Rights Movement in 1963," April 29, 1998, https://www.c-span .org/video/?104990-1/civil-rights-movement-1963. Accessed April 6, 2019.

13. Special to, the Defender. "Fight for Vote Brings Out Shotguns in Georgia, Mississippi." *Chicago Daily Defender (Daily Edition) (1960–1973),* September 12, 1962, 4. https://search-proquest-com.proxy.library.ucsb.edu:9443/docview/49391 4156?accountid=14522. Accessed June 28, 2019.

14. Prathia Hall, *This Far by Faith: African American Spiritual Journeys*, Episode 4 "Freedom Faith," PBS *Witness to Faith* in *Episode 4: Freedom Faith,* is part of the *This Far by Faith: African American Spiritual Journeys* series and is a co-production of Blackside Inc. and The Faith Project, Inc. in association with the Independent Television Service (2003).

15. Hope, 149.

16. Vincent Harding describes the long Black movement towards justice, equity, and truth and the people who have engaged in this Black struggle as a river in Vincent Harding, *There is a River: The Black Struggle for Freedom in America* (Orlando, FL: Harcourt Brace & Company, 1981), xix–xxi.

17. Hall, *Hands on the Freedom Plow*, 180.

18. Hall, *Hands on the Freedom Plow,* 176.

19. After moving away from actively serving in SNCC leadership, Hall served as a program director with the National Council of Negro Women, and fully answered her call to ministry, after which she attended Princeton Theological Seminary for her master's and PhD.

20. Hall, *Hands on the Freedom Plow*, 175.

21. Carolyn Daniels, *Hands on the Freedom Plow*, "We Just Kept Going," 155.

22. Janet Dewart Bell, *Lighting the Fires of Freedom: African American Women in the Civil Rights Movement* (New York: The New Press, 2018), 110–111.

23. Courtney Pace, *Freedom Faith: The Womanist Vision of Prathia Hall* (Athens, GA: University of Georgia Press, 2019), 1, 38.

24. "Mrs. Gregory Bound Over to Higher Court (2)." *The Chicago Defender (National Edition) (1921–1967),* Dec 28, 1963, 1.

25. SNCC News Release, January 23, 1964, CRMVET, https://www.crmvet.org/ docs/pr/640123_sncc_pr-atl.pdf. Accessed April 12, 2019.

26. Prathia Hall, 1995, Princeton Theological Seminary Archives.

27. Prathia Hall, Pre-interview with Alice Markowitz, November 13, 1999, Henry Hampton Collection, Washington University Archives, Prathia L. Hall (Faith 000111).

Chapter 3. "We Shall Not Be Moved"

1. Anne Ju, "Courage is the most important virtue, says writer and civil rights activist Maya Angelou at Convocation," *Cornell Chronicle*, May 24, 2008, http://news .cornell.edu/stories/2008/05/courage-most-important-virtue-maya-angelou-tells -seniors and Jena McGregor, "Maya Angelou on leadership, courage, and the creative process," *The Washington Post*, May 24, 2014, https://www.washingtonpost.com/ news/on-leadership/wp/2014/05/28/maya-angelou-on-leadership-courage-and-the -creative-process/?utm_term=.82dac80004f4. Accessed June 28, 2018.

2. Alison Beard, *Harvard Business Review*, https://hbr.org/2013/05/maya-angelou -on-courage-and-cr. And Jena McGregor, "Maya Angelou on leadership, courage, and the creative process," *Washington Post*, May 24, 2014, https://www.washingtonpost .com/news/on-leadership/wp/2014/05/28/maya-angelou-on-leadership-courage -and-the-creative-process/?utm_term=.b24e2e4c9c3f. Accessed June 28, 2018.

3. Courage is a virtue that many consider important in a moral life, including Aristotle, who describes courage as the first of the cardinal virtues in *Nicomachean Ethics* (Book III).

4. Cannon identifies virtue ethics of Black women as invisible dignity, quiet grace, and unshouted courage. See Katie Geneva Cannon, *Black Womanist Ethics* (Eugene, OR: Wipf and Stock Publishing, 1988), 159. Harris articulates womanist virtues of generosity, graciousness, audacious courage, compassion, spiritual wisdom, justice, and good community. See Melanie Harris, *Gifts of Virtue, Alice Walker, and Womanist Ethics* (New York: Palgrave, 2010), 66–87.

5. John Thurber, "John Blake, 89; Had Rosa Parks Arrested," *Los Angeles Times,* Obituaries, March 26, 2002.

6. Grace Jordan McFadden, "Septima P. Clark and the Struggle for Human Rights," in *Civil Rights Movement: Trailblazers & Torchbearers 1941–1965,* eds. Vicki L. Crawford, Jacqueline Anne Rouse, Barbara Woods (Bloomington: Indiana University Press, 1990), 90.

7. Adelle M. Banks, "The Spiritual Treasures of Rosa Parks," *Charlotte Observer,* https://www.charlotteobserver.com/living/religion/article8995181.html#storylink =cpy. Accessed March 29, 2019.

8. *Elizabeth Daily News*, August 9, 1963, *Jet* magazine March 31, 1960. *Atlanta Constitution*, "Spelman Girls Arrested for Disorderly Conduct in Desegregation Attempt at Local Restaurant," see Gwendolyn Zoharah Simmons in *Hands on the Freedom Plow*, 18–19.

9. Margie Davis, Interview with AnneMarie Mingo, Personal Interview, Atlanta, GA, May 10, 2010.

10. Lydia Chavez, "U.S. Steel to Close Big Alabama Mill," *New York Times*, May 22, 1982, https://www.nytimes.com/1982/05/22/business/us-steel-to-close-big

-alabama-mill.html, Accessed August 1, 2019. Charles Davidson, "Birmingham: A Powerful History Forged in Iron," Federal Reserve Bank of Atlanta, April 26, 2017, https://www.frbatlanta.org/economy-matters/2017/04/26/birmingham-a-powerful-history-forged-from-iron, Accessed August 1, 2019.

11. Albany State's President, William Dennis, made a choice that kept him in good relationships with the Georgia State Board of Regents, which fired his predecessor Aaron Brown as a result of his NAACP voter registration drives for Black residents of Albany. See *Jet* magazine, "Ousted Prexy Asks College Board to Publish Facts," March 4, 1954, 13. Black public high schools faced similar threats of closure or defunding by local leaders.

12. Margie Davis.

13. Margie Davis.

14. Professor Oliver did not live within the Fairfield community, but instead commuted thirty-two miles a day round trip from the Woodlawn community of Birmingham for forty-three years as he worked in the community. See John B. Davis, *The Fruits of His Labor* (Bloomington, IN: Xlibris Corporation, 2013), 71.

15. John B. Davis, *The Fruits of His Labor* (Bloomington, IN: Xlibris Corporation, 2013), 183.

16. According to E.J. Oliver, there were thirteen students who were recorded as leaving the school without permission and participated in the protests. Of those, eight were seniors whose graduation was put in jeopardy as a result of their absences. He notes that community leaders called a meeting at the school to request that the students who left in protest be allowed back in school without receiving any punishment. Oliver requested that a vote be taken and it was determined that the faculty could adjudicate the matter without involving the superintendent. The faculty members were said to have been sympathetic to the students' goals, but not their method of leaving school to protest instead of leaving from their homes. Oliver does not state if he was also supportive of these goals. See John B. Davis, *The Fruits of His Labor*, 151–153.

17. Margie Davis.

18. Margie Davis. Helen Ephraim mustered the strength to pull Margie to safety.

19. Large-scale arrests of children and young people in Birmingham in May 1963 were captured by newspapers throughout the North, including the *New Pittsburgh Courier, New York Times,* and *Washington Post*, but the protests were often hidden on interior pages or minimized in local southern newspapers.

20. Margie Davis.

21. Margie Davis. The process of police riding unrestrained persons around in a reckless way such that they were thrown around in the back of the vehicle foreshadows the "Rough Ride" practice that was employed in Baltimore, Maryland, on April 12, 2015, when Freddie Gray was taken into custody by police and his body was tossed from side to side in the back of the police van, sustaining injuries that later resulted in his death.

22. This memory sounded eerily familiar to me as I reflected on things that I was told in 2008 while visiting the Cape Coast and Elmina (slave castles) dungeons in

Ghana where enslaved people were held before being placed on ships to the Americas. There too, over two hundred years earlier, girls were left chained together in the courtyard while it rained, forced to sleep on concrete in crowded areas where family members did not know where they had been taken. Girls were taken away by their White Christian captors and raped, but there was limited knowledge or accounting for what happened to them afterwards.

23. Margie Davis.

24. Janice Kelsey, *I Woke Up with My Mind on Freedom* (Pittsburgh, PA: Urban Press, 2017), 14–15. Janice Kelsey, interview with author, Interview with AnneMarie Mingo, Personal Interview, Birmingham, AL, June 8, 2018.

25. Janice Kelsey, 14–16

26. Kelsey, 25.

27. Margie Davis.

28. Filed July 20, 1964. Precedential—citations—334 F.2d 369 (5th Circ. 1964). Docket Number 20875_1. https://www.courtlistener.com/opinion/264994/linda-cal-woods-a-minor-by-her-father-and-next-friend-rev-calvin-woods/?. Accessed August 6, 2019. According to court records, Wayman Matherson was the principal of the Washington School, and he received a letter from Superintendent Wright with a list of names of the students arrested for parading without a permit. On May 20, 1963, Theo R. Wright, Superintendent of Education of the City of Birmingham, Alabama, addressed a letter to Mr. Wayman Matherson, Principal of the Washington School, advising him as follows: "Attached to this letter is a list of your pupils recently arrested for parading without a permit. As you know, the policy of the Board of Education has been immediate suspension or expulsion of students who have been arrested for any offense until proper hearings can be conducted for such pupils. "Students whose names are on this list who are sixteen years old or older shall be immediately expelled for the balance of this term. Students whose names appear on the list who have not yet reached the age of sixteen shall be immediately suspended for the balance of the term. These expulsions and suspensions should be recorded on the pupil's permanent record or course card. "The Board of Education then voted to permit students to make application for summer school beginning Monday, June 3, so that they could make up the time lost and receive credit for this year's work. Those who do not enter summer school will be permitted to re-enter school in the Fall but will have to complete the full grade or semester from which they were suspended or expelled." See https://cite. case.law/f2d/334/369/ Accessed March 22, 2022. The Fifth Circuit Court of Appeals was reorganized effective October 1, 1981, during which time Alabama, Georgia, and Florida became a part of the new Eleventh Circuit. See Fifth Circuit Court of Appeals Reorganization Act of 1980 and www.ca5.uscourts.gov/about-the-court/circuit-history/brief-history.

29. Thalhammer et al., 87.

30. Soublet.

31. Soublet.

32. Soublet. Elizabeth Laizner was a Jewish woman whose family history reinforced

her commitment to doing her part in the southern freedom struggle. She was one of the Bennett College faculty members who advised the CORE chapter. See Linda Beatrice Brown, *Belles of Liberty: Gender, Bennett College, and the Civil Rights Movement in Greensboro, North Carolina* (Greensboro, NC: Women and Wisdom Press, 2013), 83.

33. AnneMarie Mingo, "Transgressive Leadership and Theo-ethical Texts of Black Protest Music," *Black Theology: An International Journal* 17, no. 2 (2019): 96–98.

34. Laizner, 16.

35. Bennett Inside, April 6, 2018, http://www.bennett.edu/inside/bennett-belles -have-storied-history-of-activism-leadership/.

36. Evelyn J. Frazier, *The Silent Warrior: An Autobiography by Evelyn J. Frazier as told to Pennye G. Hicks* (Lithonia, GA: Nia Pages II, 2008), 35.

37. Frazier, 35.

38. William Dendy, discussion with author, March 4, 2011.

39. Also see Raymond Arsenault, *Freedom Riders: 1961 and the Struggle for Racial Justice* (New York: Oxford University Press, 2006), 452–510.

40. Bethel.

41. Bethel describes Helen as her aunt but shared that she was actually her mother's first cousin.

42. Bethel.

43. "Albany Movement Formed," https://snccdigital.org/events/albany-movement -formed/. Accessed February 16, 2019.

44. Maurice C. Daniels, *Saving the Soul of Georgia: Donald L. Hollowell and the Struggle for Civil Rights* (Athens: University of Georgia Press, 2013), 140.

45. Bethel.

46. Annette Jones White, *Aspire*, Spring 2011, 18.

47. Jones White, 19.

48. Jones White, 19.

49. Jones White, 19.

50. Annette Jones White, Interview with AnneMarie Mingo, Personal Interview, Atlanta, GA, April 26, 2012

51. Francis Kennedy, Interview with AnneMarie Mingo, Personal Interview, Gainesville, FL, July 7, 2018.

52. *The Daily Journal, Elizabeth N.J.*, Friday Evening, August 9, 1963.

53. With the exception of the Lathers Union, White building trade unions refused to accept the Elizabeth NAACP's demand that two Black apprentices be hired immediately to work in each of the building trades. Tom Leonard, "Jersey Negroes Picket for Jobs," *The Militant*, September 2, 1963. https://www.themilitant.com/1963/2730/ MIL2730.pdf. Accessed August 20, 2019.

54. Rose Davis Schofield, Interview with AnneMarie Mingo, Personal Interview, Atlanta, GA, May 15, 2014. Schofield describes one father who did not want his son to participate because he was concerned about his son's future college prospects.

55. Francis Kennedy.

56. Schofield is pictured in the *Elizabeth Daily News*, August 9, 1963.

57. Rose Schofield Interview with AnneMarie Mingo, Personal Interview, Atlanta, GA, May 10, 2010.

58. Schofield, 2010.

59. Schofield, 2010.

60. Gwendolyn Robinson Simmons was given the name Zoharah in 1972 by her Bawa, and she has been known as Zoharah Simmons since that time.

61. Gwendolyn Zoharah Simmons, "From Little Memphis Girl to Mississippi Amazon," in *Hands on the Freedom Plow: Personal Accounts by Women in SNCC,* eds. Faith S. Holsaert, Martha Prescod Norman Noonan, Judy Richardson, Betty Garman Robinson, Jean Smith Young, and Dorothy M. Zellner, (Urbana: University of Illinois Press, 2010), 12–13.

62. Simmons, *Hands on the Freedom Plow,* 15.

63. Simmons, *Hands on the Freedom Plow,* 16–17.

64. There were six affiliated institutions that formed the Atlanta University Center at that time: Clark, Morehouse, Morris Brown, and Spelman Colleges, Atlanta University, and the Interdenominational Theological Center.

65. Simmons, *Hands on the Freedom Plow,* 18.

66. Simmons, *Hands on the Freedom Plow,* 19–20.

67. Simmons, *Hands on the Freedom Plow,* 20.

68. Simmons, *Hands on the Freedom Plow,* 21.

69. In the early 1960s, Atlanta became known as "a city too busy to hate," which reflected a White myth and somewhat of a public relations campaign disconnected from the daily realities of the large Black population in the city. See Virginia H. Hein, "The Image of 'A City Too Busy to Hate': Atlanta in the 1960s," *Phylon* 33, no. 3 (3rd Qtr, 1972): 205–221.

Moral Exemplar. Dr. Willa Beatrice Player

1. Willa B. Player, *Improving College Education for Women at Bennett College: A Report of a Type A Project*, EdD dissertation, Teachers College, Columbia University, 1948.

2. http://library.uncg.edu/depts/archives/civrights/detail-bio.asp?bio=95 Accessed December 15, 2018.

3. Bennett Belles organized earlier freedom struggles, including picketing the Carolina Theater in downtown Greensboro in 1937 over the practice of editing Blacks out of films who were shown as equal to Whites and boycotting theaters who supported the negative portrayal of Blacks in films in 1939. Efforts also included their successful Operation Door Knock that began in 1951 and continued into the 1960s, during which time Bennett Belles registered more than a quarter of Greensboro's Black voters. Through the initiative, classes were suspended for one week as Bennett students went door-to-door in Greensboro's Black neighborhoods registering every adult they could to vote. This ultimately created the platform for the election of the first Black

city council member that first year. Beth McMurtrie, "Bennett Activism a Tradition," October 10, 1998, https://www.greensboro.com/bennett-activism-a-tradition-as -bennett-college-enters-its-th/article_3a54e3da-dc4d-5e7c-81d5-2ac47746f526. html, accessed December 23, 2018. "Bennett Belles Have Storied History of Activism Leadership," Bennett Inside, April 6, 2018, http://www.bennett.edu/inside/bennett -belles-have-storied-history-of-activism-leadership, accessed December 23, 2018.

4. King was invited to speak by the Greensboro Branch of the National Association for the Advancement of Colored People.

5. Nancy McLaughlin, "Stand Up for Truth," *Winston-Salem Journal*, January 15, 2018, https://www.journalnow.com/news/local/the-seeds-of-the-march-on -washington-were-sown-at/article_76627f23-56df-574a-8b9c-4cda57c30053.html accessed December 23, 2018.

6. Diedre B. Flowers, "The Launching of the Student Sit-in Movement: The Role of Black Women at Bennett College," *Journal of African American History* 90, no. 1–2, (Spring 2005): 57; AnneMarie Mingo, "Just Laws, Unjust Laws, and Theo-Moral Responsibility in Traditional and Contemporary Civil Rights Activism" *Journal of Religious Ethics* 46, no. 4 (2018): 689–690.

7. Rev. John Hatchett, who served as Bennett's Chaplain from 1958 to 1962, advised the college's NAACP chapter. He describes the nightly planning and strategy meetings by Bennett students who decided to also include North Carolina A&T students during the fall 1959. Hatchett notes that the four male students from A&T had been a part of the planning meetings at Bennett before they sat-in on February 1, 1960. See Linda Beatrice Brown, *Belles of Liberty: Gender, Bennett College, and the Civil Rights Movement in Greensboro, North* Carolina (Greensboro, NC: Women and Wisdom Press, 2013), 76–77.

8. Flowers, 57.

9. Willa Player, Interview with Eugene Pfaff, 17. I have not been able to determine if Player is actually referencing the *New York Times Magazine*, which is the Sunday supplement of the newspaper, or the daily newspaper. Since the initial event by the A&T students happened on Monday, February 1st, and the *New York Times* began covering the Greensboro sit-ins on February 2, 1960, it seems unlikely that Player did not become aware of Bennett students' involvement until the following Sunday when the magazine was released.

10. Player, 17–18.

11. Laizner, 11. Larger meetings were often held at Providence Baptist Church, and the AME Zion Church pastored by Reverend Bishop, 4, 15.

12. Laizner, 4. Elizabeth Laizner was a White Jewish teacher who was actively involved as the chief of transportation officer for the protests because she had a phone at home and her office at Bennett and knew people with cars. Laizner, 7.

13. Laizner, 7–8. The students would often picket restaurants during the evening meal too.

14. Player, 21. Bennett's status as a private institution provided more options for resistance than the state-funded A&T.

15. Brown, 90–91.

16. Samuel Dewitt Proctor was the president of North Carolina A&T State from 1960 to 1964, however he took leave at times, including from January 1962 to September 1963 when he served as Peace Corps director in Nigeria, http://www.library.ncat .edu/resources/archives/leaders.html. Accessed December 26, 2018.

17. North Carolina A&T was designated a university in 1967.

18. Player, 21. Player also met with one of the Bennett faculty members, Dr. Elizabeth Laizner, who was also arrested and jailed with the students. Player assured Laizner that she had her support to see things through for her. Player, 25–26. It is not clear if any concerns regarding potential exposure to unhealthy conditions at a former polio hospital continued to be a long-term area of care for the students.

19. Player, 22.

20. Player, 18.

21. Player, 23. The point is not whether students actually shared everything. Player created the open channel for communication, and she felt connected to the planning and execution of direct actions.

22. Laizner describes a support community that could act on behalf of CORE when key members were in jail, and Dr. Player headed that committee, which would arrange which persons would stay out of jail and which would stay inside. Laizner, 22.

23. Player, 26–27.

24. Barbara R. I. Isaacs, "The Lunch Counter Struggle, 1960–1963: Women Remapping Boundaries of Race, Gender, and Vocation," in *Gender, Ethnicity, and Religion: Views from the Other Side*, ed. Rosemary Radford Ruether (Minneapolis, MN: Fortress Press, 2002), 71.

25. A copy of the May 20, 1963, Western Union telegram from Willa B. Player to Edward Strong, the father of Phyllis Strong Taylor is included in Brown, *Belles of Liberty*, 157.

26. Elizabeth Laizner, Interview with Eugene Pfaff, June 19, 1979, 24.

27. Johnsie Williams Thomas Interview with AnneMarie Mingo, Personal Interview, New York, NY, August 6, 2010.

28. Player, 23.

29. Thomas.

30. Beverly Guy-Sheftall, "A Conversation with Willa B. Player," *Sage: A Scholarly Journal on Black Women* 1, no. 1 (Spring 1984): 18.

Chapter 4. "Keep Your Eyes on the Prize, Hold On"

1. F. Eugene Heath, Moral Imagination: Ethics, *Encyclopedia Britannica*, https:// www.britannica.com/topic/moral-imagination, Accessed April 9, 2020.

2. Philip S. Keane, *Christian Ethics and Imagination: A Theological Inquiry*, (New York: Paulist Press, 1984), 81.

3. See Alasdair MacIntyre, *After Virtue;* Iris Murdoch, *Metaphysics as a Guide to*

Morals, (London: Vintage, 1992); and Lisa Tessman, *Burdened Virtues: Virtue Ethics for Liberatory Struggles* (New York: Oxford Press, 2005).

4. See Katie G. Cannon, *Black Womanist Ethics* (Eugene, OR: Wipf and Stock, 1988; Atlanta, GA: Scholars Press, 2006); and Emilie M. Townes, *Womanist Justice, Womanist Hope* (Atlanta, GA: Scholars Press, 1993).

5. Katie G. Cannon, "Moral Wisdom in the Black Women's Literary Tradition," *The Annual of the Society of Christian Ethics* 4 (1984): 171–192 [188].

6. Thelathia "Nikki" Young, *Black Queer Ethics, Family, and Philosophical Imagination,* (New York: Palgrave MacMillan, 2016), 152.

7. John Paul Lederach, *The Moral Imagination: The Art and Soul of Building Peace,* (New York: Oxford University Press, 2005), 26–27.

8. Lederach, 29.

9. Robin D. G. Kelley, *Freedom Dreams: The Black Radical Imagination* (Boston: Beacon Press, 2002), 150.

10. Alice Walker, *In Search of Our Mothers' Gardens: Womanist Prose* (San Diego: Harcourt Brace Jovanovich, 1983), xi–xii.

11. Martin Luther King's frequently referenced statement is a quote paraphrased from theologian and abolitionist Theodore Parker.

12. This song was often sung by Vincent Harding in the tune of the Spiritual "We Are Climbing Jacob's Ladder" as a way of setting the vision and encouraging the work.

13. Beatrice Perry Soublet, Interview with AnneMarie Mingo, Personal Interview, Atlanta, Georgia, April 14, 2010.

14. Margaret L. Evans, Interview with AnneMarie Mingo, Personal Interview, Atlanta, GA, August 25, 2010.

15. Schofield, 2010.

16. Romans 4:17b

17. Victor Turner, *The Forest of Symbols: Aspects of Ndembu Ritual* (Ithaca, NY: Cornell University Press, 1967), 93–111. María Lugones, "On Complex Communication," *Hypatia* 21, no. 3 (Summer 2006): 75–85, is also helpful in thinking through women as liminal beings.

18. Turner, *The Forest Symbols*, 95, 98–99.

19. It is not my aim to suggest that male leaders within the Civil Rights Movement were not also in liminal spaces as they too encountered access to new areas in the broader social and political arena. However, the women in my study could be doubly marginalized as Blacks within a White society as women within a movement with male leadership.

20. The Latin *Limen*, meaning threshold, is the root of liminal and liminality.

21. Turner, 105.

22. Although work in those places at times put Black women in danger of undesired sexual advances from White men. Also see Danielle L. McGuire, *At the Dark End of the Street: Black Women, Rape, and Resistance—A New History of the Civil Rights Movement from Rosa Parks to the Rise of Black Power* (New York: Alfred A. Knopf, 2010).

23. Jo Ann Gibson Robinson, *The Montgomery Bus Boycott and the Women Who Started It: The Memoir of Jo Ann Gibson Robinson* (Knoxville: University of Tennessee Press), 108.

24. Marjorie Wallace Smyth, January 7, 2012, 2. Parisian is an upscale department store that was founded in Birmingham and expanded throughout the Southeast and Midwest of the United States.

25. These activists acted with courage without knowing whether they would actually be successful in their efforts.

26. Crawford, 204.

27. Marjorie Wallace Smyth, Interview with AnneMarie Mingo, Personal Interview, New York, NY, August 2009.

28. Marjorie Wallace Smyth, 2012.

29. Marjorie Wallace Smyth, 2012; AnneMarie Mingo, "'They Must Have a Different God Than Our God': Towards a Lived Theology of Black Churchwomen during the United States Civil Rights Movement" in *Contesting Post-Racialism: Conflicted Churches in the United States and South Africa*, eds. R. Drew Smith, William Ackah, Anthony G. Reddie, and Rothney S. Tshaka (Jackson: University Press of Mississippi, 2015), 111–121.

30. Martin Luther King Jr., "Letter from Birmingham Jail," in *Why We Can't Wait* (New York: Signet Classics, 1963, 1964, 2000), 105–106.

31. Martin Luther King Jr., Handwritten prayer, date unknown. Transcription by AnneMarie Mingo. http://www.thekingcenter.org/archive/document/draft-prayer -given-dr-king Accessed September 18, 2012. Also see Lewis V. Baldwin, *Never to Leave Us Alone: The Prayer Life of Martin Luther King Jr.* (Minneapolis, MN: Fortress Press, 2010).

32. W. E. B. Du Bois, *The Souls of Black Folk* (New York, Dover Publications, 1903, 1994), 2

33. Doris Brunson, Interview with AnneMarie Mingo, Personal Interview, New York, NY, July 8, 2010.

34. In 1956, multiple states including Alabama, Arkansas, Florida, Georgia, Louisiana, Mississippi, South Carolina, Tennessee, Texas, and Virginia initiated court cases or passed laws with the goal of eliminating the NAACP as civil rights activities began to expand. "Southern States Try to Destroy NAACP (1956–1964)" in Civil Rights Movement Archive, https://www.crmvet.org/tim/timhis56.htm. Accessed November 9, 2019.

35. Kristen Fiscus, "Inaugural Rosa Parks Day Passes Down History," *Montgomery Advertiser,* December 1, 2018, Accessed November 8, 2019. https://www .montgomeryadvertiser.com/story/news/2018/12/01/montgomery-celebrates -inaugural-rosa-parks-day/2175542002.

36. King often spoke about the need to change the laws to help curb the actions of those for whom you could not change the heart. In King's 1963 speech at Western Michigan University, he stated, "But we must go on to say that while it may be true that morality cannot be legislated, behavior can be regulated. It may be true that

the law cannot change the heart but it can restrain the heartless. It may be true that that the law cannot make a man love me, but it can keep him from lynching me and I think that is pretty important, also." Martin Luther King Jr., Western Michigan University, December 18, 1963, Western Michigan University Archives and Regional History Collections and University Libraries, https://wmich.edu/sites/default/files/attachments/MLK.pdf. Accessed January 25, 2020.

37. Bessie Sellaway, Interview with AnneMarie Mingo, Personal Interview, Atlanta, GA, November 10, 2010

38. Bethel.

39. Bethel.

40. Lucas.

41. Jayme Coleman Williams, Interview with AnneMarie Mingo, Personal Interview, Atlanta, GA.

42. Lydia Walker, Interview with AnneMarie Mingo, Personal Interview, Atlanta, GA, April 26, 2010.

43. Barbara Ann Adams, Interview with AnneMarie Mingo, Personal Interview, Atlanta, GA, November 19, 2010.

Moral Exemplar. Eberta Lee Spinks

1. This included three sets of twins, who did not all survive.

2. Eberta Spinks, Oral History Interview with Kim Adams, Mississippi Oral History Program of the University of Southern Mississippi, Spring 1995, 1.

3. Spinks, 18.

4. Spinks, 6. James Prince Trip to Jones County, Mississippi, 1942, Book with autographs. The entry from H. B. Mott reads, "Let God ever lead and to the right be true. Thru out life give the best, And the best will come back to you. Mrs. H. B. Mott (State Evangelist)." https://sites.rootsweb.com/~msjones2/family/faprincetrip.html. Accessed January 28, 2020. Women were not often ordained as preachers Mott's denomination at that time.

5. Simmons, *Hands on the Freedom Plow*, 24–25.

6. James Chaney and Michael "Mickey" Schwerner were CORE staff and Andrew Goodman was a summer project volunteer. They were murdered in Neshoba County, Mississippi, in June 1964.

7. Cynthia Griggs Fleming, "Black Women and Black Power: The Case of Ruby Doris Smith Robinson and the Student Nonviolent Coordinating Committee," in *Sisters in the Struggle: African American Women in the Civil Rights-Black Power Movement,* eds. Bettye Collier-Thomas and V. P. Franklin (New York: New York University Press, 2001), 204–205.

8. Gwendolyn Zoharah Simmons, Panel Discussion—Consequential Impact of the Civil Rights Movement: Implications for Advancing Social Justice in the 21st Century, New York University, Washington, DC, November 20–21, 2015, https://facultyresourcenetwork.org/publications/advancing-social-justice-from-classroom-

to-community/gwendolyn-zoharah-simmons-plenary-panel-consequential-impact-of-the-civil-rights-movement-implications-for-advancing-social-justice-in-the-21st-century/. Accessed January 29, 2020.

9. Gwendolyn Zoharah Simmons, Interview with AnneMarie Mingo, Personal Interview, Gainesville, FL, July 5, 2018.

10. Spinks, 20.

11. Spinks, 20.

12. Gwendolyn Zoharah Simmons, 2018.

13. See *Akinyele* Umoja, *We Will Shoot Back: Armed Resistance in the Mississippi Freedom Movement* (New York: New York University Press, 2013), chapter 4; Lance Hill, *The Deacons for Defense: Armed Resistance and the Civil Rights Movement* (Chapel Hill: University of North Carolina Press, 2004), chapter 11.

14. Patricia Michelle Boyett, *Right to Revolt: The Crusade for Racial Justice in Mississippi's Central Piney Woods* (Jackson: University Press of Mississippi, 2015).

15. SAVF-Student Nonviolent Coordinating Committee (SNCC) (Social Action vertical file, circa 1930–2002; Archives Main Stacks, Mss 577, Box 47, Folder 10). http://content.wisconsinhistory.org/cdm/compoundobject/collection/p15932coll2/id/66257/show/66094/rec/18. Accessed January 28, 2020.

16. Spinks describes getting a driver's license after seeing a highway patrolman stopping integrated groups, and asking for their license. She went the next day and took the test for her license without the man realizing that she was a leader in the Movement. She thanked God for allowing her to get a license without any trouble. Spinks, 31–32.

17. Spinks, 21–22.

18. Spinks, 22–23.

19. Mississippi Freedom Democratic Party Newsletter, December 20, 1965, p. 5

20. Spinks, 25.

21. Spinks, 25.

22. Spinks, 32.

Chapter 5. "Which Side Are You On?"

1. Sometimes the source is explicitly named experience, at other times it may be named revelation, which I understand as an experiential act.

2. I use the term "liberative" to represent an overarching umbrella for particular liberation-oriented theologies and ethics, including Black liberation theologies and ethics, Latin American liberation theologies, womanist theologies and ethics, feminist theologies and ethics, mujerista theologies and ethics, and queer theologies and ethics. These liberative theologies and ethics represent both universal and particular claims for justice and freedom in the face of various manifestations of oppression.

3. The Movement for Black Lives is a coalition of over fifty organizations. They describe their founding in this way: "The Movement for Black Lives (M4BL) formed in December of 2014, was created as a space for Black organizations across the country

to debate and discuss the current political conditions, develop shared assessments of what political interventions were necessary in order to achieve key policy, cultural and political wins, convene organizational leadership in order to debate and co-create a shared movement wide strategy. Under the fundamental idea that we can achieve more together than we can separately." https://m4bl.org/about-us/. Accessed November 6, 2020.

4. AnneMarie Mingo, "Transgressive Leadership and Theo-ethical Texts of Black Protest Music," *Black Theology: An International Journal* 17, no. 2 (May 2019): 91–113.

5. The generation of the women may also influence the music they are drawn to and most readily associate with protest spaces.

6. In the 1940s, Baker famously said, "Give people light and they will find a way," and she held leadership conferences throughout the south titled "Give People Light and They Will Find the Way," which she drew from one of her favorite hymns. See Barbara Ransby, *Ella Baker and the Black Freedom Movement: A Radical Democratic Vision* (Chapel Hill: University of North Carolina Press, 2003), 142.

7. Callahan also later preached a version of the sermon at Louisville Presbyterian Seminary in celebration of the thirtieth anniversary of the Grawemeyer Awards on October 12, 2015. While the same key points were there, the delivery—including the illustrations and communal call-outs—changed significantly as a result of the context.

8. As a result of this training and education, the majority of these religious leaders use the New Revised Standard Version (NRSV) or New International Version (NIV), so I will use those within references in this chapter unless specifically noted differently. The Association of Theological Schools reports an increasing number of Black seminary students. Black students were 13.7 percent of the enrollment across ATS seminaries in 2012, which exceeds the national population percentage. Association of Theological School, "Racial/ethnic students represent the largest growth area for theological schools," 2012.

9. Karen Anderson, Interview with AnneMarie Mingo, Personal Interview, Memphis, TN, February 12, 2018.

10. In Ferguson, Missouri, Cathy, "Mama Cat" Daniels was an embodiment of seeing the need of physical hunger and meeting it for the activist who protested daily at the site of the killing of Michael Brown.

11. Traci Blackmon, Interview with AnneMarie Mingo, Personal Interview, Memphis, TN, February 14, 2018.

12. Charlene Carruthers, *Unapologetic: A Black Queer and Feminist Mandate for Radical Movements* (New York: Beacon Press, 2018), 63.

13. Blackmon.

14. For further discussions in the area of Black Lives Mattering to God, see: Kelly Brown Douglas, *Stand Your Ground: Black Bodies and the Justice of God*, (Maryknoll, NY: Orbis Books, 2015), Pamela R. Lightsey, *Our Lives Matter: A Womanist Queer Theology* (Eugene, OR: Pickwick Publications, 2015), Josiah Ulysses Young III, "Do Black Lives Matter to 'God'?," *Black Theology: An International Journal* 13, no. 3 (November 2015): 210–218, and Barbara Ransby, *Making All Black Lives Matter:*

Reimagining Freedom in the 21st Century (Oakland: University of California Press, 2018).

15. Assata Shakur, "To My People," *Women's Studies Quarterly* 46, no. 3–4, PRO-TEST (Fall/Winter 2018): 217–221. Also, Charlene A. Carruthers, "Hearing Assata Shakur's Call," *Women's Studies Quarterly* 46, no. 3–4, PROTEST (Fall/Winter 2018): 222–225.

16. Prathia Hall became pastor of the church her father founded, Mt. Sharon Baptist Church in Philadelphia, PA, in 1978. Very few women served as pastors of traditional Black congregations during the Civil Rights Movement. My current research has not uncovered any who pastored activist congregations in the 1950s or 1960s.

17. See "Learning from Black Lives Conversation: A Statement of Solidarity and Theological Testament," on Change.org, https://www.change.org/p/individuals-learning-from-black-lives-conversation-a-statement-of-solidarity-and-theological-testament?recruiter=24898668&utm_source=share_for_starters&utm_medium=copyLink

18. The quotes from the Black Scholars National Gathering are from personal notes taken during my attendance and participation in the gathering.

19. Leslie D. Callahan, sermon, August 23, 2015, http://1000wallace.org/sermons/.

20. Leslie D. Callahan, sermon, August 23, 2015, http://1000wallace.org/sermons/.

21. *The Christian Recorder*, "Interview with Ms. Brittany N. Packnett," April 3, 2017. https://www.thechristianrecorder.com/interview-with-ms-brittany-n-packnett/, Accessed February 11, 2021.

22. Brittany Packnett Cunningham, https://brittanypacknett.com/bio, Accessed February 10, 2021.

23. Relevant Magazine, "5 Leaders On How The Church Can Get Involved In The Fight Against Racial Injustice," May 29, 2020, https://www.relevantmagazine.com/current/5-leaders-on-how-the-church-can-get-involved-in-the-fight-against-racial-injustice/. Accessed March 2, 2021.

24. Pamela Lightsey, "Statement from Black Presidents and Deans, Schools and Departments of Theology and Religion," June 3, 2020, https://www.meadville.edu/ml-commons/details/statement-from-black-presidents-and-deans-schools-and-departments-of-theology-and-religion/. Accessed February 25, 2021.

25. Eboni Marshall Turman, "On Black Lives Matter: A Theological Statement from the Black Churches," *Color Lines*, June 19, 2020, https://www.colorlines.com/articles/theological-statement-black-church-juneteenth. Accessed February 25, 2021.

Moral Exemplar. Bree Newsome Bass

1. South Carolina Code of Laws, Chapter 10 "Removal and Placement of Confederate Flag," https://www.scstatehouse.gov/code/t01c010.php. Accessed September 10, 2020.

2. Jesse James DeConto, "Activist who took down Confederate flag drew on her faith and on new civil rights awakening," July 12, 2015. https://religionnews

.com/2015/07/12/activist-who-took-down-confederate-flag-drew-on-her-faith-and-on-new-civil-rights-awakening/. Accessed September 11, 2020

3. Bree Newsome, lecture at Penn State University, February 29, 2016.

4. Post and Courier, "Bree Newsome removes the confederate battle flag from Statehouse in 2015," February 22, 2017. https://www.youtube.com/watch?v=ilUfHV2sBNg. Accessed November 2, 2020.

5. Bree Newsome, *Blue Nation Review*, June 2015. https://bluenationreview.com/exclusive-bree-newsome-speaks-for-the-first-time-after-courageous-act-of-civil-disobedience/#ixzz3eUPYvDCg

6. Benjamin L. Corey, "Agitating and Peacemaking: The Most Important Thing We Can Learn from Bree Newsome," *Patheos*, July 13, 2015.

7. *Democracy Now!*, July 6, 2015.

8. The group identified themselves as "regular human beings, daughters, sons, mothers, fathers, Carolinians, educators, and activists—both black and white—who believe in the fundamental idea of humanity." Unfortunately, the confederate flag was replaced less than an hour after its removal by Newsome Bass. It was later permanently removed following a vote from the South Carolina legislature, the only body permitted to make that decision with at least a two-thirds affirmative vote.

9. The confederate flag was replaced less than an hour after Newsome Bass took the risk to remove it. A pro-flag rally was already planned for that day, and nearly sixty supporters of the confederate flag's placement on the Capitol grounds in Columbia, South Carolina, gathered with their flag proudly waving.

10. DeConto.

11. Rebecca Butts, "Dad: 'We Found Out Like the Rest of the World,'" *Cincinnati Enquirer*, July 1, 2015, https://www.cincinnati.com/story/news/2015/07/01/bree-newsomes-dad/29565615/

12. Kelley D. Evans, "Bree Newsome's social justice fight continues two years after taking down the confederate flag in South Carolina," *The Undefeated*, September 11, 2017, https://theundefeated.com/features/bree-newsome-social-justice-fight-two-years-after-taking-down-the-confederate-flag-in-south-carolina/

13. Goldie Taylor, "Exclusive: Bree Newsome Speaks For The First Time After Courageous Act of Civil Disobedience," *Blue Nation Review*, June 29, 2015. https://archives.bluenationreview.com/exclusive-bree-newsome-speaks-for-the-first-time-after-courageous-act-of-civil-disobedience/

14. Amy Goodman, "Bree Newsome: As SC Lawmakers Debate Removing Confederate Flag, Meet the Activist Who Took It Down," *Democracy Now!*, July 6, 2015.

Epilogue

1. Audre Lorde, *A Burst of Light*, 1988.

2. Movement for Black Lives, "The Preamble," https://m4bl.org/policy-platforms/the-preamble. Accessed May 19, 2021.

3. Movement for Black Lives, "The Preamble," https://m4bl.org/policy-platforms/the-preamble. Accessed May 19, 2021.

4. Alice Walker, *In Search of Our Mother's Gardens: Womanist Prose* (Orlando: Harvest, 1983), xi–xii.

5. Omar M. McRoberts, *Streets of Glory: Church and Community in a Black Urban Neighborhood* (Chicago: University of Chicago Press, 2003), 44–58.

6. Kelly Brown Douglas's *Stand Your Ground: Black Bodies and the Justice of God* (Maryknoll, NY: Orbis Books, 2015) provides helpful historical and theological imagining around this.

7. An earlier collection of memorial items near a pole had been reconstructed after they were burned in September 2014. Paul Hampel, "Residents rebuild Michael Brown memorial after fire; still unclear how blaze started," *St. Louis Post-Dispatch*, September 23, 2014, https://www.stltoday.com/news/local/crime-and-courts/residents-rebuild-michael-brown-memorial-after-fire-still-unclear-how-blaze-started/article_4db89442-5ea2-5345-88ac-13e3fe79e3c6.html. Accessed June 2, 2021.

8. The Brown family requested and received the asphalt where Michael Brown's body lay dying. Joshua Renaud, "Photo interactive: Ferguson then and now," *St. Louis Post-Dispatch*, August 2, 2015, https://www.stltoday.com/news/multimedia/special/photo-interactive-ferguson-then-and-now/collection_ee3b7c2e-e9dd-5ea8-b6aa-4cfb48b1c763.html#2. Accessed June 7, 2021.

9. I also noticed "R.I.P. MIKE" spray painted in Black in another area of the sidewalk.

10. When outside nationally recognized leaders such as DeRay Mckesson and Shaun King willingly acquired media platforms to speak for local efforts, they were strongly critiqued. D. Watkins, "DeRay McKesson is just one man—why do other activists criticize him so harshly?" *Salon*, September 20, 2018, https://www.salon.com/2018/09/20/deray-mckesson-is-just-one-man-why-do-other-activists-criticize-him-so-harshly/. Darren Sands, "The Success and Controversy of #CampaignZero and Its Successful, Controversial Leader, DeRay McKesson," *BuzzfeedNews*, September 13, 2015, https://www.buzzfeednews.com/article/darrensands/the-success-and-controversy-of-campaignzero-and-its-successf. Feliks Garcia, "The Rise and Fall of Shaun King, former Black Lives Matter darling," *Complex*, January 29, 2016, https://www.complex.com/life/2016/01/shaun-king-black-lives-matter/.

11. Samuel De Witt Proctor Conference, "About Us," https://sdpconference.info/about-us/.

12. Fair Fight Action, "About Fair Fight," https://fairfight.com/about-fair-fight/.

13. Adelle M. Banks, "Stacey Abrams' zeal for voting began with preacher parents," Associated Press, October 17, 2020, https://apnews.com/article/race-and-ethnicity-religion-stacey-abrams-georgia-voting-rights-9bef13d7118801d8adc9055a33ac1a76.

14. The Blaque Political Collective Facebook Group, https://www.facebook.com/BlaquePoliticalCollective.

15. Pamela Lightsey, communication with AnneMarie Mingo, June 25, 2021.

16. Anthea Butler, *White Evangelical Racism: The Politics of Morality in America* (Chapel Hill: University of North Carolina Press, 2021).

Index

ANNEMARIE MINGO is an associate professor
of ethics, culture, and moral leadership at the
Pittsburgh Theological Seminary.

The University of Illinois Press
is a founding member of the
Association of University Presses.

———————————————

Composed in 11.25/13 Adobe Garamond Pro
with Avenir display
by Jim Proefrock
at the University of Illinois Press
Manufactured by Sheridan Books, Inc.

University of Illinois Press
1325 South Oak Street
Champaign, IL 61820-6903
www.press.uillinois.edu